Behavioral Treatment
of Alcohol Problems

INDIVIDUALIZED THERAPY AND
CONTROLLED DRINKING

Behavioral Treatment of Alcohol Problems

INDIVIDUALIZED THERAPY AND CONTROLLED DRINKING

Mark B. Sobell

Vanderbilt University
Nashville, Tennessee

and Linda C. Sobell

Dede Wallace Center
and
Vanderbilt University
Nashville, Tennessee

WITHDRAWN

Department of Social and Administrative Studies,
Barnett House,
Wellington Square,
Oxford.

PLENUM PRESS • NEW YORK AND LONDON

Library of Congress Cataloging in Publication Data

Sobell, Mark B
    Behavioral treatment of alcohol problems.

    (The Plenum behavior therapy series)
    Includes index.
    1. Alcoholism. 2. Behavior therapy. I. Sobell, Linda C., joint author. II. Title.
[DNLM: 1. Behavior therapy. 2. Alcoholism—Therapy. WM274 S677b]
RC565.S6   616.8'61'06   77-12381
ISBN 0-306-31057-0

© 1978 Plenum Press, New York
A Division of Plenum Publishing Corporation
227 West 17th Street, New York, N.Y. 10011

Printed in the United States of America

To
"Cas" and Circumstance

Preface

Ideas about the nature of alcohol problems have been undergoing dramatic change over the past several years. This book summarizes the clinical research we have conducted over the past eight years; research which has evoked controversy and which, we hope, will be evaluated as having been influential in the development of a scientific approach to the clinical treatment of alcohol problems. Although we reference many studies from the general behavioral literature on alcohol problems, we make no pretense of presenting a thorough review of that literature. By and large, this book focuses on the research we have conducted, the rationale for that approach, and a detailed discussion of methods and results which cannot be presented in journal articles.

The book begins by giving the reader a perspective on traditional concepts in the alcohol field, and why those concepts are now being challenged. Within that conceptual framework, we then trace the development and sophistication of our clinical research, presenting for the first time in a single work a complete consideration of the rationale, methods, and results of the study of Individualized Behavior Therapy (IBT) for alcoholics. Following a discussion of many of the more subtle aspects of that study and its results, we describe how IBT can be used in an outpatient setting — the setting in which we have conducted clinical research for the last six years. We feel that this book has given us an opportunity to present a more thorough and integrated exposition of the IBT study and related clinical research than has been possible in scientific journals. Similarly, it has allowed us a much greater opportunity for speculation and thought sharing about the methodology, techniques, and results than previously has been possible.

We see this book as useful for two audiences: individuals who have an interest in behavior therapy, and those who are interested in the treatment and treatment outcome evaluation of alcohol problems. We believe that many of the experiences associated with developing behavioral treatment approaches to drinking problems have significance for behavior therapy in general. Finally, recognizing that the treatment of individuals with alcohol problems has met with little success in the past, we see the IBT study and related research as providing those in the alcohol field with techniques and guidelines for approaching and evaluating alcohol problems in a more systematic and pragmatic manner.

Mark B. Sobell

Linda C. Sobell

Nashville, Tennessee

Acknowledgments

Over the past eight years, we have received assistance, support, and inspiration from a great many individuals and our employers. Moreover, many of the studies described in this book were conducted in collaboration with other investigators. We would particularly like to thank the following people: Claudia Armstrong, Timothy B. Baker, Joseph V. Brady, Sebastian Casalaina, William Christelman, Kenneth C. Mills, Natalie Olsen, Fred Samuels, and Drexel B. Sheahan. We are also greatly indebted to Nancy Crow, who repeatedly typed the manuscript without complaint, and to Stephen A. Maisto, who performed the multiple regression analyses reported in Chapter 7. Lastly, we have benefited greatly from the editorial suggestions of Nathan H. Azrin and Seymour Weingarten.

M. B. S.
L. C. S.

Contents

CHAPTER 8
IBT: Interpretation of Results 155

CHAPTER 9
IBT in Retrospect 167

CHAPTER 1

The Nature of Alcohol Problems

The alcohol field is replete with paradox and irony. While this book focuses primarily on a specific behavioral treatment methodology and its results, an understanding of the context in which it developed is crucial. This particular treatment approach represented a radical departure from traditional, widely accepted notions about the nature and treatment of alcohol problems.

This chapter examines the origins of traditional concepts of alcohol problems and how empirical research and data contradict those concepts. Finally, concepts suggested by empirical evidence are briefly discussed. Taken as a whole, the intent of this chapter is twofold: to provide the reader with a general perspective for interpreting the remainder of the book and to provide an understanding of how behavioral approaches to the treatment of alcohol problems emerged.

TRADITIONAL CONCEPTS OF ALCOHOL PROBLEMS

Traditional concepts of alcohol problems do not derive from a single origin but rather from a composite of views culled from Alcoholics Anonymous (AA), the disease concept of alcoholism formulated by E. M. Jellinek, phenomenological struggles of individuals with alcohol problems, and public interpretations of those ideas. In general, traditional concepts constitute a "folk science" (Ravetz, 1971) theory of alcohol problems. They are an accretion of beliefs, values, and ideologies—a body of purported and widely accepted knowledge, developed to meet humanitarian and sociopolitical needs rather

1

than to synthesize scientific findings. This review focuses largely on the approaches of Alcoholics Anonymous and of E. M. Jellinek, as these, without doubt, have been the single most influential conceptualizations to date.

ALCOHOLICS ANONYMOUS

Alcoholics Anonymous was one of several self-help movements (Cantril, 1941) which became quite active during the post-Depression era when concerns for human welfare were championed. In part, its development can be traced to a pervasive noninvolvement by professionals with individuals suffering from alcohol problems. That is, AA filled a void—a void characterized by a lack of interest and verbalized antipathy on the part of health care providers.

Alcoholics Anonymous conceptualizes alcoholism as an "obsession of the mind" combined with an allergy to alcohol. In fact, in the book *Alcoholics Anonymous* (1939), it is said that the reason alcoholics who have suffered serious detrimental life consequences as a result of drinking engage in repeated instances of similar drinking is because they experience a powerful desire to drink in a normal or limited fashion:

> The idea that somehow, someday he will control and enjoy his liquor drinking is the great obsession of every abnormal drinker. The persistence of this illusion is astonishing. Many pursue it into the gates of insanity or death. (p. 41)

Following the initiation of drinking due to this obsession, its continuation is then ascribed to an allergic reaction. This "allergic reaction," as discussed by Jellinek (1960), essentially represents the phenomenon of physical dependence on alcohol. In order to avoid the onset of increasingly severe alcohol withdrawal symptoms, an individual who is physically dependent on alcohol experiences a felt need, described as a "craving" for more alcohol. We should point out that Jellinek's concept of this sort of craving (loss of control) has been formulated in more depth than that of AA. Further, he clearly indicated that a literal consideration of alcoholics as allergic to alcohol was scientifically untenable even by mid-century.

The allergy conceptualization put forth by AA not only implies that "alcoholism" is a distinct entity which can be described and recognized despite its variations, but also assumes that certain individuals (alcoholics or prealcoholics) have a biological predisposition toward alcohol problems, while others (nonalcoholics) do not. Quoting from the book *Alcoholics Anonymous* (1939),

> We believe ... that the action of alcohol on these chronic alcoholics is a manifestation of an allergy; that the phenomenon of craving is limited to this class and never occurs in the average temperate drinker. These allergic types can never safely use alcohol in any form at all . . .. (p. 4)

While the basic tenets of AA neither explicitly describe a developmental progression of alcohol problems nor formally state that such problems are irreversible, they do imply that there is a genetically determined and permanent allergy to alcohol. The most cogent evidence for AA's position on reversibility can be found in the book *Alcoholics Anonymous* (1939):

> But here is a man who at fifty-five years found he was just where he left off at thirty [the man having taken his first drink in twenty-five years]. We have seen the truth demonstrated again and again: "once an alcoholic, always an alcoholic." Commencing to drink after a period of sobriety, we are in short time as bad as ever. (p. 44)

JELLINEK'S DISEASE CONCEPT OF ALCOHOLISM

While the development of Alcoholics Anonymous can be viewed as primarily humanitarian in nature, the work pursued by Jellinek and his colleagues at the Yale Center for Alcohol Studies demonstrated a unique and noteworthy blend of science, humanitarianism, and sociopolitical astuteness. It should be noted that Jellinek's formulation of a disease notion of alcoholism was not the first time that such a concept was advanced. Shortly before the turn of the century, a small group of physicians had proffered a similar notion and even published a short-lived journal known as the *Journal of Inebriety* (MacAndrew, 1969). At that time, however, public concern for social welfare was not widespread. Thus, those who proselytized a disease concept of alcoholism found themselves the victims of social ostracization, both within and outside of the medical profession, and the movement became dormant.

During the first half of this century, relatively little substantive clinical research had been conducted on the topic of alcohol problems. Even though the disease concept proposed by Jellinek served to organize, synthesize, and give medical credence to the scientific and naturalistic observations of his day, he readily acknowledged that his formulation lacked a demonstrated empirical foundation. To this end, he stated that "for the time being this may suffice, but not indefinitely" (Jellinek, 1960, p. 159).

Before considering Jellinek's formulation in greater detail, two points need mention. First, he clearly presented his theory as a *working hypothesis*—a plausible explanation in need of empirical validation or disconfirmation. He deliberately noted, for instance, that:

> . . . acceptance of certain formulations on the nature of alcoholism does not necessarily equal validity. I am repeating these words at this juncture lest there should be some misunderstanding on this score. (p. 159)

Unfortunately, despite Jellinek's repeated caveats there have been frequent and continuing misunderstandings and misuses of his concepts.

Second, Jellinek acknowledged that his primary intent in advancing his disease concept of alcoholism was to influence both contemporary medical practices and sociopolitical processes. More specifically, he wanted to (a) encourage medical practitioners to assume responsibility for dealing with the serious medical complications related to alcohol problems, and (b) change societal attitudes about alcoholics from a moral and legal posture to one of concern for human welfare (e.g., treatment). As a result of efforts by Jellinek and his colleagues, these goals, for the most part, have been realized.

Jellinek plainly did not view alcohol problems as a unitary phenomenon. Rather, he spoke of *species* of alcoholism. While he described five species of alcoholism in detail, he speculated that a great many other species could exist, although he felt these would be less prevalent than the first five species. In this regard, it is unfortunate that he chose to title his book *The Disease Concept of Alcoholism*, as some have erroneously inferred that he was addressing a singular definable entity.

A second, but frequent, misinterpretation of Jellinek's work is the assumption that all his species of alcohol problems incorporate a disease process. The only species for which he actually intended such a designation are those he defined as *gamma* and *delta* alcoholism. These varieties are primarily differentiated from his other species by the characteristic of physical dependence on alcohol, as indicated by the occurrence of alcohol withdrawal symptoms upon cessation of alcohol use. In fact, he distinctly specified even more restrictive boundaries for his use of the disease concept, defining a disease process as active only when an individual was in the throes of alcohol addiction (physical dependence on alcohol):

> The excessive drinker who has been using alcohol intoxication as a means of "problem solution," while still continuing that use is, in addition—and probably more prominently—using alcohol to remedy the psychological, physiological and social stresses and strains generated by heavy drinking. *Only* when this occurs in conjunction with acquired increased tolerance, withdrawal symptoms, inability to abstain or loss of control may the excessive user of alcohol be termed an alcohol addict and his drinking behavior regarded as a disease process. (1960, p. 66, italics added)

Jellinek viewed the members of AA as representing the *gamma* and *delta* species of alcohol problems. Further, he thought that these were the predominant species of alcoholism found in the United States. The other species, which he defined but specifically identified as nondisease varieties, were psychological dependence on alcohol (*alpha* alcoholism), heavy drinking resulting in physical damage—but not physical dependence or psychological dependence (*beta* alcoholism), and episodic heavy drinking without physical dependence on alcohol (*epsilon* alcoholism). If we restrict our considerations to merely *gamma* alcoholism as defined by Jellinek, however, then he would clearly be a uniformity or single-entity theorist, since he did postulate a characteristic development for this particular syndrome.

Jellinek also found no need to postulate the existence of an *a priori* distinction between alcoholics and nonalcoholics. While he did not rule out the possibility that a biochemically mediated genetic or maturational abnormality might serve as a contributing factor to the development of drinking problems, he believed such factors, by themselves, would not be sufficient to explain the development of alcoholism. In effect, his approach to the question of which individuals might be likely to develop alcohol problems was quite similar to contemporary approaches which concentrate on determining the relative importance of various identified risk factors (e.g., Cahalan and Room, 1974). While neither Jellinek nor AA postulated the existence of characteristic preexisting personality determinants of persons prone to alcohol problems (the so-called alcoholic personality), others (e.g., Mann, 1968) have proposed such a dichotomy.

In many ways, Jellinek's hypotheses about why alcoholics repeatedly engage in instances of self-damaging drinking is quite
similar to the position of AA. Both view the onset of drinking as
having psychological determinants. While the AA approach proposes
that some persons have an obsession to drink in a social normative
fashion, Jellinek preferred the broader conceptualization that such
individuals drink as a means of coping with emotional stress. He
preferred the designation of *compulsion* to describe this strongly felt
need. An often overlooked component of Jellinek's position is that *he
distinctly viewed the onset of drinking by alcoholics as a learned behavior:*

> There remains the fact that a learning theory of drinking in the
> well-defined terms of psychological discipline is essential to all
> species of alcoholism, including addiction. The learning process
> so ably described and interpreted by Conger (1956) is a prerequis-
> ite to bring about the conditions which are necessary for the
> development of addiction in the pharmacological sense . . .. The
> learning theory . . . does not exclude any other etiological
> theories; it can be complementary to any of them. Neither would
> it conflict with a disease conception of one or the other species of
> alcoholism. (1960, p. 77)

At this juncture, it should be noted that while Jellinek and AA
attributed the onset of drinking to a psychological state, other
popular conceptions are somewhat ambiguous. For instance, Mann
(1968) describes the onset of drinking in the following manner:

> With alcoholics, choice is no longer possible, whether to drink or
> not to drink, or of the amount consumed, or the effects of that
> amount upon them, or the occasions upon which drunkenness
> occurs. (p. 9)

Again similar to AA's formulation, Jellinek hypothesized that
once "alcoholic" individuals begin to drink, a specific physiological
mechanism is responsible for the continued drinking; he termed this
process "loss of control." Based on his clinical experience, he
hypothesized that physical dependence would develop in chronic
(*gamma* or *delta*) alcoholics from the mere ingestion of one or two
drinks. That is, if the chronic alcoholic attempted to stop drinking
after having consumed just a few drinks, alcohol withdrawal
symptoms would result. However, this condition could be relieved by
the ingestion of more alcohol. In this sense, then, the drinker could
not simultaneously control his intake of alcohol and avoid withdrawal

symptoms as well and was therefore experiencing a perceived "loss of control." Specifically, Jellinek defined *loss of control* as:

> [C]haracterized by *minor withdrawal symptoms* in the presence of alcohol in the blood stream and the failure to achieve the desired euphoria for more than a few minutes. These symptoms explain superficially the behavior observed in the so-called loss of control and they suggest a combination of short-range accommodation of nervous tissue with long-range acquired increased tolerance. (1960, p. 147, italics added)

He further hypothesized that loss of control emerges progressively and does not inevitably occur each time the chronic alcoholic ingests a small amount of alcohol.

Popular interpretations of the "loss of control" phenomenon frequently quote Jellinek's statement out of context. That is, when the following passage is quoted, the first seven words are usually omitted:

> *Recovered alcoholics in Alcoholics Anonymous speak of* "loss of control" to denote that stage in the development of their drinking history when the ingestion of one alcoholic drink sets up a chain reaction so that they are unable to adhere to their intention to "have one or two drinks only" but continue to ingest more and more—often with quite some difficulty and disgust—contrary to their volition. (p. 41, italics added)

Hence, Jellinek could be considered as having interpreted and given scientific credence to the AA concept. However, one of his strongest caveats accompanied his statement of an hypothesized physiological basis of loss of control: "I repeat that I regard the above merely as a working hypothesis, but one which can be tested by means of the newer techniques in pharmacology, physiopathy, and biochemistry" (p. 155).

The idea of a characteristic train of symptoms is also central to the classification of alcoholism as a disease. Building on a data base provided by the self-reports of 98 recovered alcoholics of AA, Jellinek developed a phaseology of alcohol addiction (*gamma* and *delta* alcoholism) which has endured since 1946 (Jellinek, 1946). In 1952, he slightly revised his phaseology, attributing the changes to findings derived from a more detailed questionnaire administered to an additional 2,000 alcoholics; unfortunately, statistical documentation of this extension was not provided (Jellinek, 1952). Basically, he classified the progressive development of alcoholism into three phases

composed of a total of 43 discrete symptoms. While we will not review
the specific sequence of symptoms postulated by Jellinek, he basically
stated that individuals would first develop a psychological dependence on alcohol which then culminated in prolonged intoxications, or
"benders."

Although Jellinek did not specifically address the permanence of
biological changes in the nervous system which might occur as a result
of chronic excessive drinking, it is clear that he intended them to have
such immutability:

> . . . an "alcoholic" cannot regain the loss of control, even after
> years of abstinence the "compulsion" sets in on resumption of
> drinking . . . . there must be a grave disease process and at least its
> arrest to account for these behavior changes. (1960, p. 81)

It should be noted that an irreversibility notion is not a necessary
theoretical element in Jellinek's approach, and his theory could easily
be modified to include a proposition of reversibility—that biological
changes which result from excessive use of alcohol are largely
transient in nature and disappear over time. The idea of a reversible
disease process is commonplace in medicine.

Perhaps the single greatest point of confluence among Jellinek,
AA, and the vast majority of popular views is their total rejection of
the possibility that a person who has experienced serious alcohol
problems (particularly a person who has been physically dependent
[addicted] on alcohol) can ever again drink without incurring problems. In describing his phases of alcohol addiction, Jellinek (1952)
strongly stated that once an individual has entered the phase characterized by the development of physical dependence on alcohol
(*prodromal* phase), "It goes without saying that even at this stage the
only possible modus for this type of drinker is total abstinence"
(p. 679).

Before reviewing empirical tests of these traditional notions, we
must emphasize that *all of Jellinek's propositions discussed thus far were
founded in the retrospective self-reports of alcoholics*—mainly long-time
recovered alcoholics associated with AA. Jellinek was aware of these
limitations and even asserted that:

> By adhering strictly to our American ideas about "alcoholism"
> and "alcoholics" (created by Alcoholics Anonymous in their own
> image) and restricting the term to those ideas, we have been

continuing to overlook many other problems of alcohol which
need urgent attention. (1960, p. 35)

However, while Jellinek questioned the extension of what he viewed
as ethnocentric concepts to describe other species of alcoholism, he
cautioned time and again that his hypotheses were in need of
scientific test. On the other hand, one could easily infer with some
justification from the strength of his writings that he believed his
formulations regarding the nature of *gamma* alcoholism would be
supported and extended by empirical research.

Research conducted over the past two decades has forced a
reformulation of traditional concepts of alcohol problems. Treatment
implications suggested by empirically derived concepts often stand
contraposed to those put forth by traditional concepts. In this regard,
the behavioral studies reported in this book were empirically derived
and constitute part of the conceptual reformulation of alcohol problems. The issues involved can be better understood with an understanding of how radically these studies depart from tradition.

A CONCEPTUAL REFORMULATION

Among the benefits derived from traditional concepts, and
Jellinek's work in particular, was a rising public and professional
concern for alcoholics. For the first time, significant attention was
accorded to the study of alcohol problems by the scientific community. This attention was coupled with the advent of behavioral research
on alcohol problems. In the early 1960s, Jack Mendelson (1964) and
his colleagues pioneered the key studies in this area. Instead of
depending upon the retrospective self-reports of individuals once
physically dependent on alcohol, Mendelson and his co-workers
explicitly studied the use of alcohol by alcoholics in an experimental
setting. The enormous gains in knowledge which have resulted from
this kind of experimental work are voluminous. In large part, such
studies constitute the basis for the reformulation of concepts
suggested herein.

There now exists a prodigious body of scientific evidence which
contradicts traditional concepts of alcohol problems (Pattison, Sobell,
and Sobell, 1977). Except for the concept of irreversibility, which will
be discussed at length in Chapter 2, this impressive array of dis-

confirming evidence will not be discussed here. Instead, we will focus our attention on a proposed reformulation of concepts of alcohol problems based on the evidence available to date. Recognizing that not everyone would agree with each and every statement of traditional concepts of alcohol problems as just presented, we also acknowledge that there will be differences of opinion with the proposed, albeit tentative, reformulation of concepts. Nevertheless, current evidence suggests that new conceptualizations of the nature of alcohol problems will most likely incorporate the following major components.

The search for evidence of uniformity or homogeneity among persons having alcohol problems has, for the most part, been futile (Barry, 1974; W. R. Miller, 1976). The evidence, however, does suggest an alternative view that *alcohol problems subsume a variety of syndromes defined by drinking patterns and the presence of adverse physical, psychological and/or social consequences of that drinking*. That is, the one commonality which pervades all varieties of alcohol problems is tautological in nature—persons suffer adverse consequences related to the use of alcoholic beverages. Furthermore, there appears to be no clear preexisting dichotomy between persons susceptible to alcohol problems and persons not susceptible to such problems, and it appears that *any person who uses alcohol could under appropriate circumstances develop serious alcohol problems*. A variety of risk factors may contribute to a differential susceptibility to alcohol problems; however, these factors taken in isolation seldom appear sufficient to precipitate problems (Cahalan and Room, 1974).

The use of alcohol by an individual can have a broad range of outcomes, from no known adverse consequences to severely pathological sequelae. In fact, current evidence suggests that while some individuals in our society frequently experience minor alcohol problems, those occurrences are not necessarily predictive of increasingly severe problems (Cahalan and Room, 1974; Clark and Cahalan, 1976; Fillmore, 1974; Goodwin, Davis, and Robins, 1975). Moreover, *the development of alcohol problems by individuals appears to follow variable patterns over time and does not necessarily progress to severe or fatal states*. A progressive development of problems often occurs in a superficial sense, in that social problems and awareness of adverse consequences due to drinking often precede the explicit development of physical dependence on alcohol by an individual (Orford and Hawker, 1974). However, in many cases alcohol problems do not follow a progressive pattern of increasing severity. To this end, alcohol problems have been reversed through both naturalistic and therapeutic processes (see Chapter 2).

Assuredly, *with the continuous drinking of large doses of alcohol over an extended period of time, a process of physical dependence on alcohol will occur* and eventually will be manifested as an alcohol withdrawal syndrome upon the cessation of drinking (Gross, Lewis, and Hastey, 1974). Still, even for chronic "alcoholics" scientific investigations have determined conclusively that the consumption of small amounts of alcohol by such individuals does not initiate either physical dependence or a physiological need for more alcohol (Engle and Williams, 1972; Paredes, Hood, Seymour, and Gollob, 1973; and Sobell, Sobell, and Christelman, 1972). Therefore, Jellinek's loss of control concept (the development of physical dependence) remains viable, except that physical dependence (loss of control) is not initiated until large doses of alcohol have been continually ingested by an individual for, typically, from two to five days. Prior to that time, however, the individual may cease drinking without having to endure significant withdrawal symptoms.

As might be expected, this evidence is strongly related to studies investigating the reversibility of alcohol problems. It has been amply demonstrated that *recovery from alcohol problems bears no necessary relation to abstinence, although such a concurrence is both frequent and desirable* (Pattison, 1976). In this regard, *alcohol problems are often interrelated with other problems of life functioning*. For instance, cases have been reported where an individual has attained abstinence but has deteriorated substantially in other aspects of life health (Gerard, Saenger, and Wile, 1962). In view of the somewhat strong interrelationship between alcohol problems and other life problems, treatment should obviously address the multiple life health needs of each individual. Similarly, treatment outcome evaluation should measure changes in multiple areas of life health as well as drinking behavior.

The important differences between traditional and empirical concepts of alcohol problems are reflected in their implications for treating individuals who have alcohol problems. In large part, the reader will recognize that some of the commonly accepted implications of traditional concepts for the treatment of alcohol problems have resulted from popular interpretations of those concepts and not from their original sources. Likewise, *it is also important to prevent the inappropriate use of empirically derived formulations.*

DIFFERENCES BETWEEN TRADITIONAL AND EMPIRICALLY DERIVED CONCEPTS

One of the most perplexing indirect effects of traditional concepts involves a reification of Jellinek's disease formulation. Although Jellinek advanced his formulation for sociopolitical and medical reasons, he clearly did not view his hypotheses as validated, stating "For the time being, this may suffice, but not indefinitely" (1960, p. 159). While Jellinek considered his views as working hypotheses, others have interpreted his views as being scientifically definitive. For instance, Johnson (1973) has unequivocally stated that "alcoholism is a progressive, irreversible, and often fatal, disease" (p. 3). In a more influential volume, Mann (1968) has demonstrated a skillful blending of the scientific authority represented by Jellinek with the lay formulations of alcoholism as developed by AA:

> Alcoholism is a disease which manifests itself chiefly by the uncontrollable drinking of the victim, who is known as an alcoholic. It is a progressive disease, which, if left untreated, grows more virulent year by year, driving its victims further and further from the normal world, and deeper and deeper into an abyss which has only two outlets: insanity or death. Alcoholism, therefore, is a progressive, and often fatal disease . . . *if* it is not treated and arrested. But it can be arrested. (p. 3)

Robinson (1972), among others, has discussed the consequences of reifying the disease concept of alcoholism. He concluded that the general acceptance of this ill-defined notion has probably led to the development of false expectations about the nature of alcohol problems, their treatment, and their prognosis. At times, this reification has even appeared to function so as to hinder innovation and perhaps impede the development of more adequate and comprehensive services for individuals with alcohol problems. For instance, the need to develop appropriate services for persons experiencing minor problems with alcohol has been largely neglected or ignored. Moreover, explorations of alternative treatment goals to abstinence for some individuals with alcohol problems have on occasion been demeaned as reprehensible. For example, at a major scientific conference on alcoholism Madsen (1973) derogated those pursuing non-traditional conceptualizations in this manner: "Fortunately, these moralistic dogmatists are but a tiny minority in the field of alcohology despite the large noise they produce." The National Council on

Alcoholism, in a 1974 press release, protested that reports of research findings that some individuals who have had serious alcohol problems were able to recover and to drink in a limited, nonproblem fashion, were "misleading and dangerous." This type of rhetoric and allegiance to theoretical positions does little to encourage progress in the scientific study of alcohol problems. In fact, it can discourage innovative research developments. Ultimately, conceptualizations about the nature of alcohol problems will not be personally, anecdotally, or politically derived. Furthermore, no amount of excoriation of empirical research will fully elude the basic facts which all valid conceptualizations must eventually explain. In summary, an unintended but nevertheless potent consequence of traditional concepts has been their reification. Notions presented by Jellinek as hypotheses in need of scientific test have been treated by others as though they were demonstrated facts and have been offered as evidence supporting popular beliefs. Similarly, some individuals have developed an inordinate rigidity in defense of these reified ideas.

Several other problems have resulted from the widespread, but nevertheless erroneous, acceptance of unsupported traditional concepts. While discussed at length in several other publications (Pattison, *et. al.*, 1977; Sobell and Sobell, 1974; Sobell and Sobell, 1975a), briefly enumerated they include:

1. A reified "sick" role for the "alcoholic," which considers alcohol problems to have a primarily biological origin and to be susceptible to change only as a result of medical intervention. It has even been speculated by Roman and Trice (1968) that an individual's early acceptance of that role might even precipitate the development of more serious alcohol problems.

2. The notion of loss of control (physical dependence) occurring after ingestion of simply a small amount of alcohol may at times function as a self-fulfilling prophecy.

3. Given the implicit and generally accepted meaning which the term "alcoholic" has acquired, some individuals might unduly "deny" having any alcohol problems, based on a resistance to adopting the societal definition of an "alcoholic"—one who can never drink again.

4. Treatment services for individuals who have relatively minor alcohol problems are almost nonexistent. In view of traditional beliefs this may be partially a result of viewing alcohol problems as having an unalterably progressive development. Inasmuch as this is so, most of the existing treatment services in current alcohol programs are

inappropriately intense. That is, they are oriented only toward treating the chronic drinker.

5. Primary prevention campaigns have concentrated on describing the supposed characteristics of "alcoholics" and symptoms of "alcoholism," rather than on educating people so that they can make more responsible decisions regarding the use of alcohol in their own lives.

6. The idea that complete abstinence is the only legitimate criterion of recovery from alcohol problems forces many in the alcoholism field to ignore the important concept of varying degrees of recovery, especially over time, and, further, to ignore the interrelationship of drinking behavior with other life health functions.

7. The traditional notion of "alcoholics" never being able to drink without incurring problems may have produced unrealistic treatment expectations among those in the field. Accordingly, then, drinking and events which surround such drinking might never surface for fear of reprisal for not complying with the goal of abstinence.

CONCLUSION

The remainder of this book must be interpreted within the context of (a) the unique place of alcohol in our society (this is the only social or health problem which can claim birthright to two constitutional amendments), (b) prior humanitarian and sociopolitical efforts to help persons with alcohol problems (which resulted in wide-spread acceptance of a set of reified but now largely invalidated concepts about the nature of alcohol problems), and (c) the ever present need to improve our empirical knowledge about alcohol problems and their treatment. This book can be best understood when approached with an open mind and with the knowledge that further research is needed. As further scientific evidence is gathered, our ideas about alcohol problems will undoubtedly require revision. It is hoped that our gain will be a better understanding of this recalcitrant clinical problem.

CHAPTER 2

Alternatives to Abstinence

A DEPARTURE FROM TRADITION

The question of whether alcoholics can successfully engage in non-problem drinking has been a subject of heated debate, with arguments more often based on personal beliefs than on scientific evidence. Published reports of successful drinking outcomes by alcoholics have been continually derogated; in addition, the publication of such research has been labeled as irresponsible, perhaps unethical, and serving no useful purpose. Are these reactions reasonable and prudent? Such a determination can be made only by examining the existing evidence.

"ONCE AN ALCOHOLIC, ALWAYS AN ALCOHOLIC!": TRADITION CONTRADICTED

One consequence of rigidly adhering to generally accepted, although unsupported, positions in the alcohol field has been that many areas in need of investigation have been seriously neglected. Perhaps the most neglected area involves reports of resumed non-problem drinking by individuals once labeled "alcoholic." Certainly, one of the most entrenched beliefs in the alcoholism field is the idea that alcoholism is irreversible. The statement most exemplary of this position is "once an alcoholic, always an alcoholic!" This statement implies that once a person who has been physically dependent upon alcohol stops drinking, any further drinking by that person will over time inevitably lead to increasingly severe consequences. A necessary implication derived from this belief is that complete abstinence is the only feasible and ethical treatment objective for an alcoholic and anyone considered to be a developing alcoholic. However, this traditional belief has been repeatedly and multiply contradicted by a growing body of empirical research.

A recent review of the alcoholism literature by Pattison *et al.* (1977) presents a tabular presentation of 74 studies which report that *some* identified alcoholics have successfully demonstrated an ability to resume nonproblem drinking. (A bibliographic listing of these studies follows the References section of this book.) That review documents that the existing body of evidence is not only substantial, but includes a large number of reports about individuals who by the traditional taxonomy were unequivocally diagnosed as "alcoholic." Furthermore, since that review was prepared, 6 additional studies have been presented which document that some alcoholics can return to non-problem drinking (Armor, Polich, and Stambul, 1976; Harris and Walter, 1976; Orford, Oppenheimer, and Edwards, 1976; Pomer-leau, Pertschuk, and Stinnett, 1976; Popham and Schmidt, 1976; Vogler, Weissbach, and Compton, 1977). While it is not the intention of this book to review this myriad of studies, a number of interesting aspects of these data merit mention.

More than half of the 74 studies reported that their subjects were chronic, or *gamma*, alcoholics (Jellinek, 1960). This is an extremely important point, as *gamma* alcoholics, by definition, have experienced "loss of control" and physical dependence on alcohol. Further, one-third of the studies reported a follow-up length of at least 24 months. This is significant in view of current research findings which suggest that an 18- to 24-month follow-up interval is necessary for deriving reliable conclusions about treatment outcome data. While the number of subjects in the separate studies varied from single cases to as many as 893 subjects, information was collectively reported on a total of 11,817 subjects. Of these, 18.25% ($N = 2,157+$) were reported to have successfully engaged in nonproblem drinking after treatment. Interestingly, only 10.4% ($N = 1,234$) were reported to have been totally abstinent throughout the reported follow-up interval.

The recent proliferation of nonproblem drinking studies is most notable when publication dates are temporally analyzed. Only 7 of the 74 studies had been published prior to 1960. Over the next decade, 32 studies were reported, including three with an explicit treatment goal of controlled drinking. Most conspicuously, however, 35 of the studies were published during the present decade, including 14 with an explicit treatment goal of controlled drinking. Perhaps paramount among all other considerations is the fact that the vast majority of the 74 studies were *follow-up reports of treatment programs which had a specified treatment goal of total abstinence*. Thus, in those studies, the finding of nonproblem drinking was serendipitous. Clearly, it would be difficult to accuse the authors of those studies of finding treatment outcomes which matched their expectations or preconceptions.

The 74 studies reporting nonproblem drinking outcomes included follow-up of both inpatient and outpatient treatment programs. In fact, some of the reports derived from follow-up studies of alcoholics who had never received any treatment. Of those studies reporting treatment outcomes, the primary treatment modality (21%) associated with nonproblem drinking outcomes was behavior therapy.

In summary, these data constitute a substantial body of evidence indicating that with or without treatment, and under various treatment conditions, some proportion of alcoholics do change their drinking behavior from pathological, self-damaging drinking to some type of nonproblem drinking. Taken collectively, this large body of data directly contradicts the traditional conceptualization that "once an alcoholic, always an alcoholic."

A NEW LOOK AT AN OLD PROBLEM

Until recently, traditional concepts in the alcohol field have dictated and dominated both the treatment processes and the interpretations of outcome results. For example, traditional concepts put forth a dichotomous view of possible treatment outcomes for alcoholics—abstinent or drunk. If one accepts traditional concepts without question, then the only possible logical view of recovery is abstinence. Unfortunately, this orientation often forces alcohol treatment providers to view any drinking which occurs during or after treatment as representing treatment "failure." Interestingly, a binary view of recovery is seldom found in other health-related fields. That is, recovery from depression or pneumonia is not viewed as an "all-or-none" phenomenon, but rather in terms of degrees of recovery. The recent empirical evidence in the alcohol field suggests the value of a similar view of recovery from alcohol problems— evaluating outcome as reflecting degrees of improvement or recovery. In a related regard, *the emerging concepts of alcohol dependence*

suggest the use of a single drinking treatment goal for all individuals with
alcohol problems—a reduction in drinking to a nonproblem level. For many,
such a reduction might be achieved only through total abstinence,
while for others it might be accomplished within the context of
nonproblem drinking. Clearly, this objective directs our attention to
the *consequences* of any and all drinking.

Until 1970, nonproblem drinking was seldom pursued as a
legitimate and viable treatment objective for some alcoholics. The
reasons for this are twofold. First, as discussed earlier, traditional
concepts do not allow the consideration of nonproblem drinking as a
possible outcome. Second, the lay and professional alcohol communities have typically reacted hostilely to reports of nonproblem
drinking, at times suggesting that the communication of scientific
findings be suppressed. An exemplary case of such reaction occurred
when a study was published by D. L. Davies (1962) reporting the
results of a follow-up assessment of alcoholics who had been treated at
the Maudsley Hospital in London. In his report, Davies noted that 7
of 93 (7%) former "alcohol addicts," followed up 7 to 11 years after
discharge from treatment, were found to have been drinking "normally" for the better part of those years. An unprecedented barrage
of commentary, mostly critical, was directed at his article, and
eventually these comments appeared as a special supplement to the
Quarterly Journal of Studies on Alcohol (Davies, 1963). Most of the
critiques made it appear as if Davies had committed an act of heresy,
rather than having objectively published the findings of a scientific
investigation of treatment outcome.

Given the reaction to Davies's article, and the strongly held belief
by the lay alcoholism community that alcoholics cannot return to
nonproblem drinking, it is not surprising that for the next decade
most researchers and scientists chose to remain far removed from this
topic. While it is now apparent that nonproblem drinking outcomes
following treatment in traditional abstinence-oriented programs are
not as rare as once thought, reactions tantamount to the Davies
episode have recently occurred with the publication of what has come
to be known as the Rand Report (Armor *et al.*, 1976).

Why in 1976 was the reaction to reports of nonproblem drinking
as strong, if not stronger, than when Davies published his results in
1962? One might surmise that early reports of nonproblem drinking
were viewed not only with great skepticism but as studies which would
find no credence or support among either the lay or scientific
communities. Understandably, one would expect many alcohol

treatment providers to be initially skeptical of early reports of nonproblem drinking, simply because the majority of those therapists had ostensibly never witnessed other than a transient resumption of nonproblem drinking. In a related regard, since the majority of treatment programs do not use an explicit treatment goal of nonproblem drinking or consider such drinking by their clients to be possible, it might be expected that clients who successfully achieve nonproblem drinking would be unlikely to maintain contact with these programs. Hence, many individuals who otherwise would be evaluated as successful in terms of nonproblem drinking might well go unnoticed in traditional treatment programs.

Another popular explanation offered by some traditionalists to explain early reports of nonproblem drinking by alcoholics is the allegation that those persons who are able to return to some type of limited nonproblem drinking were not "real" alcoholics, but rather "pseudo-alcoholics" (Lemere, see Davies, 1963). The argument of misdiagnosis continues to be in vogue (Weisman, 1975), even to explain drinking by individuals who have been at one time physically dependent on alcohol. Such reasoning, however, is specious and tautological, since there is no way of *a priori* identifying those individuals who can resume drinking. This circuitous logic, consisting essentially of a *post hoc* relabeling of cases which do not conform to traditional expectations, is but one of many explantations offered in opposition to the numerous reports of nonproblem drinking by alcoholics.

A more indirect way of discounting evidence of nonproblem drinking is to suggest that these data merely reflect precursors to a full alcoholic relapse. Thus, while it is sometimes acknowledged that some alcoholics can drink in a nonproblem manner for limited periods of time, this recovery of control is viewed as a temporary sojourn before uncontrolled drinking ensues. In other words, it is stated that although alcoholics have been known to drink in a limited, nonproblem manner for periods of 6 months, a year, or even 10 years, this type of drinking inevitably develops into a pattern of alcohol dependence. For those who adhere to this line of reasoning, a similar counterargument can be made regarding abstinence. Namely, it is well known that many alcoholics have successfully attained periods of abstinence for as long as 6 months, a year, or even 10 years, only to reinitiate a pattern of self-destructive drinking. Obviously, arguments can be made to the effect that either treatment outcome, abstinence or nonproblem drinking, can be maintained over long periods of time, and *neither outcome precludes the possibility of relapse*. As might be expected, the relative efficacy of all treatment objectives will be determined only by clinical research and will very likely be found to depend largely on individual case circumstances.

At this time, we suggest the evidence is sufficient to warrant a consideration of nonproblem drinking as a treatment goal in cases where individual circumstances indicate that it might be attainable without subjecting the client to immediate serious risks and it is judged to be the treatment strategy most likely to be achieved. In this regard, it is seldom the case that individuals become totally abstinent following the completion of a treatment program. Similarly, we should expect that some individuals treated with nonproblem drinking objectives may also experience periods of excessive drinking. To this end, when abstinence is the goal and the client experiences a "slip," this does not imply that the treatment goal of abstinence be discarded, nor that treatment has "failed." In such cases, treatment is typically reinitiated with the objective of reacquiring an abstinent state. This orientation is equally applicable when individuals have been treated with an objective of nonproblem drinking.

INDIVIDUALIZED BEHAVIOR THERAPY (IBT): A NONTRADITIONAL APPROACH

A significant portion of this book is devoted to discussion of a large-scale clinical research project which incorporated use of a nonabstinence treatment goal for some alcoholics. The use of a controlled drinking treatment goal in the Individualized Behavior Therapy (IBT) for alcoholics study was a radical departure from traditional alcoholism treatment and stood in direct contradiction to basic tenets of the disease model of alcoholism and the beliefs of Alcoholics Anonymous. It would be an understatement indeed to say that the use of a controlled drinking treatment goal in 1970 was controversial.

At the time the IBT study was being designed, it was felt that the question of whether some alcoholics could, in fact, successfully engage in nonproblem drinking without a resumed dependency on alcohol was not heuristic but could be adequately tested using sound scientific methodology. It was held that within the context of a scientific evaluation, the traditional view that alcoholics could never drink again could be objectively examined, especially in light of the many existing published reports of spontaneously acquired nonproblem drinking patterns by former alcoholics.

In 1970, two lines of evidence supported the contention that *some* alcoholics could resume drinking alcohol without suffering a loss of control. First, considerable evidence had resulted from investigations of experimental intoxication. Shortly after the publication of Davies's article, Mendelson and his colleagues reported that they had experimentally studied alcoholics in the presence of alcohol (Mendelson, 1964). These studies constituted the first major series of research investigations which studied the drinking behavior of alcoholics in the presence of alcohol. They marked a change in the nature of the scientific study of alcoholism from procedures dependent upon the retrospective self-reports of alcoholics to a paradigm using scientific control and hypothesis testing. In one of the earliest studies, Mendelson and his colleagues reported that 10 alcoholics who had consumed up to 24 oz. of 86-proof alcohol daily for an extended period of time had developed no physiological cravings for alcohol. Since that time a plethora of empirical investigations (reviewed in Sobell and Sobell, 1975a; Pattison *et al.*, 1977) have resulted in similar findings which, taken in aggregate, directly challenge the traditional concepts of early onset of "craving" and "loss of control" (i.e., physical dependence on alcohol).

The second line of evidence that suggested some alcoholics could resume nonproblem drinking stemmed from 39 published studies reporting such outcomes. Lest the reader miss the significance of this point, these 39 studies were in the published literature prior to 1970. Furthermore, it will be remembered from our earlier discussion that the overwhelming majority of these studies did not employ a controlled drinking treatment goal.

The IBT study was the first research treatment program in the United States to explicitly use a treatment goal of controlled drinking for some alcoholics. In this regard, criteria for assigning subjects to a treatment goal of controlled drinking—predictors of successful treatment outcome using such a goal—were virtually nonexistent. Therefore, given the state of the art in 1970, the criteria by which subjects were selected for the controlled drinking treatment goal condition were specified by the research staff prior to the start of the IBT study. Recognizing that a preferred research design would have included random assignment of subjects to conditions, the use of an explicit treatment goal of controlled drinking at that time was experimental, innovative, and highly controversial. Therefore, pre-

selecting the criteria by which subjects would qualify for this treatment goal and then randomly assigning these subjects to either
experimental or control conditions allowed us to maintain the scientific integrity of the study while simultaneously adopting a cautious
posture in investigating a novel treatment approach.

Since the investigation of alternative treatment objectives to
abstinence is a relatively recent event, we still have very little empirically derived information regarding for whom such an objective
might be appropriate. Likewise, even though total abstinence has long
been the treatment of choice for alcoholics, we also know little about
for whom abstinence is most appropriate. Related to this issue,
Griffith Edwards (1970) has suggested that:

> it may be that the alcoholic of relatively sound personality who is a
> candidate for return to normal drinking, is also the very patient
> who is willing to take our advice, remain totally abstinent and thus
> deprive us of knowing his potential as a resumed social drinker.
> (p. 158)

In other words, perhaps the individual who is best able to maintain
abstinence may also be the best candidate for nonproblem drinking,
or, for that matter, the best candidate for any type of treatment
program. Current evidence regarding for whom nonabstinent treatment goals may be appropriate is considered in Chapter 7.

TRADITIONALISTS RESPOND TO THE MOUNTING EVIDENCE

On the basis of the existing evidence, the proportion of individuals who can return or have returned to nonproblem drinking is larger
than has up to now been recognized. Furthermore, in view of the
documented low rate of treatment success (usually considered as total
abstinence), we have little reason for complacency about the treatment of individuals with alcohol problems. Nevertheless, while our
knowledge about this complex and recalcitrant problem is limited,
there are some in the alcohol field who advocate that alternative
treatment methods for alcoholics and problem drinkers should not be
explored. For instance, in 1974, the National Council on Alcoholism
(NCA) issued the following position statement as a press release:

> "There have been claims that alcoholics can drink again,"
> Thomas G. Terbell, NCA board chairman said. "We view these as

misleading and dangerous." The NCA position statement further stated that: "Abstinence from alcohol is necessary for recovery from the disease of alcoholism . . . there is need for responsible research, carried out with proper controls as well as the judicious publication of results when pertinent. However, in the present state of our knowledge, we firmly believe and emphasize that there can be no relaxation from the stated position that no alcoholic may return with safety to any use of alcohol." (pp. 1–2)

The stated NCA position gives rise to two grave dangers. First, it appears that the use of the word "judicious" in the NCA statement is intended to discourage scientists from pursuing investigations into whether alcoholics can successfully moderate their drinking. More specifically, this can be seen as a significant threat to freedom of scientific inquiry. The question of whether *some* alcoholics are ever capable of resuming drinking in a nonproblem manner is hardly heuristic and, for that matter, has already been answered. More importantly at this time, the research questions which need further exploration involve determining *for whom such alternatives are possible and what methods are the most effective for attaining those outcomes.* The threat to scientific freedom of inquiry in this field is not moot, as attempts have been made to influence United States federal agencies to discontinue funding of such research. To this end, a United States congressional representative was recently quoted as stating that Congress should take reasonable steps to insure that "the small amounts of money made available by the federal government for alcohol abuse and alcoholism are properly used and awarded for scientific studies that will be helpful and not harmful to alcoholics." He further suggested that the National Institute on Alcohol Abuse and Alcoholism "will want to reevaluate outstanding grants for scientific research to see there is not a repeat of this type of damage (The Rand Report—a study limited to treatment outcome evaluation but reporting nonproblem drinking results)" (Alcoholism Report, 1976, p. 5).

The second and more imminent danger concerns what Dr. Morris Chafetz, former head of the National Institute on Alcohol Abuse and Alcoholism, has characterized as a "paternalistic" attitude toward the alcoholic among workers in the alcoholism field. This attitude can be summarized as: "I know what's best for them," or, sometimes, "They are poor misguided souls." It is indeed paradoxical and ironic that those very individuals who most loudly proclaim that one of their major objectives is to *remove* the moral stigma which considers alcoholism to be symptomatic of "weak willpower" or a "weak personality" are usually the same persons who would not trust the alcoholic to have access to knowledge about his disorder. One implication of such an attitude is that some persons might prefer to suppress the dissemination of knowledge, in order to preserve personal belief systems. If we are to have a greater interest in helping persons with alcohol problems than in serving our own personal agendas, then it is necessary to consider all alternatives, especially when there are early indications of success.

The National Council on Alcoholism and Alcoholics Anonymous have not only been the strongest supporters of total abstinence as a necessary treatment goal but also the most vociferous opponents of alternatives to abstinence. Their positions might in large part be attributable to the fact that the majority of their members are recovered (abstinent) alcoholics (Verden and Shatterly, 1971). By virtue of their recovery base, it could be argued that these individuals are greatly threatened by a treatment goal of nonproblem drinking. The spokesmen for NCA and AA, identified traditionalists, marshal their attacks in a variety of ways. While most, if not all, of their arguments are wrought with emotional and bitter overtones, they clearly lack a significant data base. Finally, we would suggest, as the traditionalists have suggested, that these kinds of attacks are divisive, unnecessary, and destructive to the overall growth of the alcohol field.

The recent release of the Rand Report (Armor *et al.*, 1976), which suggests that some alcoholics may be able to resume nonproblem drinking without relapse, elicited an unprecedented barrage of critical commentary. Even given several major methodological difficulties, the Rand Report raises some highly provocative questions. Similar to Davies's study (1962), the subjects in the Rand study had participated in traditional abstinence-oriented treatment programs. Furthermore, the Rand study used follow-up interviewers who were not associated with any of the treatment facilities. Additionally, the findings of the Rand study reflect the results of several different government-funded treatment programs. Attacks on the Rand study have ranged from allegations of unsound scientific methodology to statements that the field would have been better off if the study had not been published or the results had been suppressed. To this end, a spokesman for the National Council on Alcoholism has cited studies by Pittman and Tate (1972) and Ewing and Rouse (1976) as demonstrating that nonproblem drinking outcomes are impossible and stated that the methodological structure of these studies surpasses that of the Rand Report. Given that the NCA has been extremely critical of and negative toward all reported results of nonproblem drinking and has cautioned that there should be only "judicious publication of results when pertinent," it is only equitable that studies cited in support of their position be subjected to the same scrutiny as those studies they attack.

The first study the NCA used to marshal their attack against nonproblem drinking was by Pittman and Tate (1972), who reported the results of a follow-up investigation of 255 individuals who had been treated for alcoholism at a detoxification center from 1962 to 1964. Some subjects (experimental) had participated in an extensive outpatient program following detoxification, while the remaining subjects (control) received only inpatient care. Further details of the treatment are not relevant to our present discussion. The most significant finding reported by Pittman and Tate was that they " . . . found *no* patients who had returned to what may be called 'normal social drinking' during the follow-up period" (p. 188). These results, however, are subject to several alternative interpretations. First, while their conclusions may be fully valid for the sample they studied, this particular population may have been atypical. For instance, only 4.3% (3 of 78) of the control subjects and 11.7% (19 of 177) of the experimental subjects were found to have been abstinent for the full follow-up period. While follow-up abstinent rates for similar programs typically tend to be low, Pittman and Tate's findings may be unusually low. Furthermore, and contrary to numerous other studies, they found no evidence of "spontaneous recovery" among this sizable group of subjects.

The Pittman and Tate study, like several other studies in the alcoholism literature, is plagued with multiple methodological deficiencies. For instance, although follow-up interviews were stated as having begun "one year after the person's initial discharge from the treatment facility . . ." (p. 185), the reader is later informed that "the length of the follow-up period covered in the study ranged from nine to 32 months, the median being 12.9 months . . ." (p. 186). Thus, subjects sometimes had to recall events which had transpired over a lengthy interval. This might increase the probability of subjects' self-reports being inaccurate (see Chapter 6).

Another serious methodological and definitional problem creates much ambiguity in Pittman and Tate's discussion of their lack of evidence for normal drinking outcomes. Although several of their outcome variables were well defined and quantitative data were reported (e.g., median weekly income, frequency of biweekly attendance at AA meetings, employment status, place of residence, etc.), the authors inexplicably provided no quantitative data at all regarding the *drinking behavior* of their subjects, although they reported that greater than half of the subjects were drinking less following treatment than prior to treatment. That is, they described a "moderated drinking" outcome as simply involving at least seven months of abstinence during the "one year follow-up period." With regard to their concluding that no subjects were engaging in "normal social drinking," nowhere do the authors present their definition of "normal social drinking." Obviously, considerable disagreement might be found even among experts concerning what constitutes a "normal social drinking" pattern. The lack of definition and quantification of this most important variable—drinking behavior—forces the reader to either accept or dispute the authors' judgment, without benefit of evidence.

Without further explication of definitions and procedures, an evaluation of the validity of the Pittman and Tate study is impossible. Given the foregoing, it hardly seems likely that this study will be remembered for its comprehensibility, or that it will be considered as strong evidence in contradiction of the 80 studies supporting alternatives to abstinence.

The second study cited by the NCA as refuting the possibility of nonproblem drinking by former alcoholics was recently reported by Ewing and Rouse (1976). This study was a follow-up report of a project aimed at inculcating controlled drinking patterns in alcoholics who were recalcitrant to a wide range of traditional treatment approaches. While this study is plagued with several serious design problems (i.e., no control group was used, the single group of subjects was selected on the basis of poor prognosis, etc.) which would preclude its use as an evaluative test of *any* approach, the procedures used in reporting treatment outcome stand unmatched in their vulnerability to critical appraisal.

In order to evaluate subjects' functioning during follow-up, Ewing and Rouse used the poorest single day experienced by each subject at any point since the conclusion of treatment as the outcome criterion, rather than using monthly or cumulative functioning data. For example, consider an individual who may have been totally abstinent during the last 36 months of follow-up but experienced a minor drinking episode during the first 6 months of follow-up. This individual would be evaluated in the Ewing and Rouse study as having the poorest possible outcome score on the drinking behavior scale. Using this kind of evaluative system, even one episode of so-called "loss of control" represents the poorest possible outcome of treatment. Consequently, Ewing and Rouse concluded that *they* were unable to inculcate controlled drinking in all 14 of their patients. Stated in the manner that it was, Ewing and Rouse's conclusion is probably correct. However, to generalize their conclusions to the treatment of alcoholics by others would be a practice as unsound as using their treatment outcome evaluation procedures to evaluate other treatment studies. Suffice it to say that if Ewing and Rouse's evaluation measures were to be applied to all published alcoholism treatment studies, it is highly unlikely that any study would report other than the poorest of outcome results for most all clients.

These two studies, presented by the NCA as the strongest available evidence that no alcoholics can ever acquire a pattern of nonproblem drinking behavior, put the issues in a clear perspective. The question being debated concerns not whether some alcoholics *can* ever drink without incurring problems, but whether this evidence supports the *legitimacy* of a nonproblem drinking treatment objective for some individuals.

Finally, one further criticism emotionally but sincerely voiced by traditionalists is that alcoholics will relapse in droves following the publication of nonproblem drinking reports, as such studies are said to produce "false hopes" for alcoholics. Some traditionalists have even gone so far as to suggest that if the investigation of alternatives to abstinence is fostered, thousands of alcoholics will die as a result. Considering the evidence to date, it would appear that these efforts would be more effective if directed toward clarifying for the public that at this time we do not know for whom such outcomes are possible, nor how they might be best attained.

Interestingly, while critical of nonabstinence approaches, the traditionalists have either ignored or overlooked a most serious counterissue which relates to questions about how many problem drinkers or young people might refuse to enter into treatment because of the stigmatizing notion of alcoholism and its implication of lifelong abstinence. These, too, are questions that must be addressed by *all* those working in the alcohol field. The alcohol field clearly faces complex problems, and it would be ludicrous to expect that there will evolve one solution applicable for all people.

NONPROBLEM DRINKING OUTCOMES: UNEXPECTED CONSEQUENCES

For individuals who have been labeled "alcoholic," there presently exists a serious impediment to the use of nonabstinence goals. The social stigma of being an alcoholic is severe on this continent; but if there is a single condition which carries even more of a social stigma, it is being "an alcoholic who thinks he can drink without getting into trouble." Personally, we are aware of several individuals who were engaging in successful nonproblem drinking and who encountered unwarranted hostility and ostracism by various members of their family and community. As might be expected, it is not surprising that the recovered and nonproblem drinking individual might be reluctant to confide to others about his past drinking problems. There has been a great deal of speculation about the so-called hidden alcoholic. It is ironic that traditional concepts of alcoholism may actually be encouraging a great many persons to be "hidden ex-alcoholics."

From this standpoint, it would seem important that any treatment program using nonproblem drinking goals for clients should explicitly make them aware of the opinions inherent in the general populace about alcoholics returning to some form of nonproblem drinking. Finally, clients should be made aware and counseled about the possible resistance by friends and relatives, and also by unexpected sources, such as physicians and judges, to their drinking in a nonproblem manner.

CONCLUSIONS AND CAUTIONS AGAINST MISINTERPRETATION

The evidence from 80 studies which report nonproblem drinking by former alcoholics or problem drinkers strongly stands in direct contradiction of traditional concepts of alcoholism. At this time, given this large body of empirical data, we suggest that it is both justifiable and appropriate to recognize "alternatives to abstinence" as legitimate treatment objectives for *some* individuals with drinking problems. This is not to suggest, however, that alternatives to abstinence constitute a panacea. Furthermore, legitimizing alternatives to absti-

nence as viable treatment objectives for some individuals should not
be taken to imply that they are either appropriate or indicated for all
or even most persons with alcohol problems. Additionally, it does not
imply that all or even most persons currently working in the alcohol
field should pursue this goal with their clients.

The implications of the evidence reviewed in this chapter seem
clear. First, a realistic perspective requires an acceptance that at least
some of these findings, especially those arising from controlled
experimental studies, have a certain amount of validity. Given that
some alcoholics can learn to drink without incurring further problems, our efforts should now be directed at generating information
which would help predict which kinds of treatment objectives might
be more appropriate for which individuals. Second, this evidence is
directly relevant to the design of alcohol treatment programs. In the
past, a lack of recognition of alternative treatment objectives to
abstinence may have resulted in some individuals with alcohol problems being denied efficacious treatment. This limited array of treatment approaches may also have resulted in some individuals being
reluctant to become labeled as "alcoholic," and, more importantly,
may have served as a powerful deterrent to treatment for individuals
with less serious drinking problems.

While we can no longer afford to ignore alternatives to abstinence, we caution that *nonproblem drinking is probably no more or less
likely than abstinence to be attained simply through self-commitment.* Also,
striving toward nonproblem drinking could be highly detrimental,
should an individual use this to justify continued excessive drinking.
Therefore, like any other therapeutic procedure or goal, *nonproblem
drinking should be used only by trained and knowledgeable individuals* aware
of the methodology, benefits, dangers, and limitations inherent in
such an approach.

Nonproblem drinking, once viewed as a radical departure from
tradition, is now more than ever accepted by many in the alcohol field
as both legitimate and appropriate for *some* individuals with alcohol
problems. Basically, this acceptance has stemmed from the growing
dissatisfaction with traditional concepts of alcoholism and the mounting empirical evidence demonstrating that alternatives to abstinence
are possible and feasible.

CHAPTER 3

The Functional Analysis of Drinking Behavior

In our society, the use of alcohol is a frequently exhibited and highly complex behavior which involves multiple components. The majority (74%) of our adult population drinks, and, for the most part, this drinking is problem free. Thus, for most persons, drinking can be considered a socially normative, or prosocial, behavior. A functional analysis interpretation of the behavior of drinking alcohol suggests that drinking serves different functions for different individuals in different contexts. Hence, consistent with this approach, the fact that some people develop drinking problems and others do not is seen as dependent upon a given individual's internal and external environment, including biological and sociocultural factors, past learning history, and, of course, features of prevailing environmental situations.

At the present time, questions regarding whether alcoholism is most appropriately viewed as a disease, a symptom of underlying emotional conflicts, or a behavioral problem cannot be answered with certainty from scientific and clinical evidence (Pattison *et al.*, 1977). However, *regardless of etiology*, we do know that drinking problems are manifested as complex and broadly generalized behavior patterns. In this chapter, we describe how a functional analysis of drinking behavior can aid in developing individualized treatment strategies. In this regard, when discussing behavioral treatment approaches to alcohol problems, it is important to distinguish between more comprehensive behavioral orientations, such as the one described in this chapter, and less encompassing formulations which are limited to

31

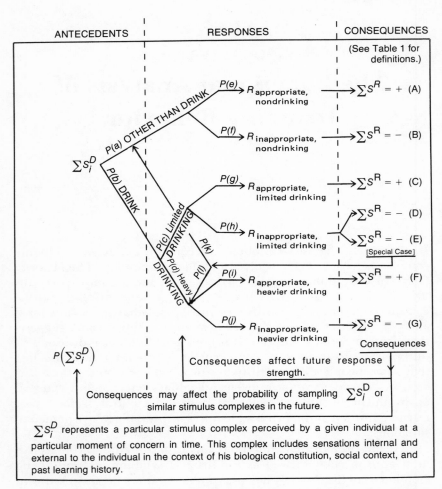

Figure 1. General model for the functional analysis of drinking. Adapted from Sobell, M. B., Sobell, L. C., and Sheahan, D. B. Functional analysis of drinking problems as an aid in developing individual treatment strategies. *Addictive Behaviors*, 1976, *1*, 127–132. Permission granted by Pergamon Press, Ltd.

superficial considerations of the drinking response and its modification (e.g., approaches limited to the use of aversive conditioning).

Applications of learning theory to the treatment of alcoholism began at least as early as 1930, long before the advent of modern behavior therapy. With few exceptions, these early approaches usually involved some form of classical aversive conditioning. Modern-day behavior therapists have continued to use classical aversive conditioning—chemical stimulants, electric shocks, or imagined aversive events—to create an aversion to alcoholic beverages (reviewed in Rachman and Teasdale, 1969; Elkins, 1975). Over the past six years, however, a variety of newer behavioral treatment approaches to alcohol problems have been developed (reviewed in Lloyd and Salzberg, 1975; P. M. Miller, 1976; Nathan and Briddell, 1977). These newer approaches share a comprehensive consideration of drinking behavior as a discriminated operant response. That is, drinking is conceptualized as occurring in certain situations and not in others (a *discriminated* behavior). More simply stated, the person whom we traditionally call an "alcoholic" is not known to drink 24 hours of the day, 365 days a year; rather, these individuals report drinking at certain times and in certain situations. Further, drinking behavior, problem and nonproblem, is hypothesized as being learned (i.e., acquired and maintained) as a function of its consequences (an *operant* behavior). More specifically, the consumption of alcohol is preceded by certain setting events (antecedents), internal and/or external, and followed by various short- and long-term consequences. If drinking behavior can be viewed as a discriminated operant response, then one would expect interventions based on learning principles to be effective in modifying that response. The first step in developing such treatment strategies lies in performing a thorough behavioral analysis of a given individual's drinking.

A FUNCTIONAL ANALYSIS MODEL OF DRINKING DECISIONS

Problems associated with the consumption of alcohol seem to be especially appropriate for behavioral analysis. For instance, drinking is a behavior that can be easily identified and quantified and has many obvious environmental antecedents and consequences. A behavioral approach to the analysis of drinking decisions appears in Figure 1 and Table 1 and will be referred to as a "functional analysis model of drinking" (Sobell, Sobell, and Sheahan, 1976). The general model in Figure 1 portrays behavioral options for a given individual within a given situation. It contrasts with single-causal models which, for example, might conceptualize that simply "stress" or "boredom" lead to problem drinking. The functional analysis model was primarily developed to simplify, classify, and arrange complex clinical data in a meaningful way. Further, since there are multiple opportunities for

Table 1. Definition of Consequence Complexes, and Examples of Responses and Consequences, to Complement Fig. 1[a]

Code	Consequence complex, definition and examples	Response examples
A	Consequences are predominantly rewarding or neutral. Typically, rewarding long-term consequences, with either rewarding or neutral short-term consequences.[b] Examples: Paycheck, promotion, praise from others, etc.	Appropriate, nondrinking: Going to work, expressing affection, being assertive, etc.
B	Consequences are predominantly aversive. Typically, aversive long-term consequences, with rewarding or neutral short-term consequences. (When such behaviors occur repetitively, short-term consequences are effective rewards in all cases.) Examples: Damaged business or personal relationships, being arrested, verbal derogation, etc.	Inappropriate nondrinking: Assault, excessive sleeping, sulking, etc.
C	Consequences are predominantly rewarding or neutral, as for code A. Examples: Social acceptance and attention, invitations to parties, etc.	Appropriate, limited drinking: Typical social drinking, religious ceremonial drinking, dinner cocktail at restaurant, etc.
D	Consequences are predominantly aversive, although control exerted by short-term rewards, as for code B. In some situations, consequences are sufficient to change ΣS_i^D complex, despite punishing elements.[c] Examples: Warned by supervisor not to drink before work again, relax but meet no new friends, etc.	Inappropriate limited drinking: Before work day, at an AA meeting, in locations where prohibited, to relax recurrent stress, to cope with loneliness, etc.
E	Similar to sequence code D, but consequences not sufficient to eliminate or make ineffective ΣS_i^D. This can lead to heavier drinking, or alternative nondrinking responses. Examples: Relaxation not sufficient, lose job, act foolish, attempting to socialize, etc.	Inappropriate, limited drinking: As for code D.

Table 1. (continued)

Code	Consequence complex, definition and examples	Response examples
F	Consequences are predominantly rewarding or neutral, as for code A. Examples: Social acceptance and praise sufficient to compensate for hangover, use of social excuse of drunkenness to rationalize flirtation, etc.	Appropriate, heavier drinking: Ritual drinking in some cultures, beer parties, drinking to drunkenness with preparations to minimize risk, such as not driving.
G	Consequences are predominantly aversive, as for code B. There is an increasing probability of highly aversive long-term consequences as physical dependence becomes more likely. Increasing threat to all areas of life functioning. *Increasing probability of being defined as Alcohol Abuse.* Examples: Being arrested, being physically ill, divorce, poor job record, death, etc.	Inappropriate, heavier drinking: Passing out to cope with stress or boredom or loneliness, morning drinking to relieve hangover, drinking to excess in any situation where performance is important, drinking to the acquisition of physical dependence, etc.

[a] The general contingency diagram model, as presented here, has been simplified and abbreviated. A more elaborate model could expand greatly on further sequence possibilities, such as the development of physical dependence on alcohol, the possibility of various arrests or medical complications, feedback loops and choice points for the termination of drinking, and so on.

[b] One common characteristic of these situations is that the response is sufficient to change the ΣS_i^D aversive intensity, deprivation levels, or other elements of the contingency so that major features of the original ΣS_i^D are either no longer present or no longer effective.

[c] In both contingency sequence codes D and E, there exists the potential for developing psychological dependence on drinking, with destructive long-term consequences influencing behavior less than short-term rewards. Sequence type *E* is particularly risky when it is followed by sequence type G—e.g., when heavier drinking *does* provide adequate sedation.

Note. Adapted from Sobell, M. B., Sobell, L. C., and Sheahan, D. B. Functional analysis of drinking problems as an aid in developing individual treatment strategies. *Addictive Behaviors*, 1976, *1*, 127–132. Permission to reprint granted by Pergamon Press, Ltd.

behavioral interventions in nearly all cases of alcohol-related problems, the model can also suggest alternative ways to effectively
promote behavior change. That is, what types of treatment strategies
and interventions are most likely to be both beneficial and efficient for
the client? Lastly, the model can also suggest where useful data might
be missing.

Unlike most other approaches to the treatment of alcohol problems, the functional analysis model as applied to drinking problems
specifically defines antecedents, responses, and consequences for any
given individual in a particular situation; that is, the treatment
approach is tailored to the client rather than vice versa. One of the
primary intents of the model is to provide a context which can help
determine which strategies of therapeutic intervention might be
maximally beneficial for a particular client. In many ways, therefore,
we are simply describing a technique for developing individual
treatment plans. The functional analysis model formed a major
component of the broad-spectrum Individualized Behavior Therapy
(IBT) study conducted at Patton State Hospital; that study is discussed at length in Chapter 5. Consideration of how the functional
analysis model was used to generate treatment plans in the IBT study
is also described in Chapter 5 in the section on Problem Solving Skills
Training.

The functional analysis of drinking is basic to all the remainder
of this book. The model has multiple advantages. One advantage of
this approach is that it demonstrates that *any* individual who uses
alcohol may engage in problem or nonproblem drinking behavior.
Further, it calls our attention to the fact that drinking is always
preceded by some complex of setting events (antecedents) and
followed by certain consequences which are related, most importantly, to the individual's own environment and the nature of the
drinking that occurs. Thus, the functional analysis of drinking, and
more specifically of problem drinking, is a highly complex and
intricate task, involving far more than consideration of the mere act
of drinking. An understanding of the breadth of this conceptualization is crucial to the development of individualized behavioral treatment plans and goals.

To reiterate, the functional analysis of drinking involves a careful
consideration of the learning history of each individual and that
person's past and present needs, resources, and deficiencies. In this
way, a treatment sequence is not only tailored to meet the needs of

each individual but also designed to maximize generalization of the treatment effects to the extratreatment environment.

WHAT CONSTITUTES A DRINKING PROBLEM

In the last few years there has been considerable discussion and little agreement regarding what constitutes "problem drinking" or "alcoholism" (Clark, 1975). Often, discussion focuses upon the frequency and quantity of drinking by an individual. For instance, the Diagnostic and Statistical Manual of Mental Disorders, Second Edition, (APA, 1968) uses the *number of times* an individual becomes drunk or recognizably intoxicated as a major diagnostic criterion. However, the adequacy of such a specification must be seriously questioned. For example, many people would say that the daily consumption of a six-pack of 12-oz. beers constitutes a drinking problem. Moreover, most people would agree that someone who drinks only one 12-oz. beer over the course of a year would not be regarded as having a drinking problem. Yet, as will be illustrated shortly, clear exceptions to these definitions exist.

The functional analysis model shown in Figure 1 dispenses with the definitional problems inherent in quantity–frequency categorizations of drinking problems. As an alternative, the functional analysis model provides an idiosyncratic definition of behavior labeled as problem drinking. *The model defines problem drinking for any individual by the total resultant consequences of that behavior.* Two examples will clearly demonstrate the appropriateness of this criterion in the assessment of alcohol-related disorders.

First, referring back to the example of an individual who drinks just one drink during an entire year, let us assume that this individual is a minister in a religious organization which proscribes drinking. Further, let us assume that this individual chooses to consume his one drink at a luncheon attended by other members of his church. Given these circumstances, should the minister order and consume just one drink, it is possible that the consequences of that drinking behavior will have resounding effects on his functions within the church, as well as on his social relationships with his parishioners. On the other hand, for most persons, ingestion of a single drink in a social setting would rarely constitute a problem. Thus, it is necessary to recognize that what constitutes a problem for one individual may not be a problem for another. That is, *drinking problems may be social determined*.

The second example involves a person with no prior history of alcohol problems who drinks a six-pack of 12-oz. beers in the confines of his home over a one-hour period. If this individual were to do nothing else but retire to bed after drinking, it is unlikely that this drinking would incur deleterious consequences. However, should this same individual decide to drive immediately after consuming the six-pack of beer, he puts himself at risk of being arrested for drunk driving. The possible consequences of a drunk-driving charge include jail time, loss of driver's license, legal fees, increased insurance costs, and so on. This example makes obvious the fact that a drinking problem may be defined by the total resultant consequences of drinking and not just the quantity of alcohol consumed. Numerous other examples could be presented to demonstrate that the definition of alcohol-related problems varies from individual to individual in terms of the factors leading to drinking, the nature of the drinking, and the nature of the ensuing consequences. As can be seen in the above examples, alcohol-related problems are not always related to quantity–frequency considerations.

For the functional analysis model to have practical value for both client and clinician, a caveat is in order. First, an overly simplified model, limited to gross generalities, may suggest too few therapeutic strategies or else overly simplified and perhaps indiscriminately applied treatment plans. Conversely, a large and complex model, incorporating an inordinate number of variables, could provide explanations for all possible behaviors but be unwieldy for practical usage. Therefore, to be of value, the functional analysis must balance comprehensiveness and complexity with pragmatism. Used in this way, the model can serve as a framework to generate ideas for individual treatment strategies. Moreover, the model provides a structure which forces the clinician to become aware of the behavioral complexities of drinking and the possibility of unanticipated consequences.

A DETAILED CONSIDERATION OF THE MODEL

In Figure 1, the symbol $\Sigma\, S_i^D$ implies that a *complex* of discriminative stimuli (S^D) are usually present for a given individual at any given time. This symbol is preferred over a single S^D, as it indicates that most situations related to drinking involve a large number of potentially effective setting events. The discriminative stimuli complex includes both internal and external factors relative to a given individual's biological makeup, present environmental contingencies, and past learning history. The emphasis on a complex of discriminative stimuli rather than on a single stimulus factor will become more salient in Chapter 5, when we consider Problem Solving Skills Training.

The center column of Figure 1 indicates classes of behavioral options. Six major classes of possible responses are delineated. These response classes include not only the full range of alternative responses (options) for a given situation but also a symbol indicating that each response class has an associated probability of occurrence in that given situation. Relative response strength, or probability, is an important consideration, as it is indicative of the individual's learning history. Self-damaging (inappropriate) nondrinking responses are included to emphasize that the adequacy of the various response possibilities must be determined by their expected consequences. Thus, while a client may report not drinking in certain situations, closer inspection may reveal that the behavior in these situations is predominantly inappropriate or self-damaging in terms of overall consequences.

The model also provides an operational definition of the relative appropriateness of behaviors in terms of the consequences likely to follow those behaviors. The range of possible consequences of behaviors is depicted in the far right column of Figure 1 and explained in greater detail in Table 1. In all likelihood, if the current model were to be expanded we would attach probabilities of occurrence to specific consequences as well. *The relative "appropriateness" of engaging in a particular behavior in a given situation is defined in terms of the total resultant consequences (outcome)—both immediate and delayed—of that behavior.* For example, the total consequences of a certain response may define that behavior as the most appropriate option in a given situation, even though the particular option may actually have enough aversive components to be considered, in an absolute sense, as punishing (e.g., paying a $500 fine, as opposed to serving six months in jail). That is, in some situations there may be no alternative responses with totally rewarding value, in which case one would then examine the relative reward value of each alternative.

In all stages of the functional analysis model, skillful interviewing and behavioral assessment and evaluation are required for obtaining sufficient and valid clinical data. The importance of in-depth interviewing to elicit descriptions of behaviors, internal states, and environmental events has been stressed by other clinical researchers (Goldfried and Davison, 1976; Goldstein, 1975; Kanfer and Grimm, 1977; Lazarus, 1971; Wolpe, 1969).

The functional analysis model can be used to develop a profile of an individual's total life dysfunction and to gain an initial perspective of his or her immediate and long-term problems. With this in mind, a needs assessment and goals profile can then be developed with the help of the client. This problem evaluation and assessment phase forms an important prologue to long-term treatment planning. A detailed assessment and evaluation of past and present alcohol- and non-alcohol-related life health dysfunction would include, but not be limited to, the following areas of life health: physical, social, marital, legal, familial, vocational, drinking, interpersonal, and recreational. In the problem evaluation and assessment stage, as in the treatment stage, the *specificity* required by the functional analysis model clearly distinguishes this behavioral approach from traditional alcoholism treatment approaches.

In using the functional analysis model of drinking in a clinical setting, we have found that clients are more proficient at describing the stimulus situations that preceded their drinking as well as the drinking itself, as opposed to delineating immediate and longer-term consequences of their drinking. As a result, in a clinical setting it is often necessary for the therapist to more actively assist the client in interpreting and considering the long-term and total resultant consequences of various behaviors. Lastly, we must not overlook the fact that consequences of behaviors generally are multiple (occur as a complex).

IMPLICATIONS: STRATEGIES FOR INTERVENTION

Since the functional analysis model has been identified as being extremely flexible, and since specific discriminative stimulus complexes, response patterns, consequence complexes, and the modification of selected behavior patterns are identified differently for different individuals, the timing and application of various intervention strategies is critical. For instance, various behavioral techniques, such as systematic desensitization, relaxation training, and discrimination training, can be used, when indicated, to modify the stimulus complex. On the other hand, for some clients merely performing a behavioral analysis of a given situation may have therapeutic benefit. That is, sometimes simply becoming aware of how certain situational factors influence one's behavior may be sufficient for an individual to modify or avoid those situations. Similarly, the information which may accrue from simply recognizing the immediate and delayed consequences associated with drinking and other behaviors may have some direct and immediate implications for a client. For example, clients are often unaware of the powerful influence of short-term consequences on their behavior. Additionally, when behaviors and situations are specified as precisely as possible, and vague terminology such as "dependency needs," "self-destructive needs," or "alcoholism" are avoided, problems may become less mysterious for clients.

An increased awareness of the delayed consequences of certain behaviors may provide the clients with a better basis for evaluating their actions. For example, consider the client who drinks in a self-damaging manner when things are described, in the client's terms, as "going well." One possible explanation for this paradox is that the client may lack sufficient behavioral skills to deal with the ostensibly improved situation. In this case, the therapeutic strategy might include helping the client learn certain necessary social and financial skills to deal with his "good life." An alternative analysis of this same situation is that while the client's life may be "going good" by conventional standards, he or she may be relatively deprived of experiences which are personally rewarding; the client may experience intense boredom and lack of adventure, although leading the proverbial "good life." In such a case, drinking to excess might provide a convenient reason for departing from that life style. In this case, the client may benefit from an awareness that various sources of personally rewarding experiences are not necessarily incompatible with having a job, home, and family.

Interestingly, some clients who label themselves as "alcoholics" report situations in which they are able to drink in a limited manner and in which their behavior is not self-damaging. Similarly, some clients never report drinking in particular situations, such as on the job or during the week. However, during weekends and holidays these very same individuals might become quite intoxicated. Several recent studies of experimental intoxication offer striking examples of stimulus control over the drinking behavior of alcoholics. (See Sobell and Sobell, 1975a, for a review of these studies.) These studies have demonstrated that even "chronic" alcoholics are capable of engaging in limited drinking behavior in the presence of appropriately designed contingencies. Similarly, if problem drinking behavior is under the control of discriminative stimuli, and if characteristics of a given case so warrant, the treatment goal most likely to be achieved might involve some type of limited, nonproblem drinking. In general, the functional analysis model of drinking suggests that the behavioral treatment goal for individuals with alcohol problems can be stated as a *reduction in drinking problems, to an ideal of no drinking problems*. In some cases, this ideal may be achieved without a full cessation of drinking; in other cases, even a prolonged period of abstinence may not be sufficient to fully ameliorate consequences which have resulted from previous drinking. As will be recalled from Chapter 2, a large body of literature documents that some alcoholics can successfully achieve some form of nonproblem drinking.

In terms of assessing the potential efficacy of treatment strategies, the functional analysis model can be used to great advantage. For example, a number of behavior therapy studies have concentrated their efforts upon simply decreasing the probability of occurrence of drinking responses. These endeavors have typically employed classical aversive conditioning procedures. Other techniques, such as avoidance conditioning, have selectively focused on decreasing the probability of excessive drinking responses. When a functional analysis suggests that a client has a response repertoire which includes sufficient appropriate nondrinking behaviors, then simply decreasing the probability of drinking may constitute a sufficient intervention, provided that the decrease in response strength is generalized to the client's daily environment. For these cases, aversive conditioning techniques might be of value. On the other hand, if a client lacks a sufficient behavioral repertoire for both problem identification and solution, then a more beneficial long-term strategy might include training in problem solving skills. As might be expected, in these cases, if treatment is limited to aversive conditioning, the client can be expected to still lack adequate means of dealing with problem situations. In fact, some nondrinking alternatives (e.g., physical violence) might even have substantially more damaging consequences than drinking.

In the field of alcohol studies, a long-held clinical impression is that some persons may have drinking problems because they lack appropriate emotional expressiveness or assertiveness. This will serve as a practical example for us, in that a number of behavioral technologies have been developed and used with alcoholics to assure that they possess necessary assertive skills to avoid further drinking problems. In particular, selection of a treatment strategy must take into account the ecological context within which the treatment will be employed. This point cannot be emphasized strongly enough. For example, if it is established that an individual lacks assertive skills, merely teaching that individual ways to be more assertive by use of procedures such as role playing, modeling, social coaching, role reversal, and social rewards may not, in and of itself, be adequate to insure that the newly acquired skills will generalize to the client's extratreatment environment. Some environmental situations (e.g., working for a rather authoritarian supervisor) may be such that the client may be severely punished (i.e., fired) as a consequence of the newly found assertiveness. While in many cases such an outcome may be evaluated as having long-term benefits, this is not always the case. Many times, other alternatives might offer a greater probability of a favorable resolution.

As can be readily seen, possible treatment strategies and points of intervention are *multiple,* and the choice of treatment is extremely important with respect to the ease of treatment and likelihood of success. It is important to recognize that in terms of time, effort, and modification of life style, various treatment strategies involve *differential costs for the client.* Therefore, it is often valuable to distinguish between treatment effectiveness and efficiency. An *effective treatment* is defined as one which promises a satisfactory resolution of current problems, with a high probability of avoiding similar problems in the future. An *efficient and effective treatment,* however, *is defined as including not only the attainment of goals, but simultaneously involving the least total change in life style for the client.* For example, for a given individual both an outpatient and a residential day-care program might be evaluated as equally likely to be effective in maintaining short-term abstinence and stabilizing familial relationships. However, if the client were employed full-time, participation in the residential day-care program might jeopardize that employment; consequently, in such a case outpatient treatment would be evaluated as most efficient.

Considerations of what constitutes effective and efficient treatment stem from an assessment of the client's needs, abilities, and immediate environment. When attempting to maximize combined effectiveness and efficiency, it is critical for the therapist to determine what personal costs a client can tolerate in pursuit of the treatment objectives. This is relevant to the issue of clients' compliance with treatment plans. Even the best treatment plan is of little value without the cooperation of the client. In this regard, an initial treatment strategy may be negotiated which delineates changes which the client agrees are attainable and likely to be personally beneficial. While some initial strategies may not be maximally effective, they may help demonstrate that short-term positive changes are possible. Either directly or indirectly, this may function to maintain clients in treatment. These initial strategies can then serve as a basis for the negotiated development of additional treatment strategies which may involve greater cost and commitment for the client. These issues will be discussed at greater length in Chapter 10.

FURTHER CONSIDERATIONS

The utility and practicality of a functional analysis model as applied to drinking behavior has been considered in great detail in this chapter. However, there remain a number of interesting issues and questions which follow from the proposed functional analysis model. For example:

1. Optimal intervention strategies may be oriented toward decreasing the frequency of all drinking responses, or only those comprising problem drinking.

2. At this time, it is unclear whether it would be easier for an individual who has never appropriately used alcohol to learn to drink in a nonproblem fashion, or whether that same nonproblem drinking repertoire might be achieved more readily by an individual who has had extensive experience with both problem and nonproblem drinking. It is possible that individuals who have never engaged in any nonproblem drinking might be better able to acquire a discrimination between nonproblem and problem drinking than persons who have had more varied drinking experiences.

3. The model suggests that not all drinking by alcoholics is necessarily of a problem nature, nor that all drinking by nonalcoholics is necessarily problem free.

4. In some cases, problem drinking may be a residual response which was effective at one time in avoiding or attaining certain consequences but is no longer necessary. This would occur if the original aversive contingencies no longer existed but the client was unaware of that fact. In the case of avoidance behavior, a familiar problem is that as long as that behavior continues to be emitted in what were once avoidance situations, the individual does not have an

opportunity to learn that aversive consequences no longer follow nonperformance of the criterion (avoidance) response.

The reader can easily derive additional issues and questions from the functional analysis model, and that is the very *purpose of the model—to suggest a variety of possible individual–environment relationships relevant to any consideration of drinking behavior.* Moreover, it is also the purpose of the model to insure that the dependent relationships among all phenomena are recognized.

CHAPTER 4

The Early Patton Studies

AN EMPIRICAL FOUNDATION

Earlier in the book we discussed the gradual emergence and acceptance over recent years of scientific investigations of alcohol problems.
The behavioral alcohol research studies conducted at Patton State
Hospital in California from July, 1969, through June, 1971, constituted part of the increasing attention given to the behavioral study of
alcohol problems. The next several chapters describe that entire
two-year research venture in some detail. In this chapter, we en-
deavor to illustrate how a series of seemingly diverse basic research
studies influenced the course of future research, eventuating in a
large-scale, broad-spectrum behavioral treatment approach—
Individualized Behavior Therapy for alcoholics.

THE RESEARCH SETTING, CIRCA 1969

Patton State Hospital is situated approximately 70 miles east of
Los Angeles, California. As of July, 1969, all admissions to the
alcoholism treatment program at the hospital were voluntary. Persons
requesting admission to the hospital typically had a long history of
alcohol problems and required medical detoxification. While alcohol
research studies at Patton began in 1968, this particular research
focused on classical aversive conditioning techniques. In the summer
of 1969 this orientation, however, changed to incorporate a more
comprehensive view of the learned components of drinking behavior.
All of the research studies discussed in the chapter were con-

beverages were stored in a heavily reinforced storage room located within the research facilities.

The simulated bar environment, while physically located within a state hospital setting, most certainly reflected an attempt to structure the research environment to promote increased generalization of treatment effects to the subjects' usual drinking environment. Actual photographs of the bar environment, control room, and beverage supplies are shown in Figures 3 through 7.

BASELINE DRINKING BEHAVIOR

Since drinking is the *sine qua non* of alcohol problems, the behavioral analysis of alcohol problems must begin with the precise definition of drinking behaviors. Prior to 1969, however, only a paucity of studies had reported actual observations of drinking behavior. Further, in those instances (e.g., McNamee, Mello, and

Figure 3. Simulated bar setting prepared for videotape replay. Seated is Dr. S. F. Casalaina, Director of the Alcoholism Treatment Program.

Figure 4. Simulated bar setting, front view.

Mendelson, 1968; Mendelson, 1964; Tamerin and Mendelson, 1969) drinking behavior had typically been observed during periods of chronic intoxication in alcoholic patients, sometimes extending beyond three weeks. Also, the dependent variables measured in those studies were more often physiological (e.g., blood alcohol levels) or clinical (e.g., mood state) in nature, rather than specific drinking behaviors (e.g., rate, volume). Furthermore, the only data available which described the drinking behavior of nonalcoholics (normal drinkers) were derived from survey interviews (Cahalan, Cisin, and Crossley, 1969). Thus, to our amazement, we found that the professional literature was greatly deficient in simple descriptive data about differences in drinking behaviors between persons labeled as alcoholics and those considered nonalcoholics.

While numerous literature references supported the notion that "alcoholics," by definition, drink to become drunk, such deductive logic could hardly be considered a sufficient foundation for further experimental studies. Furthermore, a determination of the specific characteristics of drinking behavior was of great importance at that time because considerable skepticism existed concerning whether or

Figure 5. Simulated bar setting showing refrigerator and curtain partition separating bar from simulated home environment.

not the drinking behavior of alcoholics was manipulable through the use of environmental contingencies. Therefore, within our research environment, two studies were undertaken to investigate the drinking behavior of both normal drinkers and alcoholics. These studies were not intended as epidemiological descriptions of drinking practices of various populations of drinkers, nor as an analogue of bar-room drinking. Rather, we had three main concerns: (a) to assess the drinking behavior of both normal drinkers and alcoholics as it occurred within this research setting, (b) to precisely measure the components of drinking behavior, and (c) to study those drinking behaviors related to *the act of becoming intoxicated,* rather than behaviors involved in maintaining drinking over a prolonged period of time. Surprisingly, none of these issues had ever been empirically examined.

Subjects in each of the two baseline studies were a group of inpatient alcoholics and a group of normal drinkers. In the first study (Schaefer, Sobell and Mills, 1971a), 16 male patients, ranging in age from 25 to 64 years ($\bar{X} = 45.4$ years) volunteered to serve as subjects.

On the average they had three prior alcohol-related hospitalizations, and all had previously experienced alcohol withdrawal symptoms. The 15 male normal drinkers who served in the study were recruited from the local community and ranged in age from 26 to 63 years ($\bar{X}$ = 37.0 years; not significantly different from the alcoholic subjects). None of the normal drinkers reported a history of alcohol-related incarcerations, hospitalizations, or other problems. Public bars were among the control stimuli for drinking for both groups of subjects. The two groups did differ significantly ($p < .05$) in educa-

Figure 6. Alcohol research control room. The video camera mounted in the simulated bar could be operated remotely from this location.

Figure 7. A portion of the beverages provided for research use by the California Alcoholic Beverage Control Board.

tion; normal drinkers had from 12 to 21 years of education ($\bar{X}$ = 16.5 years), while alcoholics ranged from 9 to 17 years of education ($\bar{X}$ = 11.4 years).

In the second study (Sobell, Schaefer, and Mills, 1972) 26 male patients volunteered to serve as subjects, as did 23 male normal drinkers, again recruited from the surrounding community. All of the alcoholic subjects had experienced alcohol-withdrawal symptoms, and as a group they had a mean of 5.8 past hospitalizations for alcohol problems. As in the first study, none of the normal drinker subjects had ever experienced any disruption of normal activities due to drinking. The average age for the alcoholics was 38.7 years, ranging from 24 to 54 years, while the normal drinkers had an average age of 29.8 years, ranging from 21 to 53 years ($p < .001$). The two groups also differed in educational level, alcoholics ranging from 8 to 16 years of education ($\bar{X}$ = 11.3 years) and normal drinkers ranging from 12 to 18 years of education ($\bar{X}$ = 15.4 years) ($p < .001$). In both of the studies, the alcoholic subjects (a) had consumed no alcohol for at least three weeks prior to the start of the study, (b) had been cleared for participation by the unit psychiatrist, and (c) had shown no evidence of severely disturbed liver function, organic brain syndrome, subnormal intelligence, or drug addiction. None of the patients used medication concurrent with the study, and none had a history of serious physical assaultive behavior while sober or drunk.

All sessions were conducted in the experimental bar environment, and subjects were usually run in groups of three. In the first study, subjects were instructed that during the 3-hour session they could consume as much as 6 oz. of 86-proof whiskey or its equivalent in alcohol content. After the study was completed, it was found that this particular procedure apparently resulted in an instructional artifact which will be discussed shortly. Consequently, in the second study, subjects were instructed: "Drink as much as you want; we'll stop you after 16 oz. or 4 hours, whichever comes first. You may stop sooner if you wish." The reason for using a 16-oz. limit, rather than unlimited drinking, was a concern for the safety of the subjects; blood alcohol levels resulting from consumption of more than 16 oz. within a short period of time could constitute a serious medical risk.

Research personnel were in the bar during all sessions and drank nonalcoholic beverages while recording data. They were instructed to concentrate on collecting data, while at the same time engaging in friendly social interactions with the subjects. This posture provided a more realistic bar atmosphere while assuring accurate recording of data. For each drink ordered, the type of drink, number of sips taken to consume it, time spent consuming it, and the time interval between successive sips were recorded on a data sheet. Following the drinking sessions, intoxicated normal drinker subjects were driven home by staff members.

Because of the instructional artifact which occurred in the first study, only the dependent variable measures of drink preference and sip magnitude were valid. It was found that while the normal drinkers preferred mixed drinks (81% of all drinks ordered) over straight drinks (15%) and beer (4%), the alcoholic subjects preferred straight drinks (60%) to mixed drinks (31%) and beer (9%). This preference difference was found to be statistically significant ($p < .001$). The first study also found that regardless of the drink type, alcoholics took significantly larger sips than normal drinkers ($p < .001$). However, normal drinkers consumed approximately the same number of drinks as alcoholics and drank with very similar temporal patterning. These comparable temporal patterns compelled us to interview subjects in both groups several days after their participation in the study. These interviews revealed that alcoholic subjects, aware that they would be allowed no further access to alcoholic beverages after their baseline session, tended to "savor" their last few drinks in order to make them last longer. On the other hand, normal drinkers reported that the imposed consumption limit of six drinks intrigued them, because they were uncertain about whether or not they could consume six total drinks in the allotted time period. Therefore, they tended to interpret the experimental instructions as a challenge and to drink either their first two or last two drinks very rapidly. This confounding variable which seemed to have been produced by these instructions was avoided in the second study.

In the second baseline study, which had a 16-oz consumption limit, alcoholic subjects consumed a mean of 15.3 total drinks, indicating that refusals of any of the 16 possible drinks were rare. By the conclusion of their sessions, most of the alcoholic subjects were quite noticeably drunk, having obvious motor impairment and slurred speech. Although many subjects experienced severe hangovers the following day, no subject manifested alcohol withdrawal symptoms as a result of the time-limited drinking session. Normal drinker subjects consumed a mean of 6.7 total drinks, with only one subject having more than 12 drinks. The difference between the mean number of drinks consumed by subjects in the two groups was statistically significant ($p < .001$). It should be noted that the number of drinks consumed by normal drinkers is likely to have been greater than the amount these drinkers would typically consume over such a time interval, considering that the drinks were free and transportation home was provided.

The difference between groups in terms of drink preference confirmed the findings of the 6-oz. study and are graphically displayed in Figure 8. When individual subject proportions of straight drinks ordered were statistically compared between the two groups, the difference was again found to be significant ($p < .001$).

Differences between alcoholics and normal drinkers in terms of sip magnitude similarly replicated the 6-oz. study. As illustrated in Figure 9, regardless of the type of beverage consumed, alcoholic subjects typically ingested approximately two to three times the volume per sip as did normal drinkers. The greatest sip size difference between the two groups occurred for mixed drinks; normal drinkers consumed such drinks with a mean sip size of 0.39 oz., whereas alcoholic subjects had a mean sip size of 1.25 oz. Thus, even when the alcoholic subjects consumed the type of drink most preferred by normal drinkers, their manner of consumption was substantially different. For all drinks combined, the difference between alcoholics and normal drinkers in mean sip size was statistically significant ($p < .001$). Figure 9 demonstrates that the difference between the two groups in mean sip magnitude was maintained over

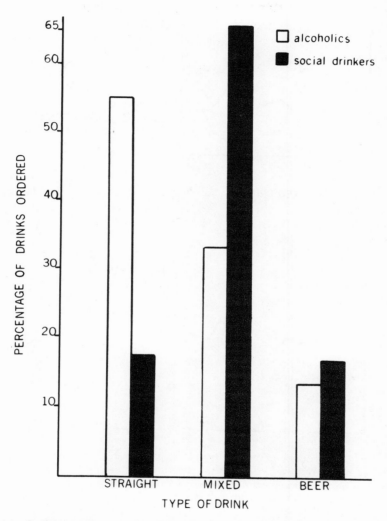

Figure 8. Drink preferences of 26 alcoholics and 23 normal (social) drinkers in the 16-oz. limit baseline drinking study.

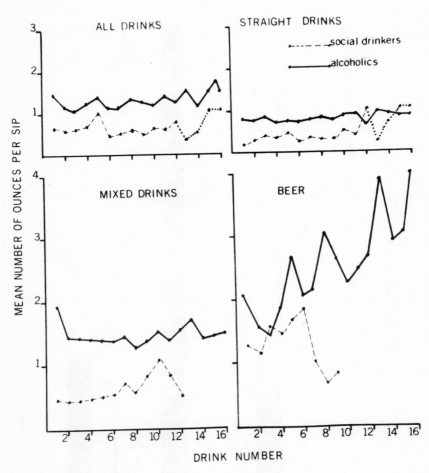

Figure 9. Mean sip magnitude for 26 alcoholics and 23 normal (social) drinkers in the 16-oz.-limit baseline drinking study as a function of drink number and type of drink ordered. Dotted lines indicate $N = 1$. Reprinted from Sobell, M. B., Schaefer, H. H., and Mills, K. C. Differences in baseline drinking behaviors between alcoholics and normal drinkers. *Behaviour Research and Therapy*, 1972, *10*, 257-267. Permission granted by Pergamon Press, Ltd.

the course of drinking, even though the values for normal (social) drinkers were computed using a base of fewer and fewer subjects as number of drinks consumed per subject increased.

As indicated in Figure 10, a large difference is clearly present between groups in terms of mean time taken to consume drinks, regardless of drink type. This difference was also statistically significant (p <.001). This dependent variable best illustrates the instructional artifact which confounded the 6-oz. baseline study. Figures 11 and 12 show the mean time per drink for the two groups of subjects in the 16-oz. and 6-oz. studies, respectively. Differences in the amount of time spent to consume early drinks in the two studies are readily apparent, with alcoholics typically consuming their first four drinks in the 16-oz. study in less than half the time they spent consuming the same number of drinks in the 6-oz. study. A detailed examination of individual normal drinker patterns in the 16-oz. study revealed no consistent temporal pattern, with 12 subjects tending to increase their time per drink as drinking progressed, 8 subjects tending to decrease their time per drink over consecutive drinks, and 3 subjects showing no definite pattern.

The finding that alcoholic subjects had a longer average intersip interval than normal drinker subjects, as shown in Figure 13, was unexpected. For all drinks combined, the difference in mean intersip interval between the two groups was statistically significant (p <.02). The apparent reversal of this trend for mixed drink data occurred only for the first few drinks ordered in a session.

Behavioral measurement, like all measurement processes, is valuable only if the measurements can be replicated. Therefore, it was vital to ascertain the reliability of the measures of drinking behavior. Circumstances did not permit us to replicate the normal drinker results; however, a replication was obtained for the alcoholic subjects in the 16-oz. study. All of the subjects participated in a second 16-oz. baseline session conducted two days after the first 16-oz. session. The results obtained were nearly identical across sessions. In the first session, the alcoholics ordered a mean of 15.3 drinks each, and in the second session they ordered a mean of 15.9 drinks each. Other measures, such as the mean number of ounces per sip and types of drinks ordered also bore a striking similarity to the results of the first session. Examples of this concordance appear in Figures 14 and 15 which respectively show mean time per drink and mean intersip times as a function of drink number and session number for the alcoholic

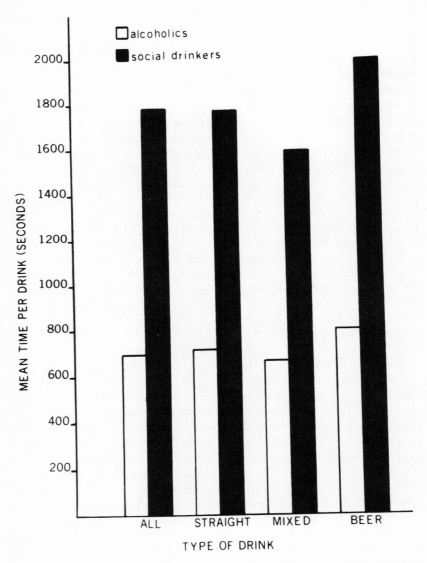

Figure 10. Drinking rates (time per drink) for 26 alcoholics and 23 normal (social) drinkers in the 16-oz.-limit baseline drinking study as a function of drink type.

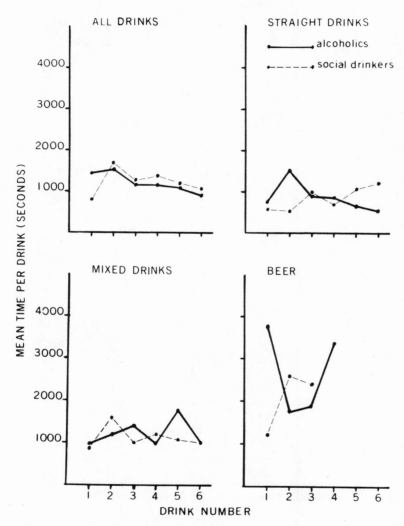

Figure 11. Drinking rates (time per drink) for 16 alcoholics and 15 normal (social) drinkers in the 6-oz.-limit baseline drinking study as a function of drink type and drink number.

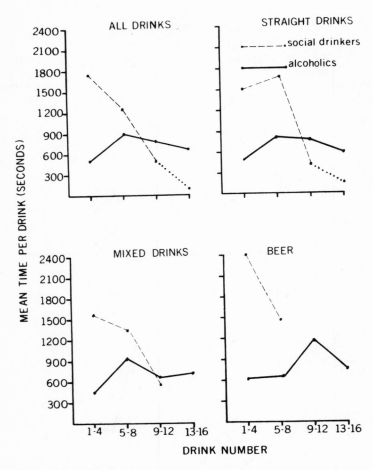

Figure 12. Drinking rates (time per drink) for 26 alcoholics and 23 normal (social) drinkers in the 16-oz.-limit baseline drinking study as a function of drink type and drink number. Means were computed from individual subject medians. Dotted lines indicate $N = 1$. Reprinted from Sobell, M. B., Schaefer, H. H., and Mills, K. C. Differences in baseline drinking behaviors between alcoholics and normal drinkers. *Behaviour Research and Therapy*, 1972, *10*, 257-267. Permission granted by Pergamon Press, Ltd.

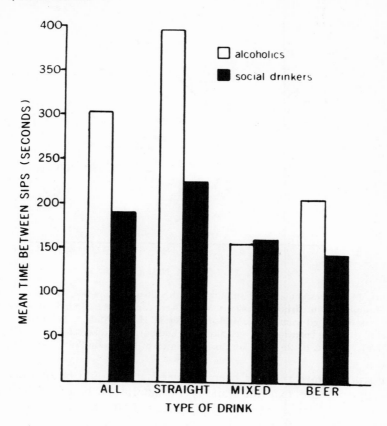

Figure 13. Sipping rates (time between sips) for 26 alcoholics and 23 normal (social) drinkers in the 16-oz.-limit baseline drinking study as a function of drink type.

subjects. We concluded from these data that reliable measurements could be obtained from alcoholic subjects within our research setting.

Combining the results of the two baseline studies, Table 2 summarizes the general drinking behavior profiles which described the drinking of alcoholics and normal drinkers within our controlled environment. Although we did not attempt to generalize these profiles to other environments, several of the problems involved in attempting to conduct an *in vivo* baseline study have been considered elsewhere (Sobell, Schaefer, and Mills, 1972). Nevertheless, some *in*

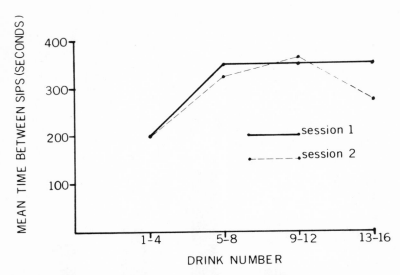

Figure 14. Correspondence of sipping rates for 26 alcoholics over two consecutive 16-oz.-limit baseline drinking sessions. Means were computed using individual subject medians. Reprinted from Sobell, M. B., Schaefer, H. H., and Mills, K. C. Differences in baseline drinking behaviors between alcoholics and normal drinkers. *Behaviour Research and Therapy*, 1972, *10*, 257-267. Permission granted by Pergamon Press, Ltd.

vivo studies have recently been reported and should be of value in interpreting the external validity of laboratory baseline findings (Billings, Weiner, Kessler, and Gomberg, 1976; Kessler and Gomberg, 1974).

Two studies by other investigators have provided a general replication of the baseline results obtained at Patton. Nathan and O'Brien (1971) studied prolonged (18-day) drinking by chronic skid-row alcoholics. Although they did not report detailed measurement of the components of drinking, they did state that their alcoholic subjects "tended to gulp rather than sip their drinks, and rarely added either a mixer or ice to them" (p. 464). More recently, Williams and Brown (1974a) reported a cross-cultural replication of the baseline studies using New Zealanders as subjects. With the exception that New Zealand alcoholics and normal drinkers both tended to prefer weaker drinks than their American counterparts, Williams and Brown found that "differences between alcoholics and normal drinkers on measures of total alcohol consumed, sip size and speed of drinking amongst New Zealand drinkers were found to be of the same order as similar differences when American alcoholics and normal drinkers were studied" (p. 293–294). This comparability of drinking behavior is striking, considering inherent cultural differences between Americans and New Zealanders.

VIDEOTAPE SELF-CONFRONTATION: A DEMONSTRATION OF THE VALUE OF SCIENTIFIC METHOD IN CLINICAL RESEARCH

The next study conducted at Patton involved relatively unobtrusive monitoring and videotape recording of the drunken behavior of alcoholics, followed by their viewing these recordings when they were

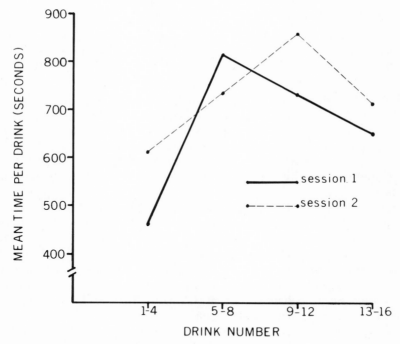

Figure 15. Correspondence of drinking rates for 26 alcoholics over two consecutive 16-oz.-limit baseline drinking sessions. Means were computed using individual subject medians. Reprinted from: Sobell, M. B., Schaefer, H. H., and Mills, K. C. Differences in baseline drinking behaviors between alcoholics and normal drinkers. *Behaviour Research and Therapy*, 1972, *10*, 257-267. Permission granted by Pergamon Press, Ltd.

Table 2. Drinking Behavior Profiles of Alcoholics and Normal Drinkers in a Research Setting[a]

Alcoholics	Normal drinkers
1. Will almost always drink more than 12 drinks within a 4-hour period.	1. Very seldom drinks more than 12 drinks within a 4-hour period.
2. Generally orders straight drinks.	2. Typically orders mixed drinks.
3. Takes a larger size sip, no matter what type of drink.	3. Takes a smaller size sip, no matter what type of drink.
4. Drinks much faster than a normal drinker; sometimes three times as fast.	4. Drinks considerably slower than an alcoholic.
5. Sips more slowly than normal drinkers but takes a larger mouthful per sip	5. Takes many rapid and small sips

[a] Adapted from Sobell, M. B., Schaefer, H. H., and Mills, K. C. Differences in baseline drinking behavior between alcoholics and normal drinkers. *Behaviour Research and Therapy*, 1972, *10*, 257–267. Permission to reprint granted by Pergamon Press, Ltd.

sober. When the study was performed, videotape self-confrontation enjoyed wide popularity in the psychotherapy literature. However, in 1970 Bailey and Sowder published a literature review which concluded that the value of videotape self-confrontation in producing beneficial behavior changes had not been adequately demonstrated and, further, that the method might even have deleterious consequences.

With these conflicting positions in mind, an experimental investigation of the efficacy of videotape self-confrontation with alcoholics was conducted (Schaefer, Sobell, and Mills, 1971b). The study was conducted in the experimental bar environment and involved 52 male alcoholic volunteer subjects. All subjects had a history of chronic alcohol problems and all had experienced alcohol withdrawal symptoms. Subjects had a mean of 5.2 prior alcohol-related hospitalizations, their mean age was 40.6 years, and their mean education was 11.5 years. Screening criteria were identical to those used for subjects who participated in the baseline studies.

Subjects were randomly assigned to one of three groups. Subjects in the first group ($N = 13$) viewed videotape replays of 30 min duration, subjects in the second group ($N = 13$) viewed videotape replays of 5 min duration, and subjects in the third group ($N = 10$)

participated in identical drinking sessions but received no videotape replay. This latter group constituted a sham-treatment condition. An additional 16 nonrandomly determined subjects comprised a statistical control group. This group was composed of subjects who had volunteered and been declared eligible for the study but for various reasons left the hospital prior to participating in the experiment; the procedures involved in conducting the videotaped drinking sessions often made it necessary to delay a subject's participation for as long as two weeks from the time he had been medically cleared. Subjects in the statistical control group differed from the other groups of subjects only in that they had left the hospital before their scheduled drinking sessions could be conducted.

Drinking sessions of 4 hours duration were conducted with groups of 3 to 4 subjects. During each session, subjects were given the opportunity to consume up to 16 oz. of 86-proof alcohol or its equivalent in alcohol content. The bartender was a patient who had worked professionally as a bartender and volunteered his services for the duration of the study. Subjects in both the 30-min and 5-min videotape replay groups were scheduled to participate in 5 drinking sessions where they would be videotape-recorded. The videotape replay sessions were scheduled to occur on the days following each drinking session. Subjects in the sham control condition were treated identically to videotape replay subjects with the exception that they were not shown any playback of their drunken comportment, and they were scheduled to participate in only 4 sessions.

An important finding for interpreting the results of this study involved attrition rates. In accordance with California law, and in keeping with federal guidelines regarding research involving human subjects, all subjects were informed that they could withdraw from participation in the experiment at any time and without a reason. Of the 10 sham control subjects, 9 completed all 4 sessions, while the remaining subject completed only 2 of the 4 scheduled sessions. In contrast, only 44% of the videotape replay subjects completed all 5 of their scheduled sessions, with approximately 14% dropping out between each successive session.

With regard to attrition rate, several points can be considered. First, the only substantial difference between subjects in the videotape replay and sham groups was viewing the videotape replays on days following the drinking sessions. Second, all subjects, including those videotaped, were aware that there was no necessity for them to consume alcoholic beverages during the drinking sessions. That is, they were aware they could determine the amount they drank, drink nothing at all, or drink nonalcoholic beverages. Rather than choosing any of these alternatives, videotape replay subjects typically requested discharge from the hospital and left within a few days of their decision not to participate in further sessions. This attrition rate was interpreted as possibly constituting indirect evidence that the video-tape self-confrontation experience was highly aversive for subjects.

By way of contrast, subjects who continued to participate in experimental drinking sessions maintained an average consumption of about 15 oz. of 86-proof alcohol per session. This occurred despite their frequent proclamations, while viewing the videotape replays, that they were never going to drink again. Subsequent to the conclusion of the study, these subjects were asked why they had continued to consume large amounts of alcohol during the sessions rather than drinking differently or not drinking at all. Typically, these subjects said they drank in such a manner because they had felt a need to aid in the ongoing "research" process.

From a clinical perspective, it was apparent to staff members that the videotape replay sessions had considerable impact on the subjects. For instance, it was not uncommon for subjects to chain smoke, sweat profusely, and exhibit many other signs of agitation when viewing their replays. These sorts of observation may have served as the basis for the strong endorsements of videotape self-confrontation proce-dures found in the clinical literature. Despite these testimonies, the effectiveness of a clinical treatment is demonstrated not by verbal proclamations of a person's intent to change, but by whether it yields any significant beneficial change in target behaviors during and, especially, following the conclusion of treatment.

In this study, beneficial changes did not occur during treatment. Even more discouraging, however, was the clear absence of any positive effect shortly after subjects left the hospital. Within 6 weeks of discharge, all 26 videotape replay subjects had returned to a pattern of heavy drinking, while 83% of sham control subjects and 75% of statistical control subjects had relapsed. While the videotape replay subjects were found to have improved slightly over a one-year follow-up evaluation period (Schaefer, Sobell, and Sobell, 1972), outcome differences among the various groups remained nonsignificant.

This study strongly reaffirmed our commitment to seek empiri-cally based answers to clinical questions. This study also serves to demonstrate the need to empirically validate all treatments, even those with appealing features (e.g., the distinct emotional impact which videotape replays had upon subjects). Moreover, the self-confrontation study fits nicely into an operant conceptualization of the drinking behavior of alcoholics. In particular, was it possible that the videotape replay sessions themselves functioned as an antecedent to the subjects' post-discharge drinking? In this regard, the follow-up data showing no difference among groups were not particularly valuable. On the other hand, 14 of the 26 videotape replay subjects had become drunk within 24 hours of discharge from the hospital, compared to a somewhat lower proportion of control subjects. At the very least, these findings supported the need for scientific clinical research and, further, compelled us to consider in greater detail the possible influence of environmental variables over drinking behavior. Finally, given the finding that videotape self-confrontation, when used in isolation, was of no particular value, and possibly even detrimental, we then became interested in whether the method could be effectively used in concert with other methods. For instance, Paredes, Ludwig, Hassenfeld, and Cornelison (1969) suggested that the technique might be effective as a way of motivating persons to participate more intensely in treatment. In retrospect, at that time the use of videotape self-confrontation had clearly raised more questions than it had answered.

MODIFYING DRINKING BEHAVIOR

One of the most steadfast elements of traditional concepts about the nature of alcohol problems has been the implicit assumption that the drinking behavior of alcoholics was a phenomenon beyond their control—the alcoholic could either be victimized by his drinking or avoid alcohol entirely. In view of the disparity between traditionalists who vehemently argued that the drinking behavior of alcoholics was unmodifiable and the experimental data which suggested quite the contrary (discussed in Chapter 2), it was of great interest to determine the extent to which environmental contingencies could shape the drinking behavior of alcoholics to approximate the drinking of normal drinkers.

The third major experiment (Mills, Sobell, and Schaefer, 1971) conducted at Patton was the first study performed in the United States to explicitly investigate the modifiability of alcoholics' drinking behavior. The study concentrated on shaping three aspects of the drinking behavior of state hospital alcoholics. The three aspects of drinking behavior selected for modification had appeared as major differences between the drinking of alcoholic subjects and normal drinkers in the two baseline studies described earlier. These target behaviors were: (a) changing drink preference from straight drinks to mixed drinks, wine, or beer; (b) changing the consumption pattern from one of gulping to one of sipping (decreasing sip magnitude); and (c) decreasing the total number of drinks consumed during a session. An electric shock avoidance schedule was chosen as the shaping method inasmuch as (a) the drinking behavior of alcoholics was reputed to be highly difficult to influence, and (b) avoidance schedules seemed appropriate for training in self-control (whether or not aversive contingencies applied would be determined solely by the subject's drinking behavior).

Thirteen alcoholic patients volunteered to serve as subjects in the study, and all met the subject selection criteria described for the earlier studies. The subjects had a mean age of 47.5 years, a mean education of 11.1 years, and a mean of 6.4 prior hospitalizations for alcoholism. Each subject was scheduled to participate in a total of 14 experimental sessions, each having a maximum duration of 2 hours. Sessions were typically conducted daily on weekdays.

All subjects were given a complete explanation of the avoidance contingencies prior to the first session of the study. During sessions, finger electrodes were attached to the thumb and ring finger of the subject's nondominant hand. Electrodes were connected by electrical cord to receptacles mounted on the outer underside of the bar. Shocks were administered, when appropriate, via three-position toggle switches. The shocks were delivered by an 800 V generator. Each of the shock generators could be controlled by either of two toggle switches wired in parallel, one mounted on the subject's side of the bar and one on the bartender's side of the bar. Shocks were generally administered by female assistants who sat next to each subject during most of the sessions. On the few occasions when one or both of the assistants could not be present, shocks were administered by the bartender. The subject's drinking behavior and the number of shocks received during each session were recorded by either the bartender or the assistant.

Two electric shock levels (1.5-sec duration) were used. A mild shock contingency was set at just above the subject's pain threshold, and a strong shock intensity was set 30% above the subject's pain threshold. Shocks seldom exceeded 5 mA. Both the delivery and the intensity of shocks administered were a direct function of the subject's drinking behavior. Disregarding avoidance contingencies, subjects could order up to five standard drinks (each drink containing the equivalent of 1 oz. of 86-proof alcohol) of their choice per session. As shown in Table 3, subjects could totally avoid shocks for the first three drinks of a session if they ordered weaker drinks and sipped these drinks. A sip was considered to be approximately one-seventh of the total volume of a given drink, and glasses were demarcated so that sip size could be easily estimated. When a subject emitted only one inappropriate drinking behavior—that is, either ordering and sipping a straight drink or gulping a mixed drink—he was administered a mild-intensity shock. If the subject emitted two inappropriate drinking behaviors—i.e., gulping a straight drink—he received a strong-intensity shock. It should be noted that even if subjects ordered a straight drink, they were under no obligation to consume that drink. After subjects had consumed three drinks during a session, a consumption-limit contingency took effect. Thus, if the subject ordered a fourth or fifth drink, he received a strong-intensity shock. He also received strong-intensity shocks each time he touched the glass, with each shock terminating when he released the glass. Nevertheless, early in training several subjects ordered and consumed both a fourth and fifth drink.

Over the sessions, the amount of social pressure on subjects to order a fourth and fifth drink was gradually increased. In early

Table 3. Shock Avoidance Contingencies During Drinking Modification Sessions[a]

Shock intensity	Drinks Number 1–3	Drinks Number 4–5
Strong	Orders straight drink and gulps.	Orders or consumes any alcoholic beverage
Mild	Either orders straight drink and sips or orders mixed drinks and gulps	
None	Orders mixed drink and sips	Orders nonalcoholic beverage

[a] Adapted from Mills, K. C., Sobell, M. B., and Schaefer, H. H. Training social drinking as an alternative to abstinence for alcoholics. *Behavior Therapy*, 1971, *2*, 18–27. Permission to reprint granted by Academic Press, Inc.

sessions, the subject was merely asked if he wanted another drink and his verbal refusal was sufficient to terminate the session. In later sessions, if the subject refused a drink, the bartender, research staff members, and/or other patients purposefully attempted to persuade the subject to order another drink. In still later sessions, if the subject continued to refuse to order additional drinks, a drink was poured and the session terminated only after the subject voluntarily left the bar without consuming the drink. The criterion for increasing social pressure was fulfilled whenever subjects had successfully refused additional drinks over 2 consecutive days. Whenever subjects terminated a session with consumption of three or fewer drinks, they were verbally praised by the bartender and others in the bar.

Over the course of the first 6 sessions, a clear dichotomy among subjects emerged. Four subjects showed an exaggerated compliance with the contingencies; they never ordered straight drinks, never ordered more than three mixed drinks, and consumed their drinks in exceedingly small sips, sometimes taking as many as 30 sips per drink. This pattern could be interpreted in one of two ways: an exaggerated avoidance of electric shock, or nonserious participation in the experiment (taking advantage of the contingencies to consume free drinks while in the hospital). A combination of both factors could also explain this pattern. Whatever, all 4 subjects left the hospital against medical advice prior to the start of their seventh session, and 3 of the 4 subjects resumed heavy drinking within 2 days after leaving the hospital.

On the other hand, the other 9 subjects demonstrated a distinct pattern of shaping over the 14 sessions. Initially, these subjects ordered an average of nearly 4 drinks per session, and approximately half of the drinks ordered were straight drinks. By the fifth session, however, most of these subjects were ordering three or fewer drinks per session, the majority of which were mixed drinks. Their sip magnitude also gradually decreased over sessions.

This study did not attempt to establish generalization of the shaped drinking behavior after hospital discharge. Although treatment outcome results were somewhat positive, the study's major purpose was to demonstrate that the drinking behavior of chronic *gamma* alcoholics was modifiable within a laboratory setting. In conclusion, this study strongly suggested that within a controlled environment and given various contingencies, even state hospital alcoholics can drink like normal drinkers in that same environment.

Similar conclusions have since been reported by several other investigators (cited in Lloyd and Salzberg, 1975; Pattison *et al.*, 1977).

REINTERPRETING THE ADAGE: "FIRST DRINK, THEN DRUNK"

The statement, "First drink, then drunk," summarizes a widely accepted phenomenon of traditional concepts of alcoholism—specifically, that certain individuals ("alcoholics") will immediately or eventually proceed to drink to drunkenness should they ingest an initial drink. The idea of avoiding a "first drink" is basic to the belief system of Alcoholics Anonymous. In fact, it so influenced Jellinek (1960) that he hypothesized a biological mechanism whereby ingestion of simply one or two drinks by an alcoholic would be sufficient to establish physical dependence on alcohol. However, Jellinek based his hypothesis on the subjective and retrospective reports of recovered alcoholics in Alcoholics Anonymous. It was not until some years later, when researchers actually administered alcohol to alcoholics under controlled conditions, that the concept was found to be invalid. As reviewed by Pattison *et al.* (1977), physical dependence on alcohol usually occurs as the result of at least 2 or more days of heavy imbibing. Regardless of empirical disconfirmation, Keller (1972) has lauded the therapeutic value of a belief in the statement "First drink, then drunk," for members of Alcoholics Anonymous. In this particular regard, he is probably correct. On the other hand, for some persons it is equally likely that this statement has functioned as a powerful self-fulfilling prophecy. That is, it is not uncommon to hear individuals at AA meetings or other traditional treatment programs attribute a period of prolonged heavy drinking to simply having taken a "first drink." While such a belief may function to help some individuals refrain from drinking totally, it may be counterproductive for others. To this end, if one has ingested a small quantity of alcohol, such a belief may actually potentiate deleterious drinking.

Concurrent with the study modifying alcoholic drinking patterns, we felt it would be of interest to interview alcoholics and gather their impressions about the possibility of modifying their own drinking behavior. It will be recalled that these patients were in a treatment facility where a series of research studies using alcohol were ongoing. Thirty male patients in treatment for alcoholism at Patton State Hospital volunteered to participate in this interview study. All subjects had previously experienced alcohol withdrawal symptoms and had not ingested alcohol for 3 to 7 days prior to the interview. Additionally, subjects who were physically ill, evidenced psychotic symptoms, had organic brain damage, or were addicted to drugs were not interviewed. Subjects had a mean age of 49.0 years and a mean of 11.9 years of education, and they reported that they had had drinking problems for an average of 12.4 years.

Interview questions and responses by the subjects are summarized in Table 4. The importance of this interview study concerns subjects' answers to questions relating to environmental control over drinking. Although 22 of the subjects believed that the expression "First drink, then drunk" was true, 19 subjects responded that at the time of the interview they would have been able to stop drinking after one drink if they had wanted to do so. Furthermore, at the time of the interview, all 30 subjects responded that on an open hospital ward, they could in fact consume one drink and not go on a drinking binge. Revealingly, only 13 subjects felt they could exercise this degree of control were they not in a hospital setting. Of the 20 subjects who reported they believed they would continue to drink to drunkenness if they were to take one drink at the time of the interview, half believed they could have one drink and stop if they were sufficiently motivated. Even when the hypothesized amount of consumed alcohol was 16 oz. of 86-proof liquor, 27 subjects still maintained that they could ingest that amount of alcohol and then stop drinking completely, so long as they were on an open hospital unit. However, only 7 subjects thought themselves capable of this behavior without the support of a therapeutic environment.

In summary, the subjects' interview responses suggested that the expression might be better stated as "First drink, then drunk, unless circumstances warrant stopping drinking." Clearly, the treatment implications of these two forms of the expression are quite different. With the added motivational qualifying statement, the statement implies that an alcoholic can intercede in his own heavy drinking even after he has begun to drink. By way of contrast, the traditional unqualified statement suggests that once a person has started to drink, only outside intervention or forceful detoxification by himself or others will suffice to terminate that drinking. Surely, most people working in the alcohol field will agree that the expression "First drink, then drunk" is not meant to be taken literally but instead is a function

Table 4. Interview Questions and Responses of Male State Hospital Alcoholics ($N = 30$)[a]

		Response	
	Interview question	Yes (%)	No (%)
1.	Do you consider yourself to have had a problem controlling your drinking of alcohol?	30 (100)	0 (0)
2.	At the present time, do you believe you have or could have control over your drinking behavior; that is, could you drink socially?	9 (30)	21 (70)
3.	A. Have you ever heard the expression, "First drink, then drunk?"	26 (87)	4 (13)
	B. Do you believe it?	22 (73)	8 (27)
4.	At the present time, after drinking one drink (1 oz. of alcohol), could you stop if you wanted to?	19 (63)	11 (37)
5.	At the present time, do you believe that if you had one drink you would continue drinking until drunk, that there is no other way?	20 (67)	10 (33)
6.	At the present time, do you believe you could have one drink and not go on a drunk:		
	A. In the hospital?	30 (100)	0 (0)
	B. On the outside (real world)?	13 (43)	17 (57)
7.	At the present time, do you believe that you could drink 16 oz. of liquor and then stop drinking completely:		
	A. In the hospital?	27 (90)	3 (10)
	B. On the outside (real world)?	7 (23)	23 (77)

[a] Adapted from Sobell, L. C., Sobell, M. B., and Christelman, W. C. The myth of "one drink." *Behaviour Research and Therapy*, 1972, *10*, 119–123. Permission to reprint granted by Pergamon Press, Ltd.

of one's motivational state. Regrettably, this connotation is usually not communicated to clients in treatment programs or to new members of Alcoholics Anonymous.

There are other reasons for challenging the concept of a special reaction to alcohol by alcoholics. For example, many individuals have probably personally tested the "First drink, then drunk" hypothesis, found that in such a planned test they did not go on drinking, and, consequently, decided that they were not actually in need of treatment for alcohol problems. Unfortunately, for those individuals actually in need of treatment, this kind of testing can be counterproductive. These and other problems strongly attest to the value of empirically based concepts opposed to those derived from "folk science." Finally, it is clear that the beliefs of alcoholic patients at Patton State Hospital were more consistent with the present empirical knowledge than are beliefs which characterize traditional concepts of alcoholism.

An additional part of the interview study went on to summarize the findings of various Patton research studies (1969 to 1971) which included drinking procedures. In interpreting these findings, it is important to recognize that following completion of experimental drinking sessions, subjects remained on a unit which was unlocked during the hours of 6 A.M. to 10 P.M. Furthermore, several bars and liquor stores were located within two blocks of the hospital. Therefore, subjects knew they could "make a run" for more liquor; but they were also aware that if they did, they would be transferred to a locked unit and subsequently discharged from the hospital. Taken collectively, 101 subjects participated in from 1 to 15 experimental drinking sessions during which they consumed between 1 and 6 oz. of 86-proof liquor or its equivalent in alcohol content. Only 2 (1.98%) of those subjects left the hospital for more alcohol. Similarly, 113 subjects participated in from 1 to 5 experimental sessions where they consumed as much as 16 oz. of 86-proof liquor or its equivalent in alcohol content. Nearly all of those subjects consumed at least 14 oz. per session. However, only 5 subjects (4.43%) left the hospital to obtain alcohol, even though they typically became quite inebriated as a result of the experimental drinking sessions. Finally, consistent with several lines of experimental evidence, none of the subjects ever experienced any symptoms more severe than a hangover following the experimental drinking sessions.

EVIDENCE FOR A LEARNING DEFICIENCY

One last study deserves brief mention, because it demonstrates how even the simplest of assumptions can be in error. Initially, we had thought chronic alcoholics, because of their vast experience with alcohol, would be quite knowledgeable about various types of alcoholic beverages and drinks. In a pilot study, however, a subject with a long history of chronic abusive drinking confessed to having no knowledge of mixed drinks. He claimed that his drinking experiences had been confined to drinking in his rented room or in skid-row bars where straight drinks, wine, and beer were the order of the day. Certainly, if some individuals were deficient in their ability to name types of mixed drinks, then that fact would need to be considered when attempting to modify drinking behavior. Once again, we were concerned with the behavior of our subject population—state hospitalized chronic alcoholics—and not the total population of individuals with alcohol problems.

Data were obtained from three groups of male subjects. Patton State Hospital patients voluntarily in treatment for alcoholism comprised two of the groups. The first group of 25 subjects consisted of men who had never sold or served alcohol professionally (Alcoholics). The second group was composed of 10 patients, each of whom had tended bar for at least 6 months with an average of 7.8 years of bartending experience (Alcoholic Bartenders). Finally, a group of 25 Normal Drinkers, matched for age and education with the first group of alcoholics, were recruited from the local community and from the hospital staff.

All subjects were interviewed and were asked to name as many mixed drinks as possible, up to a maximum of 15 total drink types. Subjects were also asked to name the type of alcohol used in each drink they named. All responses were recorded verbatim. Responses were later scored using an established bartender's guide in terms of whether the drinks were known mixed drinks and, if so, whether they contained at least one nonalcoholic component. Lastly, subjects were asked to state their drink consumption limit if they were to drink socially.

Results of this study (Sobell, Sobell, and Schaefer, 1971) appear in Table 5. Differences between the groups of alcoholics and normal drinkers were statistically significant for mean number of all mixed

Table 5. Mean Number of Mixed Drinks Named and Mean
Limit Given When Socially Drinking[a]

	Only mixed drinks having a non-alcoholic component	All mixed drinks named	Limit given when socially drinking
Social drinkers	8.56	10.32	4.56
Alcoholics	3.12	3.92	8.25
Alcoholic bartenders	8.50	12.70	9.56

[a] Adapted from Sobell, L. C., Sobell, M. B., and Schaefer, H. H. Alcoholics name fewer mixed drinks than social drinkers. *Psychological Reports*, 1971, *28*, 493-494. Permission to reprint granted by Psychological Reports.

drinks named ($p < .001$), and for mixed drinks having a nonalcoholic component ($p < .001$). The difference between these groups in their stated limit for social drinking was also statistically significant ($p < .001$). However, alcoholics who had worked as bartenders were found to possess knowledge of mixed drinks which was not discriminably different from that of normal drinkers. This finding was interpreted as reflecting a learning deficiency among our alcoholic patients who had not worked as bartenders. Unexpected as it was, this finding, including the similarity between alcoholic bartenders and normal drinkers, has now been replicated with chronic alcoholics in New Zealand (Williams and Brown, 1974b).

INTEGRATING THE EARLY RESEARCH

The studies described in this chapter, taken in concert with research being conducted and reported from other facilities, led to the formulation of a large-scale research treatment evaluation study. This major study differed from the earlier Patton studies in two respects. First, rather than being limited in focus, it had multiple components. Second, this was the only investigation which was explicitly designed as a treatment study, albeit research-oriented. At the time we designed the study, we were well aware that the long-term consequences of alcohol problems often require medical management and, further, that some day there might be substantial evidence to support a genetic or biochemical etiological theory of alcohol problems. However, given that the existing evidence did not support any one etiological orientation, our primary concern was to develop a treatment procedure which would be effective. By that time, a substantial amount of data had accumulated which indicated that regardless of the origin of alcohol problems, environmental factors were definitely influential in the maintenance of alcoholic drinking, and moreover, drinking behavior was clearly subject to modification.

In designing a large-scale study, we were also aware that studies which incorporated a variety of treatment components are often fraught with problems of interpretation. For example, if a study is successful, how does one determine which components were effective, which components were unnecessary, and which components, if any, detracted from the treatment effect? For that matter, do synergistic effects exist among certain treatment components? Taken in perspective, however, the history of treatment innovation and treatment outcome research in alcohol studies had been dismal. Therefore, we were prepared to adopt a deductive approach to the development of a treatment paradigm. If the treatment was found to be successful, further research would be necessary to establish the relative therapeutic efficacy of the various component parts. Furthermore, the need for clinical applications of the mounting behavioral evidence was immediate. If successful, a treatment program could always be refined to become more efficient through continuing research efforts. On this basis, a major clinical research treatment trial was undertaken—*Individualized Behavior Therapy (IBT) for alcoholics.*

CHAPTER 5

Individualized Behavior Therapy (IBT)

A BROAD-SPECTRUM BEHAVIORAL APPROACH

The studies described in Chapter 4 collectively formed the basis of a major research treatment study, henceforth to be referred to as Individualized Behavior Therapy (IBT) for alcoholics. This study was conducted at Patton State Hospital during 1970 and early 1971. Whereas all the earlier Patton research studies had been rather limited in focus, the IBT study was designed as a multiple-component research treatment-evaluation project.

While many of the findings and components of the earlier research greatly influenced the design of the IBT study, the rationale for the experimental treatment was based on a working hypothesis that problem drinking can be considered to be a *discriminated, operant behavior.* That is, problem drinking is presumed to occur in selective situations and to be acquired and maintained primarily as a result of its consequences (see Chapter 3). Prior to designing the IBT study, we reviewed the existing literature, which suggested that the drinking behavior of alcoholics seemed to have characteristics typical of operant responses (e.g., Bandura, 1969; Lazarus, 1965; Mello and Mendelson, 1965; Nathan, Titler, Lowenstein, Solomon, and Rossi, 1970). Rather than continuing to perform basic research documenting the operant nature of alcoholics' drinking responses, the IBT study was designed to examine specific treatment implications derived from an operant conceptualization. Several of these implications were discussed in Chapter 3. The major treatment implications the IBT study was designed to examine included: (a) treatment sessions should deal directly with the behavior of excessive drinking; (b) whenever possible, treatment conditions should be designed to maximize generalization of the treatment effects; (c) in order for drinking to become a less probable response in certain stimulus situations, clients may need to learn to employ alternative responses for dealing with those situations; (d) an optimal treatment should recognize the unique learning history of each client and be specifically tailored to each individual case; and (e) treatment goals should be those which individuals are most likely to attain and maintain with respect to their particular extratreatment environment.

The IBT study was a broad-spectrum behavioral treatment approach. The use of a broad-spectrum behavioral approach in the treatment of alcohol problems was first reported in a case study by Lazarus in 1965. This approach emphasizes that no single method or combination of methods is optimal for treating all problems and all persons.

Lazarus (1971) has described two general treatment orientations in the field of behavior therapy—a broad-spectrum approach and a narrow-band approach. The "narrow-band" approach refers to depending upon a highly limited array of therapeutic tools (i.e., using only systematic desensitization and/or assertion training) for treating all cases. Although a narrow-band approach has obvious value when used with some particular pathologies (i.e., phobias), the population of persons with alcohol problems has been found to be extremely diverse (reviewed in Pattison *et al.*, 1977). Thus, a broad-spectrum approach appears to be appropriate as a general orientation for behavioral treatment of individuals with alcohol problems.

EXPERIMENTAL DESIGN

SUBJECTS

A group of 70 male *gamma* (Jellinek, 1960) alcoholic patients who had voluntarily admitted themselves to Patton State Hospital for treatment of alcoholism served as subjects in the IBT study. All subjects had experienced physical dependence on alcohol and had several previous alcohol-related arrests and hospitalizations. No subject had any past history of drug abuse other than alcohol.

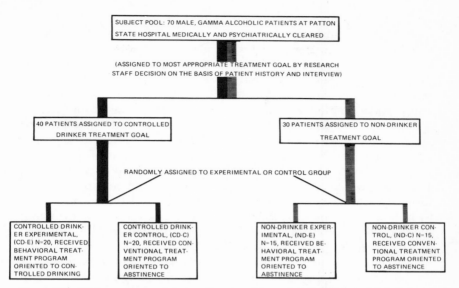

Figure 16. IBT experimental design. Reprinted from Sobell, M. B. and Sobell, L. C. Alcoholics treated by individualized behavior therapy: One year treatment outcome. *Behaviour Research and Therapy*, 1973b, *11*, 599-618. Permission granted by Pergamon Press, Ltd.

After subjects had volunteered for the study and received medical and psychiatric clearance for participation, they were carefully interviewed by the research staff. This screening interview determined (a) the reasons that subjects were seeking treatment in this particular study, and (b) whether they were likely to complete a treatment program lasting approximately four weeks. Since the assignment of subjects to the four treatment conditions is important for understanding the experimental treatments and for the interpretation of results, Figure 16 presents a schematic diagram of the IBT experimental design.

ASSIGNMENT TO EXPERIMENTAL CONDITIONS

After subjects were accepted for participation in the IBT study, they were individually assigned to a treatment goal condition of either controlled (nonproblem) drinking or non-drinking (abstinence). This treatment goal decision was determined by a majority vote of the research staff and was based on information derived from an extensive interview conducted with each subject by the full research staff, as well as a social and drinking history questionnaire completed by each subject. Selection of a treatment goal of controlled drinking was largely based on the following criteria: (a) that some form of nonproblem, limited drinking was requested as a goal by the subject; (b) that the subject could reasonably be expected to learn new drinking behaviors (e.g., screening factors included a reported minimal history of impulsiveness and past indications of exercise of self-control over other behaviors); (c) that the environment to which the subject would return after hospitalization could be expected to be supportive of controlled drinking (e.g., family support, especially from a spouse; religious affiliation which did not proscribe drinking; stable residential setting—one's own home or apartment as opposed to a halfway house or transient lodging; minimal or no expected future contacts with a group of heavy drinkers); and (d) evidence of having practiced moderate, problem-free drinking at some time in the past (while this information was derived from the subjects' self-reports, only credible reports were considered—e.g., a report of drinking a case of beer per day was not considered as indicating past nonproblem, moderate drinking). The staff also considered various other factors when deciding whether a subject might be a candidate for the controlled drinking treatment goal condition. These factors included subjects having relatively few alcohol-related hospitalizations and arrests, being younger, reporting a shorter history of drinking problems, and having greater educational attainment.

All subjects who requested abstinence as a treatment goal were assigned to that condition. Furthermore, those subjects who could socially identify with Alcoholics Anonymous, had extended periods of past sobriety, and/or were evaluated as lacking sufficient social support to maintain a controlled drinking pattern outside of the hospital (e.g., living in half-way houses or other abstinence-oriented supportive care residences) were likely to be assigned to the nondrinking treatment goal condition. After assignment to one of the two treatment goal groups (controlled drinking or nondrinking), subjects were then *randomly assigned* to either a control group or experimental group. The conventional state hospital alcohol treatment program at Patton State Hospital served as a comparison control treatment. Earlier unpublished reports of alcoholism treatment outcome for this same program had found outcome results similar to those of other traditional state hospital inpatient programs (typically between 20 and 40% success, evaluated by various criteria). *The control* (conventional) *treatment, which was totally abstinence oriented,* consisted of large group therapy meetings, AA meetings, chemotherapy, physiotherapy, and industrial therapy. The experimentally treated subjects received 17 experimental treatment sessions in addition to the conventional state hospital treatment.

The IBT experimental design outlined in Figure 16 traces the derivation of the four treatment conditions. The design can also be interpreted as two concurrent experimental treatment programs—nondrinking and controlled drinking—each with an appropriate control group. As can be seen in Figure 16, *only the Controlled Drinker Experimental (CD–E) subjects received treatment specifically oriented toward a goal of controlled drinking.* That is, subjects selected as qualifying for a controlled drinking treatment goal but who were assigned to that control group (CD–C) were strongly advised that complete abstinence would be in their best interest and informed that they would not be receiving any treatment oriented toward attainment of a controlled drinking treatment goal. Both of the nondrinker groups, experimental and control, had a treatment goal of abstinence. Thus, *three of the four groups of subjects in the IBT study had a treatment goal of abstinence.*

A summary of the descriptive characteristics of subjects in each of the four groups appears in Table 6. All subjects reported having experienced major dysfunction in most areas of life health as a result of their drinking, and all had experienced alcohol withdrawal symptoms and other alcohol-related physical health problems. No statistically significant differences in subject characteristics were found between respective experimental and control groups, with the exception that Nondrinker Experimental (ND–E) subjects had a singificantly ($p < .05$) higher level of education than Nondrinker Control (ND–C) subjects. Typically, subjects were 40 years of age, had completed or nearly completed high school, and worked in blue-collar occupations. Further, subjects in the nondrinking treatment groups reported a greater number of alcohol-related incarcerations and a somewhat longer history of problem drinking than subjects assigned to the controlled drinking treatment groups.

Table 6. Summary of Descriptive Statistics for the Four Groups of Subjects in the IBT Study[a]

		Groups[b]			
Descriptive variable		CD–E	CD–C	ND–E	ND–C
Age (yrs.):	Mean	40.30	41.25	40.40	43.27
	SD	9.42	10.58	9.32	10.06
Education (yrs.):	Mean	12.60	12.45	13.03	11.27
	SD	1.54	2.35	2.29	2.09
Drinking problem (yrs.):	Mean	9.70	8.65	11.33	11.86
	SD	6.21	4.51	6.95	8.16
Alcohol-associated	Mean	6.25	5.70	8.85	9.86
arrests (No.):	SD	6.99	5.33	10.06	13.96
Prior hospitalizations for	Mean	2.10	1.90	3.43	4.13
alcoholism (No.):	SD	2.83	1.29	4.97	2.83
Marital status:	Married	6	4	3	6
	Single	4	5	3	2
	Divorced, separated	10	11	9	6
	Widower	0	0	0	1
Religion:	Protestant	16	13	13	13
	Catholic	2	5	1	1
	LDS	1	1	1	1
	Agnostic	1	1	0	0
Occupation:	Blue-collar	17	16	11	15
	White-collar	1	2	3	0
	Retired	1	1	1	0
	Student	1	1	0	0
Withdrawal symptoms:					
	Tremors, sweating	9	12	5	5
	Convulsions, blackouts	4	4	3	2
	Hallucinations, d.t.'s	7	4	7	8
	$N =$	20	20	15	15

[a] Adapted from Sobell, M. B. and Sobell, L. C. *Individualized behavior therapy for alcoholics: Rationale, procedures, preliminary results and appendix. California Mental Health Research Monograph, No. 13.* Sacramento: California Dept. of Mental Hygiene, 1972. Permission granted by California State Department of Health; and from Sobell, M. B. and Sobell, L. C. Individualized behavior therapy for alcoholics. *Behavior Therapy,* 1973a, *4*, 49-72. Permission granted by Academic Press, Inc.

[b] Groups were Controlled Drinker, Experimental (CD–E); Controlled Drinker, Control (CD–C), Nondrinker, Experimental (ND–E); and Nondrinker, Control (ND–C).

TREATMENT PROCEDURES

FACILITIES

The alcohol research unit at Patton State Hospital contained the central research facilities, simulated bar and cocktail lounge, and a simulated home environment. The bar environment, video recording apparatus, and operant conditioning equipment were described in Chapter 4. The simulated home environment was primarily constructed for use in the IBT study and was located immediately adjacent to the bar but separated from it by heavy, floor-length draperies. Furnishings included two sofas, a soft chair, two end tables with table lamps, two coffee tables, a pole lamp, a television set, a phonograph, and wall-to-wall carpeting. Its location is illustrated in Figure 2. Figure 17 shows a portion of the actual simulated home environment used in the IBT study. The shock generators located behind the bar were used in the home environment by attaching 25-foot extension cables to both the electrodes and switches. Similar

Figure 17. Simulated home environment at the Patton State Hospital Alcohol Research Facilities, circa 1970.

to earlier studies, a large variety of confiscated alcoholic beverages were supplied for research use by the California State Alcoholic Beverage Control Board.

OVERVIEW

Irrespective of an experimental subject's treatment goal— controlled drinking (CD–E) or nondrinking (ND–E)—the 17 experimental treatment sessions focused directly on drinking behavior and emphasized helping the subject to identify functions served by his problem drinking and to develop alternative, more appropriate (self-defined) ways of dealing with those situations. Within a general framework, the treatment was tailored as specifically as possible to each subject's case history and eventual extratreatment environment. In this regard, Problem Solving Skills Training was a central element of the experimental treatment in all instances. The problem solving skills training procedures, derived from the functional analysis model of drinking (see Chapter 3), are based on the assumption that the functions of drinking are relatively unique for each individual.

The only explicit treatment difference between the ND–E and CD–E groups was that the CD–E subjects were trained in nonproblem (controlled) drinking skills and allowed to practice these behaviors during certain treatment sessions. On the other hand, while ND–E subjects were allowed the opportunity to consume alcohol (as is usually the case in the extratreatment environment), they were instructed that drinking was not only inappropriate but in direct conflict with their selected treatment goal of nondrinking. Consequently, these subjects were informed that certain aversive contingencies might sometimes be in effect if they ordered or consumed any alcohol.

Except for the first two sessions, all sessions were 90 minutes in length, and the majority of sessions were conducted in the simulated environment—experimental bar or home environment—whichever most closely approximated the subjects' usual drinking environment. In Sessions 3 through 17, the subjects were run individually with one staff member (determined on a rotating basis) assigned to each session. All sessions were highly structured and very intense in application.

MODIFICATION OF THE DRINKING RESPONSE—AVOIDANCE CONTINGENCIES

One of the Patton studies (Mills, Sobell, and Schaefer, 1971) described in Chapter 4 demonstrated that in a controlled research setting and under certain contingencies, the drinking behavior of chronic alcoholics could be shaped to approximate normal drinking patterns. Given the results of that study and the uncertainty that existed in 1970 regarding what would constitute both an efficient and effective method for shaping appropriate drinking behavior in alcoholics, it was decided to use shock avoidance contingencies as part of the IBT study. During Sessions 4 through 16, except for "probe" sessions (Sessions 8, 12, and 16), an electric shock was administered to the subject on a variable ratio 2 (VR 2) avoidance schedule when inappropriate drinking behaviors (as defined by the subject's treatment goal) were emitted. In order to increase resistance to extinction, a VR 2 schedule was used rather than a continuous reinforcement schedule. A larger ratio schedule (e.g., VR 3, VR 10) was not used because we suspected that the reinforcing effects of drinking might be sufficient to completely nullify the effects of the few shocks which would be occasioned by such schedules.

During the probe sessions (Sessions 8, 12, and 16), shock avoidance contingencies were not in effect and electrodes were not connected to the subjects' hands. Probe sessions were intended to assess whether the drinking or nondrinking patterns acquired in shock avoidance contingency sessions would generalize to situations where there were no shock avoidance contingencies in effect for inappropriate drinking. We hoped that the data gathered during probe sessions would be useful in predicting whether the changes in drinking behaviors which occurred in the highly structured laboratory situation would generalize to situations where such conditions did not exist or, more importantly, would generalize to the client's postdischarge environment.

At the start of Session 3 ("education" session), subjects were instructed about why, when, and what shock avoidance contingencies would be in effect during the remaining sessions. Also, in Session 3 an initial shock level was determined for each subject. The actual shock levels, which generally ranged from 2 mA to 5 mA, were painful but harmless. Shocks were delivered across the little and index fingers of the subject's nondominant hand.

When shock avoidance contingencies were in effect, ND–E subjects *occasioned* a 1-sec shock (delivered on a VR 2 schedule) for ordering any type of drink. That is, whenever a ND–E subject ordered a drink, there was a 50% chance that he would receive a shock. The drink was then served, and each time the subject touched the glass he would occasion a shock which would continue until he released the glass (however, the drink could be consumed). Additionally, during Sessions 4 through 16, when an ND–E subject ordered no drinks for two consecutive sessions, a "priming prompt" (no shock) of a free drink was offered at the start of the next session. If the subject consumed the free drink, then any applicable shock contingencies were immediately reinstated. If the subject chose not to consume the free drink, he was asked to pour it down the sink, and this procedure continued at 15-minute intervals throughout the entire treatment session.

Shock contingencies for CD–E subjects were similar to those used by Mills *et al.* (1971) (see Chapter 4). Thus, the CD–E subjects occasioned a 1-sec shock (delivered on a VR 2 schedule) for the following inappropriate drinking behaviors: (a) ordering a straight drink; (b) taking a sip larger than one-sixth of the total volume of a mixed drink, one-twelfth of a 12-oz. beer, or one-sixth of either 2½ oz. (20% alcohol content) or 4 oz. (12% alcohol content) of wine (glasses were demarcated by a strip of premarked tape to be of equal sip proportions with respect to drink type); (c) ordering a drink within 20 minutes of having previously ordered a drink; or (d) ordering more than three total drinks during a 90-minute treatment session. After consuming three drinks within a treatment session, CD–E subjects were placed on the same shock contingencies as applied to ND–E subjects.

Since a variety of alcoholic beverages were available throughout all drinking sessions, it was necessary to develop a standardized conversion equivalency to account for the varying percent of alcohol content in different beverages. The standard drink equivalency used in the IBT study was as follows: (a) mixed drinks—1 oz. liquor (43–48% alcohol content) combined with 2 oz. mixer; (b) beer—12 oz. (3–4% alcohol content); (c) malt or stout beer—8 oz. (6–8% alcohol content); (d) dinner wine—4 oz. (12% alcohol content); (e) fortified, sweet wines—2½ oz. (20% alcohol content); and (f) straight drinks—1 oz. liquor (43–48% alcohol content). In the IBT study, all straight drinks were served in three ⅓-oz. portions in order to guard against subjects taking advantage of the variable shock schedule. This obviously necessitated subjects taking a minimum of three sips to finish the drink.

VIDEOTAPED DRINKING: SESSIONS 1 AND 2

Another component used in an earlier Patton study (Schaefer *et al.*, 1971b) (see Chapter 4) was the relatively unobtrusive videotape monitoring and recording of events which occurred in the simulated bar. While the earlier study found that videotape replay, when used in isolation, was not effective in changing drinking or associated behaviors (Schaefer *et al.*, 1971b; Schaefer *et al.*, 1972), it was felt that this procedure might be effective when incorporated into a broad-spectrum treatment sequence.

Sessions 1 and 2 were the only sessions where subjects were run in pairs. During these sessions, subjects were allowed to consume up to 16 oz. of 86-proof liquor or its equivalent in alcohol content. The sessions were 3 hours in length, were always conducted in the experimental bar, and were always separated by one nondrinking day. That is, these two sessions were never run on two consecutive days. The final 90 min of each session were videotaped. However, unlike the earlier study, these videotape sessions were specifically designed as part of the initial treatment sequence. Thus, during the drinking sessions we took advantage of the subjects' sedation and familiarity with the drunken situation to probe for stimulus materials (both past and present setting events for drinking) which would be useful in later treatment sessions. These two drinking sessions were structured to identify specific antecedents of drinking, and it was felt that the use of alcohol facilitated the identification of such situations. In this regard, while we cannot provide direct evidence, we believe that the sedative effect of alcohol helped to moderate the physiological components of anxiety which accompanied subjects' discussing of embarrassing, fear-laden, or problem situations. Similarly, the sessions were structured to take advantage of what has been suggested to be a cultural phenomenon involving a broadening of social norms (MacAndrew and Edgerton, 1969); namely, that when one is intoxicated, it is socially permissible to talk with others about personal problems or otherwise embarrassing topics.

During these sessions staff members also evaluated the subjects' nonverbal reactions to various potential problem situations (e.g., confrontation by an assertive male or female, group pressures, being ignored, etc.). Lastly, an ancillary function of Sessions 1 and 2 was that they served to demonstrate to each subject that he could, in fact, become quite drunk and then sober up on the next day without suffering from withdrawal symptoms or severe cravings for more alcohol. This information was communicated to the subject in Session 3 when the "myth of one drink" was discussed.

EDUCATION: SESSION 3

Session 3 was multifaceted, with a central purpose of preparing the subject for the remainder of the treatment program. Regardless of treatment goal, all subjects were: (a) instructed that during certain sessions various shock contingencies would apply for inappropriate drinking behaviors (the contingencies defined were a function of each subject's treatment goal); (b) instructed that during some sessions they could drink with no possibility of shock (probe sessions); (c) presented a detailed explanation of the treatment rationale, emphasizing that drinking would be considered as a learned behavior which occurs in certain situations and not in others and is acquired and maintained as a result of its consequences; in this regard, the functional analysis of drinking was explained, emphasizing the need to consider both short-term and long-term consequences of drinking and other behaviors; and (d) evaluated for an individual electric shock pain threshold level.

The final component of Session 3 involved training subjects in certain response repertoires. Based on our previous experience, it was evident that many of our state hospital alcoholics were deficient in their ability to refuse drinks. To increase their response repertoire in this regard, both groups of experimental subjects were exposed to a series of situations where they were socially pressured to drink. In these situations they were taught and practiced ways of resisting such pressures. Appropriate responses could range from well-known euphemisms (e.g., "I've got an ulcer and should not be drinking") to direct confrontations (e.g., "I don't care to drink today," "I have a drinking problem"). To this end, other investigators have recently documented that chronic alcoholics may be deficient in ways of refusing drinks in social situations (Foy, Miller, Eisler, and O'Toole, 1976). Further, all CD–E subjects were trained in a response repertoire for mixed drinks using a "mini-drink" procedure, whereby subjects actually sampled small amounts (½ oz.) of various types of mixed drinks. The rationale for this procedure derived from one of our earlier studies (Sobell, Sobell, and Schaefer, 1971), which had demonstrated that many state hospital alcoholics have a gross deficiency in familiarity with mixed drinks.

VIDEOTAPE REPLAY: SESSIONS 4 AND 5

During Sessions 4 and 5, subjects viewed the videotape replays of Sessions 1 and 2, respectively. Prior to the start of Sessions 4 and 5, the staff member who was to conduct the session reviewed the respective videotape, carefully noting behavioral deficiencies (e.g., emotional expressiveness, assertiveness) and excesses (e.g., aggressiveness), as well as identifying setting events which the subject had mentioned as likely to result in drinking (e.g., confrontations with one's spouse; situations involving job performance; inability to relate to one's children). Then, when the subject viewed the videotape during the session, the staff member would point out to him the identified deficiencies, excesses, and setting events. Subjects' reactions to these videotaped sequences were recorded in research notes so They could be dealt with later, in the problem solving skills training sessions.

While our earlier work suggested that videotape self-confrontation of drunken behavior was quite stress-inducing for sober alcoholics, later pilot studies led us to believe that videotape self-confrontation increased a subject's motivation for changing his drinking behavior. We also found the method to be extremely effective for rapidly demonstrating to the subject various behavioral problems and setting events for problem drinking. Finally, as previously mentioned, alcohol was available to all subjects during these two sessions and shock avoidance contingencies appropriate to each treatment condition were in effect.

ANALOGUE FAILURE EXPERIENCE: SESSION 6

Twenty minutes before the start of Session 6, subjects were administered an artificial failure experience—a series of plausible but impossible to complete tasks. After the staff member who had administered the tasks informed the subject of his poor test performance, another staff member conducted the actual treatment session. The session then focused on failure experiences, both past and present, how the subject had previously responded to such situations, and the consequences of those responses. All subjects were subsequently debriefed as to the exact nature of the session. Alcohol was available to subjects in this session, and shock avoidance contingencies were in effect.

PROBLEM SOLVING SKILLS TRAINING: SESSIONS 7 THROUGH 16

The major treatment component used in Sessions 7 through 16 was a behavioral technology we now call "Problem Solving Skills Training." Problem solving skills training was a broad-spectrum behavioral treatment procedure which largely focused on identifying and evaluating multiple opportunities for treatment intervention. Basically, the training incorporated the following four-stage process:

Stage 1—Problem Identification. Subjects were first trained in ways to operationally define (identify) specific circumstances and events which had resulted in drinking problems in the past or were likely to do so in the future. That is, what particular environmental factors and/or internal (physical or emotional) states set the occasion for problem drinking behavior? Unlike textbook examples, most problem situations are not simply restricted to a single factor, such as a divorce or a job loss, but usually involve a complex of factors. The primary objective of this stage was to gain sufficient information about problem situations so that appropriate treatment strategies could be delineated and instituted. For instance, if a client labeled lack of job advancement as a problem but failed to mention that he lacked the necessary educational background to qualify for a desired position, the resulting treatment strategies would probably have been inappropriate and nonbeneficial. Essentially, this stage can be conceptualized as an ecological orientation to describing problem situations (defining a problem in terms of how it related to the subject's total life functioning).

The following hypothetical clinical dialogue illustrates the advantage of operationally defining a problem. That is, the client begins by describing a problem in vague and abstract terms, but through the interaction with the therapist a very concrete and specific statement of the problem situation eventuates.

SUBJECT: I've been very anxious and nervous for about the last two months.

THERAPIST: Has anyone else noticed or commented that you've seemed nervous or anxious?

SUBJECT: Well, my wife mentioned it, but she always says I'm nervous. Then again, my boss also mentioned it once or twice recently. It's really bothering me, because it keeps me from working at my best.

THERAPIST: In what ways does it keep you from working effectively?

SUBJECT: Well, I've been feeling more irritable and worried at work, and I just can't seem to sit down and get my ledgers or monthly reports completed on time, and this has never happened before.

THERAPIST: Has anything happened to you in the last two months, any kinds of major life changes or traumatic situations, which might be associated with the anxiety that you're describing?

SUBJECT: Nothing's happened. I go home every night and everything's the same. I don't have any particular worries, such as bills, and our children are doing fine. In fact, in another month or so I'm probably going to get a promotion, and then I'll even have some spare money.

THERAPIST: Tell me about the promotion.

SUBJECT: Well, the boss has been considering me for a promotion to a supervisory job. I'm really excited by it. I'll be supervising about 10 other clerks. On the other hand, it also scares me as I've never really had that many people under me. But I've been with the company a good 15 years now, and the boss knows I'm dependable and should do a good job. I'm really worried about this nervousness problem. If it wasn't bugging me, I'd really be feeling great.

THERAPIST: When did your employer first talk to you about the planned promotion?

SUBJECT: Oh, the vacancy was first announced about three months ago. Then, early last month the boss called me in and told me that I was being considered for the position. You know, come to think of it now, a lot of my anxiety started just about the time when he told me that I was being considered for the job.

THERAPIST: Have you ever worked in a supervisory job before?

SUBJECT: Well, not exactly. You know that bothers me, too, because I'm not really sure how to deal with that many people. Don't get me wrong. I can do my job fine; I have no problem there. But lots of these people I'd be supervising are the same people I've been working with for the last 15 years. You know; they're my friends. In some ways, I guess I wouldn't know how to say no to them. Maybe that's got me a little bothered. I've never really—I'm just not sure how to be a supervisor. I mean, I can deal with the work, but I don't know about handling people.

THERAPIST: Have you discussed this with your boss?

SUBJECT: No. I think I know him pretty well. If I brought it up, he probably wouldn't consider me qualified for the job.

THERAPIST: Well, do you think that this possible lack of supervisory skills that you've identified might eventually surface and perhaps

cause you serious problems after you've been promoted into
the job? Maybe you need some more information about
whether the way you see the situation is accurate.

SUBJECT: I suppose it might come back to haunt me. While I want the
job, I'm not even sure that I can handle it, or if I can learn
how to handle it. I guess I'm going to have to decide what to
do about it. I've got a friend who's a supervisor for one of our
competitors. Maybe I'll talk to him. I can find out what he
does at work and the kinds of problems he comes up against.
Maybe I'm worrying over nothing, or maybe it's rougher than
I think. You know, the more I think about it, the easier I think
it will be to decide what to do after I have some idea of what to
expect.

Once the situation has been operationally defined, it is possible
for the subject to begin formulating possible alternative strategies for
dealing with the problem. With respect to the foregoing example,
these will be enumerated shortly. The problem identification stage is
crucial, and even the foregoing clinical example has been simplified as
regards the specificity which can occur when delineating a particular
problem.

*Stage 2—Delineation of Behavioral Options (Alternative Responses) to
Problem Drinking.* Subjects were assisted in generating a series of
alternative behavioral responses to identified problem situations. It is
important to note that *in this stage value judgments regarding the
delineated options were specifically avoided.* Therefore, any determination
of the relative "goodness" or "badness" of various behavioral options
was not relevant to this stage of problem solving. To deal with indebt-
edness, for instance, options could include, but not be limited to, de-
claring bankruptcy, obtaining a consolidation loan, robbing a bank,
drinking, taking drugs, or taking a second job. In using this or similar
examples, it was explained to subjects that while all of the alternative
behaviors have varied short- and long-term anticipated consequences,
they nevertheless are actual behaviors which have been engaged in by
some individuals in similar situations.

In their recent book, *Clinical Behavior Therapy* (1976), Goldfried
and Davison equate the enumeration of alternative responses with
Osborn's (1963) method of "brainstorming." This is an excellent
comparison, as the four basic rules of brainstorming describe very
nicely what takes place in Stage 2 of the problem solving skills training
procedure—criticism is ruled out, freewheeling is welcomed, quantity
is welcomed, and combinations and improvements of ideas are

sought. Goldfried and Davison (1976) report that "brainstorming is more likely to generate effective responses than is the attempt to produce *only* good quality alternatives" (p. 190).

In the hypothetical clinical example described earlier, our subject was able to identify an impending job promotion as a setting event for his drinking. More precisely, he felt that the promotion would carry with it an assumption that he possessed supervisory skills which he believed he might lack. In the second stage of the process, the therapist assists the subject in generating a variety of behavioral options which might help him to deal with his problem situation:

SUBJECT: I really want this job, and it'll mean a lot more money for me, not only now but also at retirement. Besides, if I refused the promotion, what would I tell my wife or my boss?

THERAPIST: Rather than worrying about that for the moment, why don't we explore what kinds of possible behavioral options you have regarding this job promotion. Remember, don't evaluate the options now. Alternatives, at this point, can include anything even remotely possible; what we want you to do is come up with a range of possible alternatives. You don't have to carry out an alternative just because you consider it.

SUBJECT: You know, I could do what I usually do in these kinds of situations. In fact, being as nervous as I've been these past couple of months, I've done that quite often.

THERAPIST: You mean drinking?

SUBJECT: Yeah, I've been drinking quite heavily some nights when I get home, and my wife is really complaining.

THERAPIST: Well, OK, drinking is one option. What other ways could you deal with this problem?

SUBJECT: Well, I could take the job, and on the side I could take some night courses in business at a local college. That way I could learn how to be a supervisor. But, gee, that would be a lot of work. I don't even know if I have the time. Besides, I don't know if they offer the kind of training I need.

THERAPIST: At this point, it's really not necessary to worry about how to carry out the options, but simply to identify them. You're doing fine. What are some other ways you might handle the situation?

SUBJECT: Well, another thing I could do is to simply tell the boss that I'm not sure I'm qualified, and either tell him that I don't want the job or ask him if he could give me some time to learn my new role.

THERAPIST: OK. Go on, you're doing fine.

SUBJECT: But what if the boss tells me that I have to take the job, I don't have any choice?

THERAPIST: Well, what general kinds of things might happen in that case?
SUBJECT: Oh, I could take the job and fail. That's one option. I could take the job and learn how to be a supervisor. I could refuse the job, risk being fired, and maybe end up having to look for another job. You know, I could just go and talk to my supervisor right now and explain the problem to him and see what comes of that.
THERAPIST: Well, you've delineated a lot of options. Let's take some time to evaluate them before you reach any decision.
SUBJECT: OK, but I'm getting really worried just thinking about the problem. I guess what I have to do is sit down and think this out and decide what's going to be best for me and my family in the long run. I really like working for this company, and I've been there a long time. I definitely don't want to jeopardize my retirement benefits, but then again, I'm still worried about whether or not I could really supervise all of those people.

Stage 3—Evaluation of Each Behavioral Option for Its Possible Outcomes. In this stage, subjects were asked to evaluate each of the behavioral options delineated in Stage 2 for their probable short-term (immediate), long-term, and total (short- and long-term) consequences. Thus, an emphasis was placed on determining the relative appropriateness of behavioral alternatives. In this context, *relative "appropriateness" was defined in terms of the total anticipated consequences of an option, the most "appropriate" alternative being that having the most beneficial total anticipated consequences.* Subjects were made aware that it was important to evaluate all behavioral options *before* deciding which particular behaviors were most appropriate.

Using the functional analysis model format, it was explained to subjects that some behavioral options, although not involving drinking, could still cause serious life health dysfunction. For example, again consider the individual who has financial difficulties. Robbing a bank is an extreme example of trying to solve this problem. Proceeding from there, it is quite likely that this individual will suffer severe life dysfunction (i.e., prison sentence) as a result of engaging in this behavior, irrespective of not drinking.

It was also explained to the subject that while the behavioral option of prolonged intemperate alcohol consumption is usually associated with long-term deleterious consequences, engaging in such behavior is often initially (short-term) rewarding. The most significant point communicated to subjects in this stage, however, was that *the best behavioral option is often not immediately rewarding.* For example, while taking a second job might be evaluated as the behavioral option having the best total anticipated consequences for solving a financial dilemma, the immediate consequences of working a second job are somewhat punishing (e.g., decreased recreational time, increased fatigue, less time to spend with friends and family, etc.). As is readily apparent, a *focus on the total consequences* of behaviors is the crux of the functional analysis model of drinking.

While all of the short- and long-term consequences associated with all possible options cannot always be predicted, for most options the major anticipated consequences can be readily estimated and evaluated. In this stage, the subject (not the therapist, although the therapist will naturally be involved to some degree) was expected to make value judgments regarding the personal "goodness" or "badness" of particular consequences, and, thus, of particular options. The more detailed the evaluation, the better able the subject was to delide among particular options. After carefully examining the various alternatives, the subject then arranged by priority the alternatives in terms of those having the best *total* anticipated consequences for him, emphasizing long-term expected outcomes. The following clinical example, with our hypothetical subject, illustrates the process involved in this stage:

THERAPIST: In discussing this problem of job promotion, you've generated quite a few alternatives. What's necessary at this point is for you to decide which particular option or options you're going to select to deal with this problem. First, are there any that you think are really so wild and bizarre that there's no use considering them further?

SUBJECT: Yes, in the long run I really don't think that drinking is going to solve the problem for me. We've discussed that before. It would only let me temporarily avoid the situation, and if I continued to drink I just might find myself out of a job, much less a promotion. Also, I really can't see myself accepting the job without at least mentioning to my boss that I feel I will need some guidance in being a supervisor. If I didn't do that, I could probably survive for a month or two. You know, when you start on a new job it's sort of easy to explain away poor performance as getting adjusted to a new situation. But in reality, I'd probably be as nervous and anxious, if not more, than I am right now. Eventually, I'd probably end up being fired or demoted. That would really be embarrassing; probably even more embarrassing than just admitting that I might not be able to handle the new job.

THERAPIST: OK, you've eliminated a few options. Now are there any that immediately strike you as making sense?

SUBJECT: I don't know. Some of them sound all right, but if they were that good I would have engaged in them right away. I just don't know. I'm not really sure how to go about doing all of those kinds of things.

THERAPIST: Remember, you don't have to put any of these options into action right now. We're just evaluating them from the standpoint of which would have the best probable outcomes for you.

SUBJECT: Well, the one that seems most appealing, I mean overall, is just going in and talking to my boss—explaining to him that while I would like the promotion, I'm not really sure what would be expected of me if I took the new supervising position. When I think about it, you know, I've known my boss for a long time. I really don't think that he'd actually fire me or anything because he thought I wasn't immediately qualified to take the new position.

THERAPIST: Is it possible that your supervisor expects you to feel a little anxious but believes that you will learn to function as a supervisor?

SUBJECT: I don't know. I've never really asked him.

THERAPIST: What if you were to ask him on what basis he made his decision to offer you the job?

SUBJECT: That might be a good way to handle it. That way if he said he knew that I would have to grow into the job, then I could explain to him that I don't know how fast I can learn the ropes, but that I'd like to give it a try. I think that's what I'll do.

THERAPIST: We're still just evaluating alternatives for the time being. Why not consider some other alternatives before you decide? What if your boss doesn't expect you to have any problems as a supervisor? Then what do you think his response might be if you tell him that you may lack the necessary experience for this new job?

SUBJECT: Well, I'm not sure. I mean, I wouldn't want to miss out on the opportunity just because I made a bad impression on him.

THERAPIST: Well, I'm also wondering if there aren't perhaps some different strategies for discussing these problems with him.

SUBJECT: I'm not sure if I follow you. What can I do, other than level with him?

THERAPIST: Well, I'm just thinking that there might be other ways of communicating to him that you possibly don't have the necessary experience. Especially, some alternative way of communicating that information which would be less likely to jeopardize your getting the promotion. Do you have any idea what I mean?

SUBJECT: No. If I don't get some training before I start the new job, I just know I'll end up blowing the whole thing. If only I had a year or so to take some courses and get myself ready.

THERAPIST: Well, let's look at another alternative. Suppose you went in and talked to your boss about the impending job promotion and mentioned to him that you're very pleased with the job promotion and that, since you haven't been a supervisor before, you are considering possibly taking some night courses at a local college in order to be more effective.

SUBJECT: That sounds like a really good idea. Then I wouldn't really be putting myself down, and he'd know I would be learning while I'm on the job. Also, he'd know that I was working hard to improve my performance.

THERAPIST: What do you see as the added responsibility that you'd take on if you present this alternative to your boss?

SUBJECT: Well, I'm just going to have to spend some time hitting the books and in classes. That's about it!

THERAPIST: Yes, but if you're going to be going to school, and studying, and taking on a new job all at the same time, that's a pretty big load. Something may have to give. Do you have any idea of what that might be?

SUBJECT: Well, I'm going to be a lot more tired, I guess. But that's nothing new.

THERAPIST: You know, all of what you've said makes sense; but there may be some other consequences you haven't fully evaluated. For instance, what about having less time to relax from job pressures, or you might have less time to spend with your family and friends as a result of going to school, or you might be a little more irritable with your family, and, of course, there's the possibility that you might have some difficulty in school.

SUBJECT: Well, I guess all of those things are possible, but I wasn't looking at it that way. Still, I guess you don't get something for nothing. It's not quite as positive as it all looked at first. But I look at it this way. While there aren't a lot of rewards in going to school, if it all works out I'll have a new job with better pay, I'll be a supervisor instead of taking orders all the time, and my benefits toward retirement will be increased. That's a pretty big payoff and worth working for.

At this time, the subject would be encouraged to continue to evaluate several of the other behavioral options in detail, so that he would have seriously considered many different ways of possibly dealing with the particular situation. Then, the options would be arranged in order of priority by the subject in terms of their total anticipated consequences.

Before leaving the discussion of this stage of the procedure, it should be mentioned that there are at least two general types of problem situations which are unique and, consequently, for which there are really no "best" outcomes. The first of these involves handling a situation when nothing constructive can be done until the actual situation occurs (e.g., an impending court date, open-heart surgery). In such cases, the only adequate option is "waiting" and not engaging in any self-destructive behaviors. That is, rather than dwelling on the impending "crisis" or possible outcome, the client must learn to constructively view being patient and waiting as having the best probable outcome in these kinds of situation. The second unique example involves handling a traumatic or crisis situation (e.g., the death of a relative, partial paralysis). Again, in this case it cannot really be said that there is any "right" way of dealing with these types of situations. Yet, behavioral options can still be evaluated to determine which are likely to incur the least negative consequences. For example, if the individual assesses the traumatic situation as putting him at risk of drinking excessively, it may be in his best interests for him to arrange to be in the presence of close friends who are aware of his drinking problem and will help to occupy his time.

Stage 4 – Employing the Behavioral Options(s) Evaluated to Have the Best Probable Total Outcome. Finally, subjects were actually trained in and practiced the behavioral option(s) evaluated as having the best total consequences, even if in some cases the chosen alternative was expected to incur some negative consequences. In this stage, various psychotherapeutic and behavioral techniques (i.e., shaping, role playing, relaxation training, etc.) were used when indicated. In some cases, subjects were given homework assignments to complete prior to their next session. As has been reiterated throughout this chapter, the specific treatment methods and techniques were tailored to both the individual and the chosen behavioral options. During the treatment sequence, subjects were encouraged to use the problem solving skills procedure whenever necessary, both in the hospital and when they went home on weekend visits or were visited by friends or relatives.

As described earlier in this chapter, alcohol was available to all subjects in Sessions 7 through 16. Of course, the availability of alcohol and the appropriateness of any drinking was a function of the subjects' treatment group and various other conditions that existed through-out the treatment sequence (e.g., probe sessions and priming prompts). While alcohol was available and served on request during the treatment sessions, it did not interfere with the problem solving skills training procedure. Lastly, 30 min of Session 16 (a probe session) were videotaped.

VIDEOTAPE CONTRAST AND SUMMARY: SESSION 17

Session 17 was a summary session, and alcohol was not available to the subjects. The session had several component parts. First, selected videotape replays of drunken behavior which had occurred during Sessions 1 and 2 were contrasted with videotapes of the subject's sober behavior recorded during Session 16. The subject's progress throughout the treatment program was then discussed, and he was presented with a wallet-sized, plastic-coated card which specified on one side that he had participated in the IBT research program at Patton; the other side of the card contained a list of *Do's* and *Do Not's* specific to his treatment. *Do's* usually referred to patterns of appropriate limited drinking and to socially appropriate responses to setting events which had previously been associated with his past heavy drinking. Examples of *Do's* which were listed on subjects' cards included: (a) talk things over with your wife when you feel jealous; (b) use alternative methods of relaxing besides booze; (c) refuse a drink without being apologetic; (d) drink only when your wife is around; (e) discuss problems with your wife; and (f) keep up with child support. *Do Not's* were typically specific cautions, such as *Do Not Drink:* (a) after a quarrel with your wife; (b) if you have to work overtime; (c) after talking with your mother; (d) on the night that you pay your bills; (e) with American Legion or Purple Heart buddies; and (f) when stood up by your girl friend. While constituting a minor component of the entire IBT treatment sequence, the intent of the *Do's and Do Not's* card was twofold: (a) to serve as a reminder of certain personal issues which were highlighted for each subject throughout the treatment program; and, most importantly, (b) to provide the subject with the research program's address and phone number and with instructions to call the program collect when necessary. This latter element was included in hopes of facilitating follow-up contacts between subjects and the program.

Finally, the last part of Session 17 was devoted to encouraging the subject to extend the basic principles of the problem solving skills approach to other phases of his life. After this session, subjects were told they could request discharge from the hospital at any time. In almost all cases, discharge occurred within two weeks after Session 17.

CHAPTER 6

IBT: Emergence of New Treatment Evaluation Measures and Procedures

Traditional concepts of alcoholism not only prescribe certain treatment goals but also have strongly influenced treatment outcome evaluation. For example, traditional concepts usually portray the alcoholic as unable to control his or her drinking. Consequently, in evaluations of treatment effectiveness, drinking behavior is often portrayed as either abstinent (sober) or drunk. This dichotomous representation of drinking behavior is typically characteristic of most alcoholism treatment outcome studies (see reviews by Crawford and Chalupsky, 1977; Hill and Blane, 1967; Sobell and Sobell, 1975a). A host of similar problems have plagued the evaluation of all alcohol treatment outcome variables. Until recently, this can be attributed partly to the nearly nonexistent involvement of professionals and scientists in this field.

For years, investigators have laboriously documented a plethora of methodological deficiencies and inadequacies which pervade published reports of alcohol treatment outcome studies (reviewed in L. C. Sobell, 1977). However, while these deficiencies have long been noted, in the last few years there have been marked advances in the areas of treatment evaluation measures and techniques. The development of more adequate outcome evaluation methods and measures can be attributed, in large part, to two major influences: (a) the recent development and evaluation of an alternative treatment goal to abstinence—controlled drinking; and (b) the critical examination of traditional concepts of alcohol dependence. The emergence of new outcome techniques and measures can also be traced one step further, to the Individualized Behavior Therapy (IBT) study (Sobell and Sobell, 1972, 1973a, 1973b, 1976). This study, by virtue of its radical and controversial departure from the traditional alcoholism treatment orientation—an unorthodox treatment paradigm, including the goal of controlled drinking—made necessary the development of more sensitive and valid treatment outcome measures and follow-up procedures. Lest the reader be confused, we are not suggesting that the development of more adequate outcome evaluation measures could only have been accomplished *vis-à-vis* an unorthodox treatment paradigm, but rather that this radical approach made necessary the immediate development of alternative methods.

Clearly, the traditional dichotomous view of alcoholics' drinking behavior as either drunk or abstinent cannot reflect varying degrees of control over drinking. This, taken in concert with the controlled drinking treatment goal in the IBT study, compelled the development of a more sensitive and quantifiable posttreatment measure of drinking behavior. This suggested alternative dependent variable measure for evaluating drinking behavior was *daily drinking disposition* (Sobell and Sobell, 1972, 1973a). This measure will be defined shortly. To our knowledge, the IBT study was the first investigation which reported using daily drinking measures to evaluate posttreatment drinking behavior.

The traditional emphasis on "sobriety" (abstinence) as the primary indicator of treatment outcome, or in some cases the only such indicator, further limits the comprehensive interpretation of outcome findings. For instance, as early as 1962, Gerard, Saenger, and Wile presented findings which suggested that an alcoholic who had become totally abstinent after treatment could still suffer marked deterioration in other areas of life health concomitant with the abstinent state. Such findings have drawn attention to the need for interpreting outcome in terms of an individual's overall life health functioning. That is, in most cases, alcohol abuse is integrally related to one's total life functioning. However, an outcome whereby a person no longer drinks but develops or continues to have other serious life health problems (i.e., strong avoidance of social relationships, inability to maintain employment, aberrant behavior, etc.) should be seriously questioned if evaluated as "successful."

A number of investigators (Belasco, 1971; Emrick, 1974; Lowe and Thomas, 1976; Pattison, Headly, Gleser, and Gottschalk, 1968;

Sobell and Sobell, 1976) have, in fact, suggested that alcoholism treatment evaluation research should include multiple treatment outcome measures. Essentially, these authors' cumulative findings have suggested that *improvement in one area of life functioning does not necessarily imply or predict improvement in other areas of life functioning*. Given this evidence, the IBT study included a broad array of outcome evaluation measures which assessed multiple areas of life health. These *adjunctive measures of life health outcome* will be described in detail later in this chapter. First, however, it is necessary to consider the importance of using efficacious data-gathering procedures and techniques.

The utility of all treatment outcome evaluation measures is highly dependent upon the follow-up procedures used. It is well documented that most published alcoholism treatment studies report complete outcome data for only about 30 to 75% of all subjects in any given study (Crawford and Chalupsky, 1977; Hill and Blane, 1967; Miller, Pokorny, Valles, and Cleveland, 1970). Recent evidence (Barr, Rosen, Antes, and Ottenberg, 1973; Sobell and Sobell, 1976) suggests, however, that unless outcome data are gathered for a large proportion of subjects in a given study, the results might be biased in a positive direction. For example, Barr and his colleagues (1973) reported obtaining treatment outcome information on 81% of all subjects. Unsatisfied with this retrieval rate, they then implemented a second wave of follow-up to obtain a more complete subject sample. This second effort located an additional 10% of the subjects for whom no data had been previously collected, and "virtually none of this group was doing well" (p. 6). Bowen and Androes (1968) and Moos and Bliss (1977) have reported similar findings. Data from the IBT study (Sobell and Sobell, 1976) further support the conclusion that subjects who are difficult to locate for follow-up are typically functioning less well than subjects easily located (see Chapter 7).

While adequate assessment of any treatment program requires that data be gathered for a sufficiently representative sample of treated clients, numerous investigators have reported extreme difficulty in locating and maintaining contact with subjects over an extended period of time (i.e., Rhodes and Hudson, 1969). In fact, the number of published treatment studies with retrieval rates greater than 10% is so limited that it prompted Pittman and Tate (1972) to suggest that "considerable skepticism should be attached to any follow-up study with a retrieval rate of less than 90 percent" (p. 185). Needless to say, the use of the unorthodox treatment goal of controlled drinking in the IBT study made it imperative to obtain as complete follow-up data as possible. In this regard, we found 98.6% of all IBT subjects (69 of 70 subjects) throughout a two-year follow-up period.

IBT FOLLOW-UP PROCEDURES

Tracking subjects and their collaterals (significant others) to obtain adequate follow-up data has been viewed as a nearly impossible task by most experienced treatment providers in the alcohol field. Realistically, follow-up takes a good deal of time and persistence. Thus, one prerequisite for conducting an adequate treatment outcome study is planning the evaluation component prior to implementing the treatment program.

The outcome evaluation component of the IBT study was a planned rather than retrospective venture; consequently, comprehensive follow-up tracking information was obtained on all IBT subjects prior to their hospital discharge. The reason the follow-up evaluation component of the study was carefully planned was to minimize the difficulty of locating and tracking subjects for follow-up. Prior to their hospital discharge, an intensive individual follow-up planning interview was conducted with all subjects, both experimental and control. This interview was designed to obtain follow-up tracking information (e.g., addresses, phone numbers, places of employment, residence, personal identifying information, etc.) which could be used to locate subjects and their respective collaterals over a long time period. In this regard, detailed information on at least three collateral information sources (CISs) was obtained from each subject.

All subjects, both experimentals and controls, were told the reasons for the intensive nature of the follow-up—that the investigation was an experimental study funded by a federal grant, and that it was necessary to conduct the follow-up for an extended period of time to determine the effectiveness of the various treatments. Further, subjects were told that the follow-up was to be conducted with both themselves and their CISs approximately every month. They were told that the mode of contact (phone, letter, or personal) would be the method deemed easiest to obtain the necessary information. While subjects were not aware of the specific kinds of questions to be asked, nor the particular criteria used to evaluate their functioning, they were aware that questions would be asked about the specific amounts of alcohol they consumed each day and about other areas of life health functioning. They were also aware that their CISs would be asked similar kinds of questions. Most importantly, all subjects were assured that all information obtained during follow-up would be kept confidential and would not affect their welfare. They were further informed that no names would ever be associated with the publication of the study. Finally, all subjects were told they could telephone collect to report information about their functioning.

TRACKING PROCEDURES

Extensive tracking procedures were used to follow subjects and their CISs throughout the two-year follow-up interval. Subjects and their respective CISs were generally contacted each month for follow-up interviews for a total period of two years. Collateral information sources included individuals and/or agencies who had had any contact with the subjects in the preceding follow-up period. Subjects and CISs were always unaware of the exact dates and times when they would be contacted. While complete two-year follow-up information was obtained on 69 of the 70 subjects, some subjects, usually those functioning very poorly, were more difficult to locate for follow-up. Consequently, follow-up interviews for those subjects were occasionally conducted less frequently than scheduled.

As indicated throughout the book, the IBT study differed from other alcoholism treatment outcome studies in several respects. One of the most notable differences concerns the intense and frequent follow-up contacts with subjects and their CISs. A myriad of federal, state, and local agencies and individuals provided invaluable assistance in tracking subjects. The following examples best demonstrate the intensive nature of the follow-up which was conducted: (a) criminal records ("rap sheets") were obtained for all subjects every three to six months throughout the follow-up interval; (b) a copy of each subject's driver record was routinely obtained from the state where he resided; (c) all jail or hospital incarcerations reported by subjects and/or CISs were verified by contacting the respective facility; (d) routine checks of the local jails and hospitals in the area where the subject resided were also made to check for arrests or hospitalizations not reported; (e) subjects were traced to locations as disparate as Virginia, Texas, Montana, Louisiana, Hawaii, the Canary Islands, Italy, and Spain; (f) in some cases as many as 10 or 12

CISs were used to corroborate follow-up information for subjects; (g) reported deaths were always verified, and copies of death certificates and autopsy reports, if performed, were obtained; and (h) a listing of some of the major and more frequently used public and private agencies includes the California Department of Human Resources, Veterans Administration, Social Security Administration, bureaus of vital statistics and records, welfare departments, municipal courts, local halfway houses, Salvation Army facilities, and state mental hospitals.

Finally, the example which best illustrates the extensive and successful tracking procedures used in the IBT study involves a single subject. This subject, who had a prior history of transient behavior, amassed a total of 61 hospital and jail incarcerations during the two-year follow-up period (Sobell and Sobell, 1974). Despite this subject's transient life style, and as a direct result of the follow-up briefing procedures described earlier—collect phone calls and his understanding for the need to keep in contact—we were able to verify each of the 61 jail and hospital incarcerations.

IBT OUTCOME MEASURES: DRINKING BEHAVIOR

Follow-up interviews with subjects and CISs were structured so that specific data were obtained regarding the subject's functioning since the time of the last follow-up contact. As mentioned earlier, the primary dependent variable measure of treatment outcome used in the IBT study was *Daily Drinking Disposition*. Subjects and collaterals were not aware of the definitional criteria (i.e., operational definitions of drinking disposition categories) used by the investigators and were only asked, "How many days since our last contact have you had anything to drink and how much did you drink on each day?" Specific drinking reported by subjects and CISs were recorded verbatim. Alcohol consumption for each day of the follow-up interval was then coded into one of five mutually exclusive categories: (a) *Drunk Days*—usually consumption of greater than 6 oz. of 86-proof liquor or its equivalent in alcohol content (in earlier reports [Sobell and Sobell, 1972; 1973a, 1973b] *drunk days* had been defined as any day during which 10 or more oz. of 86-proof liquor or its equivalent in alcohol content were consumed, or any sequence longer than two consecutive days when between 7 and 9 oz. were consumed on each day. This particular criterion was used so infrequently, however, that we now prefer to describe drunk days as consumption of greater than 6 oz. of 86-proof liquor); (b) *Controlled Drinking Days*—usually consumption of 6 oz. or less of 86-proof liquor or its equivalent in alcohol content (as mentioned above, originally this was defined so that if a subject had consumed between 7 and 9 oz. during an isolated one- or two-day sequence, this would have been considered to constitute a controlled drinking day; it had been thought that this special contingency would allow for weekend or holiday indulgence, but it proved to be virtually unnecessary for categorizing treatment outcome); (c) *Abstinent Days*—no consumption of any type of alcohol; (d) *Incarcerated Days, Jail*—days spent in jail for alcohol-related arrests; (e) *Incarcerated Days, Hospital*—days spent in a hospital for alcohol-related health problems, usually detoxification.

IBT ADJUNCTIVE OUTCOME MEASURES OF LIFE HEALTH

GENERAL ADJUSTMENT

This measure was obtained every six months from the CIS who had had the most frequent and extended contact with the subject and the best opportunity to evaluate his total functioning during that interval. The CIS was asked to evaluate whether the subject's general adjustment to interpersonal relationships and problem situations during that period was either "improved," "same," or "worse," as compared to the year preceding his hospitalization.

VOCATIONAL STATUS

This measure consisted of the subject's evaluation of his vocational functioning as either "improved," "same," or "worse," as compared to the year preceding his hospitalization. Evaluations could be based on changes in job activities, hours worked, supervision, etc. which occurred in each six-month follow-up interval.

OCCUPATIONAL STATUS

This measure was an objective assessment of each subject's vocational activities during the majority of each six-month interval. Occupational status was categorized as either full-time employment, part-time employment, retired, physically disabled, student, on welfare, or unemployed. Whenever possible, corroboration of occupational status by CISs was obtained. Although rare, when contradictory ratings were found, the best documented rating was used.

RESIDENTIAL STATUS AND STABILITY INDEX (RSSI)

This measure summarized the subject's residential status and stability over each full year of follow-up. A "Residential Status and Stability Index (RSSI)" was computed for each subject, using the formula:

$$\text{RSSI} = \frac{\dfrac{1}{\Sigma_i \, [\, (L_i \times S_i) \,]}}{\text{Opportunity to reside}} \tag{1}$$

In Equation 1, L_i represents a subject's length of residence at any particular shelter (i), coded as:

(1) = Residence greater than or equal to 6 months (30 days/month).

(2) = Residence less than 6 months, but greater than or equal to 4 months.

(3) = Residence less than 4 months, but greater than or equal to 1 month.

(4) = Residence of less than 1 month.

Also in Equation 1, S_i represents the status of a particular shelter (i), coded as:

(1) = Permanent housing, defined as any residence where rent or payment occurred on a monthly basis (usually a house or apartment).

(2) = Transitional housing, defined as any residence where rent was usually required on a weekly or daily basis and where there was an expectancy that residence would be ephemeral (e.g., recovery houses, non-skid-row motels and hotels, Salvation Army, Rescue Missions, YMCA, etc.).

(3) = Transient housing, defined as an identifiable skid-row hotel or motel, a car, or no shelter.

Finally, in Equation 1, "Opportunity to reside" represents the opportunity of a given subject to seek shelter over the interval, computed as:

Opportunity to reside = 1 − (proportion of follow-up interval incarcerated in jail or hospital).

Thus defined, the RSSI has a range from 1 (highest residential status and stability) to approaching 0 (lowest residential status and stability).

VALID DRIVER'S LICENSE STATUS

This measure indicated the number of subjects who possessed valid driver's licenses at the end of the two-year follow-up interval, as compared with the number who possessed valid driver's licenses at the time of hospital discharge.

MARITAL STATUS

Each subject's marital status at the end of the two-year follow-up interval was compared with his marital status at the time of hospital discharge.

USE OF THERAPEUTIC SUPPORTS

This measure was obtained by recording a subject's use of any type of outpatient therapeutic supports (including AA) during each six-month follow-up interval.

POSSESSION OF RESEARCH PROGRAM DO'S AND DO NOT'S CARD

At the end of each six-month interval, both groups of experimental subjects were asked if they still retained their Research Program Card. Control group subjects had not been given these cards.

PHYSICAL HEALTH EVALUATION

At the end of the second year of follow-up, each subject was asked to evaluate whether, in his opinion, his physical health was "improved," "same," or "worse," as compared with his physical condition during the year or two before he entered the hospital.

In all cases and for all measures of outcome, discrepancies among (a) reports of subjects and their CISs, (b) reports of different CISs, and (c) reports of subjects or CISs and official records were always probed, with final data derived from the most verifiable source of information.

SUMMARY MEASURES OF IBT OUTCOME

Rather than evaluating treatment outcome results using several separate dependent variable measures, it is sometimes preferable to use a single index of outcome which combines the results of several outcome dimensions. For this purpose, we developed two such measures to evaluate the treatment outcome results of the IBT study. However, we caution that these general measures are preliminary in nature; their validity has yet to be determined. The interpretation of each general evaluation measure is discussed in Chapter 7.

The first general indicator of outcome, a *Factor Success* method, incorporates the second-year follow-up variables of drinking behavior, general adjustment as evaluated by a CIS, and vocational status as evaluated by the subject. For this measure, we somewhat arbitrarily defined criteria for success as follows: (a) successful drinking behavior defined as either abstinent and/or controlled drinking for greater than or equal to at least 75% of all days of the follow-up interval, (b) an evaluation of "improved" general adjustment, and (c) an evaluation of "improved" vocational status. Thus, a subject evaluated as successful on all three of these criterion variables could be considered a "three-factor success," a subject evaluated as successful on two variables would be a "two-factor success," etc. This method of combining factors equally weights outcome on drinking, general adjustment, and vocational adjustment dimensions and can only be statistically analyzed using nonparametric tests.

The second general indicator of treatment outcome was a single parametric index of success which could be used to compare individual outcomes. Using the same three dependent variables as the first general measure of outcome, a *General Index of Outcome* (GIO) was calculated for each subject, having a range from 0.00 (representing the poorest possible outcome) to 1.00 (representing the best possible outcome). The formula for calculating the GIO was as follows:

$$\text{GIO} = \frac{\begin{aligned}&[(\text{Proportion of days abstinent}) + (\text{proportion of days controlled drinking})]\\ &+ [\text{general adjustment weight } (1.0 = \text{Improved}, 0.5 = \text{Same}, 0.0 = \text{Worse})]\\ &+ [\text{vocational status weight } (1.0 = \text{Improved}, 0.5 = \text{Same}, 0.0 = \text{Worse})]\end{aligned}}{3}$$

$$(2)$$

LENGTH OF FOLLOW-UP: HOW LONG IS LONG ENOUGH?

How many years of follow-up data must be collected before an investigator can feel reasonably assured that outcome results are stable and conclusions valid? Research to date suggests that while changes may continue to occur in the status of individual clients, the number of clients in specific status categories at any given time remains relatively constant after about 18 months of follow-up. Thus, the length of the follow-up interval for the IBT study was chosen to be 24 months. This topic will be discussed in more depth in Chapter 7.

A LOOK BACK AT IBT FOLLOW-UP AND A LOOK AHEAD

Despite the intensity and depth of the outcome evaluation measures and procedures developed and used in the IBT study, the field of alcohol treatment outcome evaluation is still in its infancy. That is, there continues to be a need to develop more comprehensive and verifiable outcome measures with which to evaluate critical areas of life functioning. For instance, whenever possible, all measures of treatment outcome should be continuous and quantifiable. In this regard, Hunt and Azrin (1973) have provided an excellent example of novel outcome measures, using variables of "percent of time employed" and "percent of time away from home." Such measures are far more sensitive to intersubject differences than simple categorical measures such as "employed" or "not employed." Further, it is important that all treatment outcome measures be quantifiable and operationally defined.

Since the implementation of the IBT study follow-up, we have made several modifications and additions to our original battery of outcome measures. Since it is necessary to use a consistent set of measures to evaluate a given study over time, these changes were not incorporated into the IBT follow-up. We would, nevertheless, suggest that these changes be incorporated in further outcome evaluation studies. In fact, we are currently testing several of these modified outcome measures in another treatment evaluation project.

It is suggested that the following areas of life health be considered when evaluating alcohol treatment outcome:

1. *Daily drinking behavior*—while reports of drinking behavior are usually obtained from the subject or collaterals, this method of data

collection has been criticized as being extremely difficult to quantify and validate; to this end, it is suggested that investigators also use measurements of an individual's blood alcohol level, obtained through the use of breath, blood, or urine tests. Several studies have recently made use of in-field breath tests on a probe day basis to assess drinking (Miller, Hersen, Eisler, and Watts, 1974; Sobell and Sobell, 1975b; Sobell, Sobell, and VanderSpek, 1976).

2. *Vocational assessment*—number of days employed, type of employment, number of days missed work, amount of money earned, etc.

3. *Physical health*—liver function tests, evaluation of other types of physical impairment or problems resulting from consuming alcohol, etc.

4. *Time incarcerated as a result of alcohol use*—time in jail and hospital.

5. *Use of therapeutic supports after treatment*—psychotherapy, AA, pastoral counseling, etc.

6. *Residential status and stability*—how long one has lived at a residence, the type of residence, time spent away from home, etc.

7. *Social and familial adjustments*—time spent with spouse, children, and/or other relatives, types of social and recreational activities in which one engages, etc.

8. *Legal problems resulting from alcohol use*—incarcerations, divorce, loss of driver's license, etc.

9. *Financial*—monetary losses as a result of excessive drinking, gains as a result of not abusing alcohol, etc.

ON THE USE OF SELF-REPORTED DATA

A final concern of this chapter is with the reliability and validity of subjects' self-reports. Most of the descriptive, comparative, and evaluative data published about alcoholics are derived from self-reports. Furthermore, most of the pretreatment history information and treatment outcome measures in the IBT study were obtained from both subjects' and collaterals' self-reports. Unfortunately, despite the frequent and extensive use of self-reports in the alcoholism field, only a few studies have actually investigated the reliability and validity of such reports (see review by L. C. Sobell, 1976).

Largely because of the use of the nontraditional treatment goal of controlled drinking in the IBT study, several investigators have begun to question the reliability and validity of self-reports of drinking behavior, especially as regards the IBT study. Since the finding that some alcoholics can drink in a nonproblem manner directly contradicts the traditional concept that no alcoholic can ever drink again, it is not surprising that the validity of IBT subjects' self-reports of drinking behavior is being questioned. The reason is simple: many believe such results to be impossible. Interestingly, however, the existing limited evidence on the reliability and validity of self-reports suggests that self-reports by alcoholics who are interviewed when sober are surprisingly accurate and acceptable for use as outcome data, at least concerning alcohol-related events which can be verified by official record information and collateral interviews (L. C. Sobell, 1976; Sobell and Sobell, 1975a; Sobell, Sobell, and Samuels, 1974; Sobell, Sobell, and VanderSpek, 1976). In fact, one of those studies (Sobell, Sobell, and Samuels, 1974) actually found the self-reported incarceration histories of the IBT subjects to be remarkably valid.

Regardless of the outcome measures used, self-reports by subjects and their collaterals have been and probably will continue to be the major source of data describing drinking behavior and adjunctive measures of treatment outcome. For the present time, we suggest that alcoholics' self-reports be checked and supported for their reliability and validity in the following ways: (a) multiple collateral sources of information—friends, relatives, employers, neighbors—should be interviewed, as was done in the IBT study; this kind of validation can serve to increase confidence in treatment outcome results; (b) daily drinking reports can, in part, be verified on a probe day basis by obtaining unannounced, in-field breath tests of subjects' blood alcohol levels; (c) official records (i.e., jail, hospital, welfare, drivers' records, etc.) can be used to corroborate or disconfirm subjects' self-reports, as was done in the IBT study; and (d) periodic liver function tests should be used to assess recent (within three to four weeks of the interview) episodes of heavy drinking.

CONCLUDING COMMENTS

Throughout this chapter, we have stressed that the use of a controlled drinking treatment goal in the IBT study forced a radical departure from traditional ways of measuring and evaluating treatment effectiveness with alcoholics. In brief, these departures are as follows:

1. The use of a controlled drinking treatment goal forced the development of a more sensitive and quantifiable measure of drinking behavior—daily drinking disposition. Quite obviously, if varying degrees of control over drinking were to be assessed, the traditional binary nomenclature of abstinent vs. drunk would not suffice.

2. In the alcoholism field, follow-up has usually been conducted six months to five years after subjects leave treatment programs. In this respect, the use of daily drinking disposition measures raised serious questions about the accuracy of subjects' recall concerning the amount of drinking they had engaged in during a six-month interval. Accordingly, we selected a monthly follow-up interval in an effort to help all subjects recall events more accurately. While frequent follow-up contacts are uncommon in published reports of alcoholism treatment outcome studies, they may well have contributed to the successful tracking of the IBT subjects, in that complete follow-up data were obtained for 98.6% of the subjects. To date, this is the highest documented follow-up rate in the alcoholism literature.

3. As a direct result of the published reports of controlled drinking from the IBT study, long overdue questions regarding the reliability and validity of alcoholics' self-reports were raised. Investigators have now begun to systematically investigate this topic. Concomitant with the use of a controlled drinking treatment goal in the IBT study, several procedures were developed to aid in evaluating the reliability and validity of subjects' self-reports, including multiple contacts with collateral sources of information and the use of official records.

4. A broad range of treatment outcome measures were used to assess various areas of life health in the IBT study. These measures were developed consistent with the suggestion that multiple measures of treatment outcome need to be obtained in all alcohol treatment studies.

Because the treatment outcome measures and methods used in the IBT study are different from almost all other alcoholism treatment outcome evaluation studies, it is difficult to compare the results of the study with other published studies. For example, since this was the first study to assess drinking outcome using daily drinking disposition measures, we do not know whether the IBT drinking behavior data may be more sensitive and reflective of drinking as contrasted with the way drinking has been measured in other published studies. For that matter, many studies have never even questioned subjects about any limited drinking in which they may have engaged during follow-up. Therefore, comparison of the results of the IBT study with other alcohol treatment studies is extremely difficult, if not impossible. One might liken this task to that of comparing apples and oranges. In addition, the IBT study differs from other alcoholism outcome evaluation studies in that the follow-up measures and tracking procedures are more detailed and intensive than any reported to date.

In conclusion, while the IBT study was unique in a number of ways, one of its most important contributions to the alcohol field has been the development and implementation of more comprehensive and sophisticated treatment outcome measures and follow-up procedures. Finally, it should be noted that *regardless of the treatment method or goal, adequate outcome evaluation procedures and measures must be used to adequately determine alcohol treatment effectiveness.*

IBT: Results

This chapter presents a summary of the results of the IBT study and the major implications of those results. For a more technical and extensive presentation of those results, the reader is referred to the original reports of the study (Sobell and Sobell, 1972, 1973a, 1973b, 1976).

WITHIN-TREATMENT RESULTS

NONDRINKER EXPERIMENTAL (ND–E) SUBJECTS

Any ND–E subject who chose to drink alcoholic beverages during the treatment sessions could minimize the number of electric shocks received by ordering straight drinks (the smallest possible drink volume) and consuming those drinks in the smallest possible number of sips (straight drinks were served as three separate 1/3-oz. portions). In fact, the majority of ND–E subjects who ordered drinks followed this pattern. Four of the 15 ND–E subjects never ordered any drinks during Sessions 4 through 16. Although the remaining 11 subjects ordered some drinks, none ordered drinks during more than 6 of the 13 therapy sessions. The average number of sessions during which individual subjects ordered drinks was 2.1. Of the 59 total drinks ordered by the 11 subjects, 75% were straight drinks, 15% were beer, and 10% were mixed drinks. No ND–E subject ever ordered wine. Further, in 11 of the 31 total sessions when subjects ordered drinks, they did not consume all of the drinks they ordered. Additionally, of the 44 straight drinks ordered by subjects, all but 1 were consumed in the minimum number (3) of possible sips.

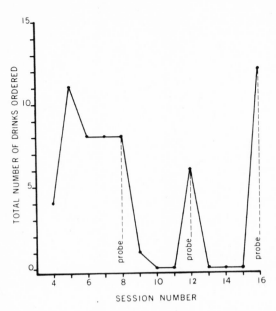

Figure 18. Total number of drinks ordered per session by nondrinker experimental subjects ($N = 15$) during experimental treatment sessions 4 through 16. Reprinted from Sobell, M. B. and Sobell, L. C. Individualized behavior therapy for alcoholics. *Behavior Therapy*, 1973a, *4*, 49-72. Permission granted by Academic Press, Inc.

Since shocks were programmed on a VR 2 avoidance schedule, ND–E subjects received only 61 of the 120 total shocks occasioned. However, a shaping effect over sessions was evident, as 116 of the 120 shocks occasioned and 58 of the 61 shocks received occurred prior to Session 8. Figure 18, which presents the total number of drinks ordered by ND–E subjects as a function of treatment sessions, indicates that some subjects (4 in Session 12, 3 in Session 16) formed a discrimination between shock contingency sessions and probe (no shock) sessions. Even though up to 6 free drinks were available during the probe sessions, all 4 subjects who drank in Session 12 and 1 of 3 subjects who drank in Session 16 ordered only 1 or 2 drinks. During Session 16, 2 subjects ordered 5 and 6 drinks, respectively.

While there was evidence that some subjects developed a discrimination between shock contingency sessions and probe sessions, no single subject drank during all three probe sessions, and no subject who drank during Session 12 ordered drinks during Session 16. Four subjects ordered drinks during two of the three probe sessions, and three subjects ordered drinks during only one of the three probe sessions. For most of the ND–E subjects, therefore, these results suggest that drinking responses were effectively suppressed over the course of treatment, even though alcohol was readily available throughout all sessions.

Drinks which were offered and consumed as priming prompts (ND–E subjects only, see description in Chapter 5) were not included in the data summaries. While priming prompt drinks were given to 11 subjects during 17 total sessions, only 3 subjects consumed those drinks. On each occasion when a priming prompt drink was consumed, the subject then proceeded to order and fully consume only one additional drink. Thus, there was no evidence that priming prompts, as used in this experiment, were effective in producing increased drinking. If anything, these occasions simply functioned as learning experiences where subjects practiced refusing free drinks.

In summary, ND–E subjects ordered few drinks throughout their treatment sessions. When drinks were ordered or consumed, this usually occurred so as to minimize the number of shocks occasioned. Some shaping of nondrinking behavior was apparent over Sessions 4 through 7. After Session 7, however, only one drink was ordered during a shock contingency session (Session 9).

CONTROLLED DRINKER EXPERIMENTAL (CD–E) SUBJECTS

All 20 CD–E subjects ordered drinks at some time during Sessions 4 through 16. The mean total number of drinks ordered by CD–E subjects over all treatment sessions was 27.8, ranging from 9 to 43. Like the ND–E subjects, CD–E subjects drank in a manner which somewhat minimized the number of shocks occasioned according to the respective avoidance contingencies. For example, no CD–E subject ever ordered a straight drink during any treatment session. Of the 556 total drinks ordered, 80.8% were mixed drinks, 13.5% were beer, and 6.6% were wine. In the 248 sessions (of a possible 260) where drinks were ordered, the mean number of drinks ordered by subjects per session was 2.2. Subjects ordered more than 3 drinks in a session on 14 occasions; 11 of these occurred during probe sessions, and 3 occurred during Session 6.

Altogether, CD–E subjects occasioned 63 ($\bar{X} = 3.2$) electric shocks and received only 30 ($\bar{X} = 1.5$) shocks. Fourteen of the 20 subjects received 2 or fewer shocks throughout the entire experiment, and the greatest number of shocks received by any single subject was 6. Furthermore, 7 subjects never emitted an inappropriate drinking behavior throughout the treatment sessions. On the basis of these data it seems highly unlikely that a conditioned aversion to electric shock was important in controlling these subjects' drinking behaviors. It is apparent, however, that the mere threat of shock effectively suppressed inappropriate drinking behaviors, as the number of inappropriate drinking behaviors emitted during probe sessions ($\bar{X} = 18.7$) was significantly ($p < .001$) greater than during shock contingency sessions ($\bar{X} = 2.2$). Similar to the ND–E subjects, the increase in inappropriate drinking during probe sessions could not be attributed to any small group of subjects; 2 subjects emitted inappropriate drinking behaviors during all 3 probe sessions, 2 subjects emitted such behaviors during 2 probe sessions, and 7 subjects did so in just 1 probe session.

With the exception that CD–E subjects learned to take smaller sips, little or no shaping of drinking behavior was evident over sessions. This finding was not unexpected as subjects had been explicitly instructed in Session 3 (the education session) about the differences between appropriate and inappropriate drinking behaviors. In this regard, the data could be interpreted as subjects simply following the instructions they were given in Session 3. The fact that no subject ordered straight drinks, even during probe sessions, further suggests that subjects earnestly practiced controlled drinking patterns. This interpretation is also supported in Figure 19, which presents the mean number of ounces of 86-proof alcohol (or equivalent alcohol content) which were consumed during each treatment session by those CD–E subjects who ordered drinks. While the mean number of ounces of alcohol consumed by subjects per session increased slightly over the course of the treatment sessions, the mean number of ounces consumed per session by subjects never exceeded 3 (the maximum for appropriate drinking behavior as defined in this study). Figure 19 also shows a significant ($p < .01$) increase of drinking during probe sessions (mean of 2.5 oz. consumed by those subjects drinking) as compared with shock contingency sessions (mean of 1.9 oz. consumed by those subjects drinking).

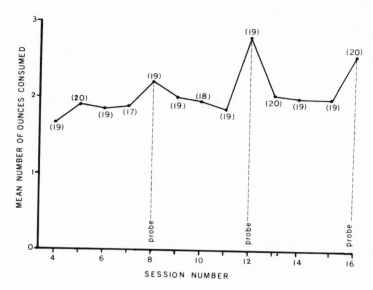

Figure 19. Mean number of ounces of 86-proof alcohol (or the equivalent in alcohol content) consumed per session by controlled drinker experimental subjects who ordered drinks during experimental treatment sessions 4 through 16. Numbers in parentheses indicate the number of subjects who ordered drinks during each session. Reprinted from Sobell, M. B. and Sobell, L. C. Individualized behavior therapy for alcoholics. *Behavior Therapy*, 1973a, *4*, 49-72. Permission granted by Academic Press, Inc.

The initial drinking pattern of most CD–E subjects was one of exaggerated sipping (more than six sips per drink) which subsequently decreased over treatment sessions to the minimum level necessary to avoid shocks. Thus, the majority of CD–E subjects, like the ND–E subjects, appeared to adjust their drinking behaviors during the treatment sessions to minimize the number of shocks they occasioned. This conclusion is supported by the fact that over the 13 treatment sessions each CD–E subject received on the average only 1.5 shocks.

FOLLOW-UP RESULTS

A perennial concern in the alcohol field has been what period of time is both necessary and adequate to gather outcome data which will be stable. In 1966, Gerard and Saenger addressed this issue in detail.

They reviewed the findings of three long-term follow-up studies conducted in disparate locations (England, Canada, and Connecticut). These studies used different outcome criteria, different patient populations, and different follow-up methodologies (Davies, Shepard, and Myers, 1956; Gerard and Saenger, 1959; Gibbins and Armstrong, 1957). They concluded that after a one-year follow-up interval ". . . the time interval does not influence the statistical patterning of the patients' status at follow-up" (p. 101). Thus, while the status of individual subjects may change throughout the interval, *the number of subjects in specific status categories at any given time remains relatively constant after one year*. As will be seen shortly, the IBT data lend support to this conclusion. Lastly, one of the studies (Gerard and Saenger, 1959) referred to by Gerard and Saenger (1966) used controlled drinking as an outcome category, with subjects compared at two-, five-, and eight-year follow-up intervals.

DATA SOURCES

Treatment outcome data were obtained for 69 of the 70 total subjects. No outcome data were obtained for one CD–C subject. (Throughout the first, second, and even a third year of follow-up, this subject was not reported arrested or imprisoned within the United States, nor had any state reported him as deceased to the Social Security Administration. Further, the Social Security Administration had no record of his having been employed during that time interval.) At least one collateral information source (CIS) was interviewed for each subject found during the first year of follow-up (Year 1), and at least two CISs were interviewed for each subject during the second year of follow-up (Year 2). Two subjects died before the end of the two-year follow-up period. Circumstances related to their deaths will be discussed later in this chapter. Tape-recorded interviews were also conducted with 67 of the 68 living subjects at the end of the two-year follow-up period. Results of those interviews will be discussed in Chapter 9.

DRINKING OUTCOME: FUNCTIONING WELL

For purposes of statistical comparisons, the daily drinking disposition categories of *abstinent* and *controlled drinking* (see Chapter 6) were combined and operationally defined as days *functioning well*. This was compared to days *not functioning well*, operationally defined as the sum of *drunk* days and days *incarcerated* in a hospital or jail as a result of drinking. During Year 1, CD–E subjects (N = 20) functioned well for a mean of 70.5% of all days, as compared to 35.2% for CD–C subjects (N = 19). This difference was significant (p <. 005) and continued through Year 2, with CD–E subjects functioning well for 85.2% of all days, compared to 42.3% for CD–C subjects (p < .001). During the final 6-month follow-up interval (months 19–24), 17 of the 20 total CD–E subjects functioned well for greater than 85% of all days. Only 4 of the 19 CD–C subjects met this criterion, and only 5 of the CD–C subjects functioned well for even the majority of the final 6-month follow-up period.

Differences in days functioning well were also significantly different (p < .005) between ND–E (N = 15, $\bar{X}$ = 68.4% of days) and ND–C (N = 14, $\bar{X}$ = 38.5% of days) subjects over Year 1. However, the difference between these groups was not statistically significant during Year 2 (ND–E, $\bar{X}$ = 64.2% of days; ND–C, $\bar{X}$ = 43.2% of days; .10 < p < .05). While one is tempted to describe the second-year follow-up data for the nondrinker groups as approaching statistical significance, our reasons for not doing this will become clear as we examine adjunctive measures of treatment outcome.

One ND–C subject died in an automobile accident 10 weeks after his hospital discharge, and consequently his data were not included in the statistical analyses. Although this subject had remained abstinent until he died, an autopsy report indicated a barbiturate blood level of 0.4 mgm. This finding confirmed reports by CISs that the subject had been using drugs prior to the accident. While driving alone, his car apparently veered off the road and crashed into a road divider. One additional ND–E subject was not included in the data tabulation for Year 2, as he had died a few days following the completion of his first year of follow-up. According to the autopsy report, this subject died as the result of a subdural hematoma sustained in a fall. The autopsy report found no evidence of alcohol or drugs in the subject's blood.

Although group data is frequently used for statistical analyses and presentation of results, Sidman (1960) and others have noted that reports based solely on group data may obscure important individual subject differences. Therefore, the percentage of days that each individual subject functioned well during each successive 6-month follow-up interval is graphically presented in Figures 20 and 21 for controlled drinker subjects and Figures 22 and 23 for nondrinker subjects.

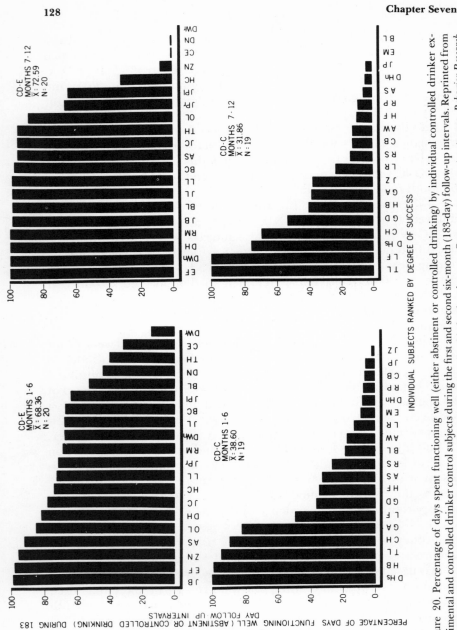

Figure 20. Percentage of days spent functioning well (either abstinent or controlled drinking) by individual controlled drinker experimental and controlled drinker control subjects during the first and second six-month (183-day) follow-up intervals. Reprinted from Sobell, M. B. and Sobell, L. C. Alcoholics treated by individualized behavior therapy: One year treatment outcome. *Behavior Research and Therapy*, 1973b, *11*, 599-618. Permission granted by Pergamon Press, Ltd.

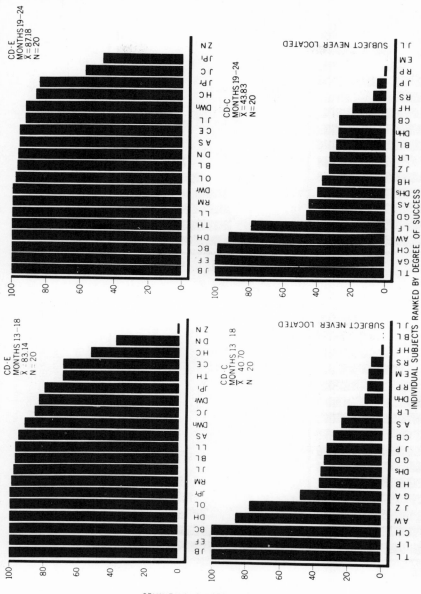

Figure 21. Percentage of days spent functioning well (either abstinent or controlled drinking) by individual controlled drinker experimental and controlled drinker control subjects during the third and fourth six-month (183-day) follow-up intervals. Reprinted from Sobell, M. B. and Sobell, L. C. Second year treatment outcome of alcoholics treated by individualized behavior therapy: Results. *Behaviour Research and Therapy*, 1976, *14*, 195-215. Permission granted by Pergamon Press, Ltd.

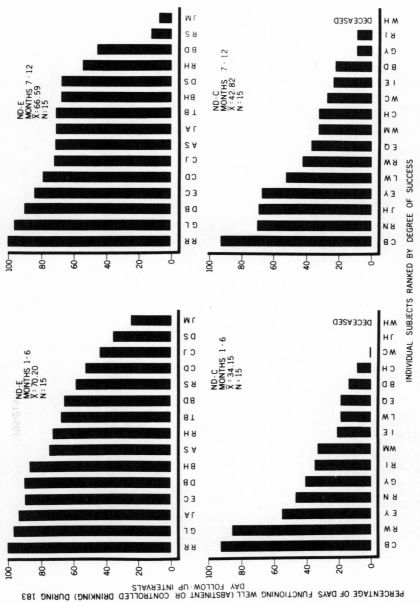

INDIVIDUAL SUBJECTS RANKED BY DEGREE OF SUCCESS

PERCENTAGE OF DAYS FUNCTIONING WELL (ABSTINENT OR CONTROLLED DRINKING) DURING 183 DAY FOLLOW-UP INTERVALS

Figure 22. Percentage of days spent functioning well (either abstinent or controlled drinking) by individual nondrinker experimental and nondrinker control subjects during the first and second six-month (183-day) follow-up intervals. Reprinted from Sobell, M. B. and Sobell, L. C. Alcoholics treated by individualized behavior therapy: One year treatment outcome. *Behaviour Research and Therapy,* 1973b, *11,* 599-618. Permission granted by Pergamon Press, Ltd.

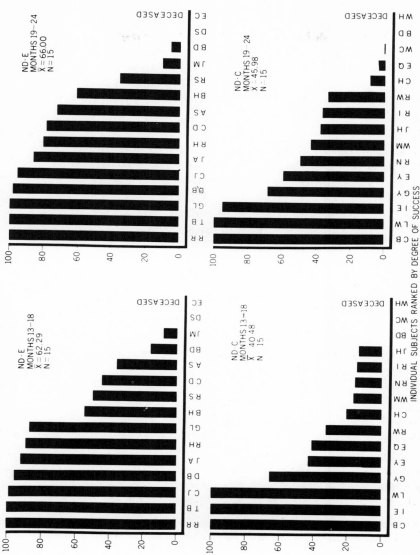

Figure 23. Percentage of days spent functioning well (either abstinent or controlled drinking) by individual nondrinker experimental and nondrinker control subjects during the third and fourth six-month (183-day) follow-up intervals. Reprinted from Sobell, M. B. and Sobell, L. C. Second year treatment outcome of alcoholics treated by individualized behavior therapy: Results. *Behaviour Research and Therapy*, 1976, *14*, 195-215. Permission granted by Pergamon Press, Ltd.

Using group data, Table 7 presents drinking outcomes for subjects in each of the groups over each of the two follow-up years using the mean percentage of days spent in each of the five mutually exclusive drinking disposition categories. Experimental subjects were abstinent a substantially greater number of days during each follow-up year than were their respective control subjects. Surprisingly, CD–E subjects as a group engaged in more abstinent days in Year 2 than any of the other three groups.

Table 7. Mean Percentage of Days Spent in Different Drinking Dispositions by Subjects in Four Experimental Groups, Displayed Separately for the First and Second Year of Follow-Up[a]

Drinking disposition	Experimental condition[b]			
	CD–E	CD–C	ND–E[c]	ND–C[d]
Follow-up Year 1 (months 1—12):				
Controlled drinking	25.19	9.56	3.33	6.13
Abstinent, not incarcerated	45.29	25.66	65.06	32.35
Drunk	14.02	49.88	13.99	39.85
Incarcerated, alcohol-related				
Hospital	11.34	5.55	11.77	6.29
Jail	4.16	9.35	5.85	15.38
Total	100.00	100.00	100.00	100.00
Follow-up Year 2 (months 13—24):				
Controlled drinking	22.57	5.81	3.65	1.56
Abstinent, not incarcerated	62.60	36.46	60.50	41.67
Drunk	12.27	49.25	20.37	37.47
Incarcerated, alcohol-related:				
Hospital	1.58	2.49	6.13	8.82
Jail	0.98	5.99	9.35	10.48
Total	100.00	100.00	100.00	100.00

[a] Adapted from Sobell, M. B. and Sobell, L. C. Alcoholics treated by individualized behavior therapy: One year treatment outcome. *Behaviour Research and Therapy,* 1973b, *11*, 599–618, and from Sobell, M. B. and Sobell, L. C. Second year treatment outcome of alcoholics treated by individualized behavior therapy: Results. *Behaviour Research and Therapy,* 1976, *14*, 195–215. Permission for use granted by Pergamon Press, Ltd.

[b] Experimental conditions were Controlled Drinker Experimental (CD–E), N = 20; Controlled Drinker Control (CD–C), N = 19; Nondrinker Experimental (ND–E), N = 14; and Nondrinker Control (ND–C), N = 14.

[c] Second-year summary does not include data for one deceased subject.

[d] Does not include data for one deceased subject.

[e] Nondrinker group incarceration data tends to reflect extreme scores of a few individual subjects.

The reported incidence of controlled drinking among subjects in *all* treatment groups was not surprising. In fact, it is consistent with a number of other follow-up studies in the literature (reviewed in Sobell and Sobell, 1975a; Pattison *et al.*, 1977) which have found a small proportion of subjects in abstinence-oriented treatment programs able to engage in limited drinking without incurring problems. Over the course of follow-up, however, the incidence of controlled drinking decreased for all groups except CD–E subjects. Similar to the abstinence data, clear differences were present between respective experimental and control groups in terms of mean percentage of drunk days, with control subjects experiencing far more drunk days. Over the total follow-up period, CD–E subjects experienced the fewest drunk days.

The mean percentage of days that nondrinker subjects were incarcerated remained relatively stable over the two-year follow-up interval. However, while in Year 1 ND–E subjects had been incarcerated more frequently in hospitals and ND–C subjects more frequently in jails, this difference was not evident in Year 2. Incarcerations for both groups of controlled drinker subjects decreased over the course of follow-up; the most impressive decrease occurred for the CD–E subjects who were hardly ever incarcerated during the final months of follow-up. Throughout the course of follow-up, CD–C subjects were incarcerated more frequently in jail, and CD–E subjects more frequently in hospitals. Since no treatment outcome studies have heretofore used daily drinking disposition measures, it is impossible at this time to evaluate whether the incarceration rate for the various groups of subjects was unique to this study or typical of similar populations.

DRINKING OUTCOME: CONTROLLED DRINKING

The nature and frequency of controlled drinking outcomes in this study is one of its most controversial aspects. Since some subjects in all groups engaged in some controlled drinking days, we can evaluate how controlled drinking behavior relates to functioning throughout the various follow-up intervals. Elsewhere (Sobell and Sobell, 1973b, 1976), it has been demonstrated that subjects, regardless of experimental condition, who were able to engage in 5% or more controlled drinking days during follow-up typically functioned better than other subjects in their respective group.

Some have suggested that one reason subjects in the other three groups did not function as well as CD–E subjects may have been a

Table 8. Individual Drinking Profiles Summarizing Subjects' Predominant Drinking Patterns during the Second Year (366 Days) of Follow-Up[a]

Group[b] and subject's initials	Abstinent days Total no.	Controlled drinking days Total no.	Type drinks[c]	No. drinks	Days/ wk.	Soc. env.[d]	Where[e]	Drunk days Total no.	Style[f]	Max. binge[a] drinks	Type drinks[c]	No. drinks	Soc. env.[d]	Where[e]	No. of days in abstinence oriented env.[h]
Controlled Drinker Experimental:															
J. B.	162	204	W	1–2	4	S	R	0	—	—	—	—	—	—	0
E. F.	252	112	M	3–5	2–3	S	R,O	2	1	—	M	10	S	R,O	0
D. H.	363	3	B	2–3	<1	S	R	0	—	—	—	—	S	—	0
O. L.	236	127	B	3–4	2–3	S	R,O	3	1	—	B	10–16	A	O	0
L. L.	164	197	B	2–4	3–5	S,A	R,O	5	1	—	B,M	10–12	S	R	0
B. C.	99	258	B	3–5	5	S,A	R	9	C	3	B	9	S	R	0
B. L.	302	55	B	3–5	5–6	S	R	9	1	—	B	10–15	S	R	0
J. L.	295	58	M	4–5	1	S	R,O	13	1	—	B	12	S	R,O	0
A. S.	255	97	B,M	1–4	2	S	R	14	1	—	B,M	10	S	R	0
J. Pr.	282	57	B,M	2–3	2	S	R,O	27	C	7	H	>20	S	R,O	0
D. Wn.	327	12	M	2–3	<1	S	R,O	27	C	3	W	12	S	R,O	0
D. Wr.	336	0	—	—	—	—	—	0	—	—	0	0	—	R,O	—
R. M.	175	140	M	2	4–5	S	R	1	1	—	M	10	A	R	0
T. H.	311	0	—	—	—	—	—	48	C	48	H	16	S	O	0
C. E.	272	33	B	5–6	<1	A	R	29	C	14	B	12–15	A	O	0
J. C.	93	170	B	4	3–4	S,A	R	89	C	85	H	8->20	S	R	0
H. C.	211	44	B	3–4	<1	A	R	104	C	2	B,W	12->20	A	R	0
D. N.	208	38	B	4–6	C[i]	S	R	69	C	64	W	>20	A	R	0
J. Pl.	221	12	B	2–3	<1	S	R	96	C	34	W	12	A	O	0
Z. N.	3	0	—	—	—	—	—	351	C	351	H,W	>20	S	O	0

Controlled Drinker Control:

T. L.	366	0	—	—	—	—	—	0	—	—	—	—	—	—	0
C. H.	292	73	M	3–4	1–2	S	R	1	1	—	—	16	S	R	0
L. F.	329	0	—	—	—	—	—	35	C	29	H.	12	S	R	291
A. W.	329	0	—	—	—	—	—	23	C	8	W	>20	A	R	143
G. A.	271	0	—	—	—	—	—	91	C	91	H	>20	A	O	0
J. Z.	206	0	—	—	—	—	—	150	C	49	H	12	S	O	171
C. B.	172	0	—	—	—	—	—	211	C	67	B,W	>20	A	R,O	68
G. D.	43	105	B	3–4	2	S	R	217	C	21	H,B,W	7–12	S	O	0
D. Hs.	26	114	B	3–4	2	S	O	226	C	92	B	9–16	S	R	0
H. B.	93	43	H	6	<1	A	R	230	C	60	H,B	8–10	A	O	93
A. S.	80	48	B,W	1–3	1	S	R	236	C	5	H	8–12	S	R	0
L. R.	98	2	B,M	1–4	<1	A	O	157	C	39	H	>20	A	R	3
D. Hn.	82	0	—	—	—	—	—	63	C	42	H,B	>20	A,S	R,O	19
J. P.	71	0	—	—	—	—	—	248	C	70	H	>20	S	O	0
B. L.	38	16	B	2–6	<1	A	O	285	C	116	B	>20j	A	R	0
H. F.	43	0	—	—	—	—	—	316	C	45	W	8–10	A	R,O	0
R. S.	29	0	—	5	—	—	—	337	C	16	H	>16	A	R,O	0
R. P.	19	3	B	—	<1	A	R	249	C	49	B	15–20	A	R,O	0
E. M.	16	0	—	—	—	—	—	350	C	350	H	8–16	A	R	0
J. L.	—	0	—	—	—	—	—	—	—	—	—	—	—	—	NEVER LOCATED

Nondrinker Experimental:

T. B.	366	0	—	—	—	—	—	0	—	—	—	—	—	—	0
R. R.	366	0	—	—	—	—	R	0	1	—	—	—	—	—	0
D. B.	344	11	M	8	<1	S	O	8	C	—	H	10	A	R	0
C. J.	284	67	B,M,W	2–7	1	S	R	15	C	6	W,B	8	S	R	60
G. L.	285	57	B	2–3	1	S	—	22	C	20	H	16	S	O	0
J. A.	327	0	—	—	—	—	—	21	C	21	H	>20	A	R	0
R. H.	311	0	—	—	—	—	R	45	C	19	H	>20	A	R	150
C. D.	221	3	B	1	C[i]	A	R	140	C	28	W,H	>20	A	R	0
B. H.	184	29	B	2	<1	S	O	149	C	28	H,B	>20	A	R	0
A. S.	179	20	B	6	<1	S	—	56	C	21	W	>20	S	O	68
R. S.	158	0	—	—	—	—	—	153	C	28	W	>20	S,A	R	44
J. M.	107	0	—	—	—	—	—	82	C	16	W,B	12j	A	O	25
B. D.	39	0	—	—	—	—	—	51	C	7	H	9–12	S	R	0
D. S.	0	0	—	—	—	—	—	304	C	163	H	20	—	—	0
E. C.	DECEASED—NOT ALCOHOL-RELATED														

Table 8 (continued)

Group[b] and subject's initials	Abstinent days Total no.	Controlled drinking days — Total no.	Type drinks[c]	No. drinks	Days/wk.	Soc. env.[d]	Where[e]	Drunk days — Total no.	Style[f]	Max. binge[g]	Type drinks[c]	No. drinks	Soc. env.[d]	Where[e]	No. of days in abstinence oriented env.[h]
Nondrinker Control:															
C. B.	341	25	B	2–3	<1	S	R	0	—	—	—	—	—	—	0
L. W.	366	0	—	—	—	—	—	0	—	—	—	—	—	—	0
I. E.	350	7	B	1	<1	A	R	8	I	—	B	12–18	A	R	0
G. Y.	246	0	—	—	—	—	—	61	C	7	H	>20[j]	A	O	230
E. Y.	187	17	B	1–2	<1	S	—	103	C	21	H	>20	A	O	93
R. N.	114	0	—	—	—	—	O	53	C	36	B	9–12	S	O	0
R. W.	122	1	B	2	—	A	R	241	C	97	H	>20	A	R	0
W. M.	110	30	B	1–2	<1	A	R,O	186	C	30	W	18	A	R	0
R. I.	66	0	—	—	—	—	—	266	C	49	B	14–18	A	R,O	0
J. H.	95	0	—	—	—	—	—	113	C	22	W	18	S	O	95
E. Q.	82	0	—	—	—	—	—	254	C	173	H,W	>20	A	O	0
C. H.	54	0	—	—	—	—	—	285	C	91	W,B	18	A	R	39
W. C.	2	0	—	—	—	—	—	4	C	4	H.B	>10	S	O	0
B. D.	0	0	—	—	—	—	—	346	C	190	H,W	>20	A	R	0
W. H.	DECEASED—BARBITURATE-RELATED														

[a] Adapted from Sobell, M. B and Sobell, L. C. Second year treatment outcome of alcoholics treated by individualized behavior therapy: Results. *Behaviour Research and Therapy*, 1976, *14*, 195-215. Permission granted by Pergamon Press, Ltd.

[b] Subjects within groups are ranked according to the percentage of days they "functioned well" (operationally defined as the algebraic sum of abstinent and controlled drinking days) during the second year of follow-up.

[c] Type of beverage typically consumed was coded as: H = straight whiskey or other high-proof (i.e., over 40% alcohol) beverage, M = mixed drink consisting of hard liquor plus a nonalcoholic mixer, W = wine with 12% alcohol content, and B = beer with 4% alcohol content.

[d] The nature of the social environment where drinking typically occurred was coded as: A = drinking alone and S = drinking in the presence of others.

[e] The location where drinking typically occurred was coded as: R = in the subject's own residence and O = in a location other than the subject's residence.

[f] Drunk days which typically occurred in a continuous (i.e., daily drinking) fashion were coded as C, whereas drunk days which occurred in isolation were coded as I.

[g] When drunk days were continuous for a subject, the entry in this column indicates the length of the longest drinking binge recorded for that subject.

[h] Days spent in an explicitly abstinence-oriented environment included any days when a subject was living at a halfway house, Twelfth Step House, Salvation Army, or other similar residential program.

[i] In these cases, use of the code C indicates that the controlled drinking days consisted of continuous daily drinking.

[j] In these cases, concurrent use of barbiturates and alcohol was reported by subjects.

result of subjects other than CD–E subjects attempting to drink moderately, which resulted in their drinking to excess. The data considered thus far are not useful in dealing with this criticism. However, two additional analyses provide a more thorough description of the subjects' controlled drinking behavior.

A statistical index to evaluate the extent of control that subjects demonstrated over their drinking was first suggested by Madsen (Doherty, 1974). This index, which we call a Drinking Control Index (DCI), is computed by dividing the number of days during which a subject engaged in controlled drinking by the total number of days during which the subject drank at all. The DCI value for any given subject, therefore, can range from 1.00 (indicating totally controlled drinking) to 0.00 (indicating totally uncontrolled drinking). While Madsen suggested computing a single index for each group of subjects based on their combined raw data, such an application would clearly be unrepresentative of actual group results (extreme scores by a few subjects would be vastly overrepresented in the group DCI). However, the index can be used to compute individual subject DCI values which then can form group data which can be meaningfully analyzed by statistical techniques. Indices were computed for CD–E and CD–C subjects for both the third and fourth 6-month follow-up intervals. In each case, differences between these two groups were statistically significant ($p < .001$). Similar analyses were performed comparing ND–E and ND–C subject indices for these follow-up intervals, but no statistically significant differences were found.

A second way of examining the relationship of controlled drinking days to total drinking days is to examine individual subject data. Thus, detailed Year 2 drinking profiles for each of the 69 subjects for whom data were gathered appear in Table 8. In some ways, the use of individual subject profiles is preferable to descriptive summaries of group data because the profiles provide a more complete portrayal of each subject's functioning.

The profiles in Table 8 provide strong evidence that those subjects who successfully engaged in controlled drinking typically did not initiate extended periods of drunk days as a result of that drinking. For example, only CD–E subjects had a high incidence of *isolated* drunk days, as compared to the predominant pattern of extended periods of continuous drunk days shown by other subjects. These findings have been independently supported by Oki (1974), who investigated the drinking of skid-row alcoholics living in a therapeutic community in Canada. He found that skid-row alcoholics who engaged in limited drinking were no more likely to get drunk on succeeding days than those alcoholics who did not drink at all. The data contained in the individual drinking profiles also lend support to Orford's (1973) assertion that some alcoholics are capable of controlling their drinking nearly all of the time, others are capable of controlling their drinking on some or most drinking occasions, and still others appear to never engage in drinking without drinking to excess.

The individual drinking profiles also suggest that situational determinants may have frequently influenced whether individuals engaged in controlled drinking. For example, only one subject, a CD–E, engaged in a substantial number of controlled drinking days which involved the consumption of straight drinks. Also, controlled drinking days occurred more often when subjects were at their own residences and in a social context, as compared to when alone or away from home. Lastly, no CD–E subject spent time in an explicitly abstinence-oriented environment (e.g., a halfway house, Twelfth Step House, Salvation Army, or similar residential setting) during Year 2, while several subjects in the other groups lived in such an environment for a substantial number of days during that period.

ADJUNCTIVE OUTCOMES: GENERAL ADJUSTMENT

Group differences in CIS evaluations of controlled drinker subjects' general adjustment were significant for both years of follow-up ($p < .05$), with between 80 and 90% of CD–E subjects rated as "improved," compared to between 32 and 47% of CD–C subjects (results were analyzed over sequential 6-month intervals; see original references for details). For nondrinker subjects, differences between the ND–E and ND–C groups were statistically significant throughout the entire first year of follow-up ($p < .05$); these differences, however, did not retain significance during Year 2. Between 50 and 73% of ND–E subjects were rated as "improved" over various quarters of follow-up, as compared to between 21 and 50% of ND–C subjects.

This measure is of interest, as the treatment procedures used with both groups of experimental subjects (CD–E and ND–E) stressed their learning to respond to problem situations in more beneficial ways than in the past. The lack of significant differences between nondrinker groups during the second year of follow-up, coupled with not finding differences between these two groups for other adjunctive measures, is the reason we are unwilling to even suggest that the drinking outcomes of nondrinker subjects approached statistical significance.

ADJUNCTIVE OUTCOMES: OCCUPATIONAL STATUS

"Occupational Status" refers to whether a subject was (a) employed, (b) nonemployed (retired, disabled, or student), or (c) unemployed, during the majority of each follow-up interval. The one noteworthy trend in these data is that the CD–E subjects became less unemployed over the course of follow-up. No differences between respective experimental and control groups were statistically significant during the first year of follow-up. While differences between the ND–E and ND–C groups continued to be nonsignificant over Year 2, differences between CD–E and CD–C groups approached significance for months 13–18 ($p < .09$) and were statistically significant during the final 6 months of follow-up (CD–E, $\bar{X} = 5.0\%$ unemployed; CD–C, $\bar{X} = 42.1\%$ unemployed; $p < .01$).

ADJUNCTIVE OUTCOMES: VOCATIONAL STATUS

"Vocational Status" refers to a subject's own evaluation of his job satisfaction during the majority of each 6-month follow-up interval. As might be expected, the results parallel the findings for the variable of occupational status. During the first year of follow-up, no group differences were statistically significant, although experimental groups ranged from 40 to 53% improved, whereas control subjects ranged from 7 to 26% improved. During Year 2, ND–E and ND–C differences again were not statistically significant (ND–E, 50.0% improved; ND–C, 28.6% improved); however, differences between CD–E (70.0% improved) and CD–C (26.3 to 31.6% improved) groups were found to be significant over the third and fourth 6-month follow-up intervals (mos. 13–18, $p < .02$; mos. 19–24, $p < .01$).

ADJUNCTIVE OUTCOMES: RESIDENTIAL STABILITY AND STATUS

An index of Residential Stability and Status (RSSI) was computed for each subject over each year of follow-up according to the procedures described in Chapter 6. The difference in RSSI between CD–E and CD–C groups was not statistically significant during the first year of follow-up and approached but did not attain significance for the second year of follow-up ($p < .09$). The difference between the nondrinker groups was not significant for either year of follow-up. Since this measure has never been used by other investigators, it is difficult to interpret. It may be that the RSSI is not sufficiently sensitive for general use as an outcome measure. For example, if only residential status had been evaluated and subjects were grouped according to whether they had spent the majority of an interval in a permanent residence as opposed to a nonpermanent residence, then controlled drinker group differences would have reached statistical significance. However, considering the lack of available quantifiable measures for assessing treatment outcome, continued investigation of this variable is recommended.

ADJUNCTIVE OUTCOMES: DRIVING STATUS

The number of subjects who possessed a valid driver's license after two years of follow-up was fewer for all groups than at the time of their hospital discharge. None of the differences were statistically significant. This variable, too, is difficult to interpret, as subjects could have lost their driving privileges for a variety of reasons not necessarily related to drinking, such as being cited for driving on an already suspended or revoked license.

Another driving outcome variable was the incidence of drinking-related driving violations (e.g., drunk driving, open container in car, etc.) per driver. However, such violations occurred so infrequently throughout follow-up that no meaningful statistical evaluation of these data was possible. Several alcohol-related events, including automobile accidents which caused subjects personal tragedy, will be discussed later.

ADJUNCTIVE OUTCOMES: PHYSICAL HEALTH STATUS

At the end of their second year of follow-up, subjects were asked to retrospectively evaluate their physical health status as compared with their physical health during the year or two preceding their hospitalization. Differences between the controlled drinker groups approached statistical significance ($p < .08$); 65.0% of CD–E subjects reported "improved" physical health, compared with 36.8% of CD–C subjects. Differences between nondrinker groups were not statistically significant; 60.0% of ND–E subjects reported "improved" physical health, as did 46.7% of ND–C subjects.

ADJUNCTIVE OUTCOMES: MARITAL STATUS

The percentage of subjects who were married increased substantially over the follow-up interval for both experimental groups (+20% for CD–E subjects; +25.3% for ND–E subjects), and either remained stable (CD–C subjects) or decreased (−16.2% for ND–C subjects) for the control groups. However, little empirical data exist to suggest that getting married should be unequivocally accepted as beneficial for subjects. Therefore, no statistical analyses were performed using these data, and their interpretation is left to the reader's discretion.

ADJUNCTIVE OUTCOMES: USE OF THERAPEUTIC SUPPORTS

The use of outpatient therapeutic supports by subjects during the follow-up interval is another variable which is interesting but not clearly interpretable. Consequently, no statistical analyses were performed using these data; however, the types of supports used by subjects will be discussed. Since very few after-care services exist which support other than abstinence, there was some question about the appropriateness of using this variable to evaluate CD–E subjects. Unexpectedly, however, CD–E subjects made slightly more use of therapeutic supports than CD–C subjects over each follow-up period. During the first year of follow-up, 8 of the 20 CD–E subjects used therapeutic supports: only 1 of those subjects used AA, 5 used psychotherapeutically oriented services, 1 used a recovery house not affiliated with AA, and 1 saw a private physician. During the second year of follow-up, 7 of the 20 CD–E subjects utilized therapeutic supports: 1 attended AA, 2 used other self-help groups (e.g., Neurotics Anonymous), 2 sought outpatient therapy, 1 saw a private psychotherapist, and 1 used multiple supports.

During the first year of follow-up (mostly the latter part—months 7 through 12) 7 of the 19 CD–C subjects used therapeutic supports: 2 subjects used AA while staying at an AA oriented recovery house, 1 subject used outpatient counseling, 1 used both outpatient and religious counseling, and 3 subjects used other resources (e.g., Salvation Army). During the second year of follow-up, 6 of the 19 CD–C subjects used therapeutic supports: 3 attended AA meetings, 1 joined another self-help group, 1 used Antabuse, and 1 received religious counseling. Although CD–C subjects had participated in treatment oriented toward abstinence, the relatively low use of AA by both CD–E and CD–C subjects is not surprising, as both groups had expressed a dissatisfaction with that organization and with traditional treatment modalities in general. In fact, such an expressed dissatisfaction was one of the major criteria used for assigning subjects to the controlled drinking goal.

All 15 of the ND–E subjects used therapeutic supports during the first follow-up year: 11 subjects used AA in addition to other types of services, such as recovery houses, outpatient counseling, Antabuse, and so on; an additional 3 ND–E subjects sought outpatient therapy; and 1 used a recovery house not affiliated with AA. In the second year of follow-up, 10 of the 15 ND–E subjects used therapeutic supports: 3 attended AA, 2 participated in outpatient therapy sessions, 2 received private counseling, and 3 used multiple supports.

Only 8 of the 14 ND–C subjects used therapeutic supports during the first year of follow-up: 6 subjects used AA in combination with other services, 1 used oupatient counseling, and 1 stayed in a recovery house not affiliated with AA. Over the second year of follow-up, 6 of the 14 ND–C subjects used therapeutic supports: 5 attended AA and 1 used another self-help group.

In summary, two comments about the subjects' use of therapeutic supports seem warranted. First, a greater proportion of nondrinker subjects than controlled drinker subjects made use of outpatient therapeutic supports over the two-year follow-up period. Second, consistent with treatment goal assignments, a substantially larger number of nondrinker subjects made use of AA compared to controlled drinker subjects.

ADJUNCTIVE OUTCOMES: ANCILLARY EVIDENCE

Some subjects experienced serious debilitation during the follow-up intervals. However, because of the outcome measures used, this could not be reflected in the quantitative outcome data just presented. Nevertheless, these events related to the subjects' drinking.

Earlier we mentioned that shortly after hospital discharge 1 ND–C subject died in a single-car traffic accident. Another ND–C subject was involved in a felony hit-and-run accident when drunk and received over 150 stitches for facial lacerations. A third ND–C subject, who was intoxicated while driving along a mountain road, failed to negotiate a curve and plummeted into a deep roadside ditch. As a result, he was hospitalized for four and one-half months in a full body cast. Another ND–C subject was hospitalized for 11 days with a broken jaw when he drove his car into a telephone pole. While no blood alcohol level was ascertained in this case, he and his friends reported he was drinking on the day of the accident. Finally, another ND–C subject fell off a two-story building while drunk and broke his neck, causing a temporary paralysis. He was hospitalized for three months. Thus, five ND–C subjects suffered serious alcohol- or drug-related personal tragedies during the follow-up interval. In contrast, only one ND–E subject suffered a traffic injury, having broken his leg in a fall off a motorcycle. At the time of the accident, however, the subject had not been drinking. Further, one ND–E subject died 33 months after hospital discharge. Although his death did not occur during the two-year follow-up interval, the death certificate listed the causes of death as broncho-pneumonia, hepatic coma, and cirrhosis of the liver. It appears that excessive drinking was definitely a contributing factor in this subject's death.

Controlled drinker control subjects were also involved in some serious incidents, although not as frequently as nondrinker subjects. One CD–C subject who was driving in foggy weather while intoxicated was involved in a multiple-car collision. As a result, he suffered severe facial cuts and a partially severed optic nerve. The latter condition left him permanently blind in one eye and with only 10% vision in his other eye. Another CD–C subject died 33 months after hospital discharge as a result of thermal burns over 50% of his body. He had apparently fallen asleep while smoking in bed in his room in a boardinghouse. At autopsy, he was found to have a blood alcohol concentration of 0.28% (ml/100cc). Over the duration of the follow-up, no CD–E subjects suffered similar injuries. These results, although anecdotal, perhaps indicate more clearly than quantitative data the extensive personal cost and seriousness of the subjects' alcohol problems.

ADJUNCTIVE OUTCOMES: RESEARCH PROGRAM CARD

A final variable of ancillary interest involved only experimental subjects. This variable simply measured whether these subjects retained their research program card (*Do's and Do Not's* card) following discharge from the hospital. At the end of the first year of follow-up, 90% of CD–E subjects and 86.7% of ND–E subjects retained their research program card. At the end of the second year of follow-up, 65.0% of the CD–E subjects and 78.5% of the ND–E subjects still had their cards. The large number of subjects who retained their program cards suggests that the cards were of some value for those subjects.

GENERAL MEASURES OF TREATMENT OUTCOME

Sometimes it is valuable to consider a single measure of outcome which incorporates several outcome dimensions. To this end, we developed two general measures of treatment outcome. While these measures were discussed in Chapter 6, we again stress that they are preliminary formulations and have not yet been validated. We computed these general measures of outcome for the second-year follow-up data only, as that interval seems best suited as a basis for deriving general outcome conclusions.

The first measure, *General Index of Outcome (GIO)*, provides a single parametric index ranging form 0.00 to 1.00, with 1.00 representing the highest attainable outcome. The measure incorporates drinking behavior, general adjustment, and vocational status. Consistent with the majority of aforementioned results, CD–E subjects (mean GIO = 0.8589) differed significantly from CD–C subjects (mean GIO = 0.4786) during the second year of follow-up ($p < .001$). Also consistent with earlier findings, ND–E (mean GIO = 0.6722) and ND–C (mean GIO = 0.5370) groups did not differ significantly from one another during Year 2.

The second general measure of outcome was a *Factor Success Method* and incorporated the same three variables as the General Index of Outcome. While this method can be evaluated only by nonparametric analysis, it provides less of a relative comparison between groups, as success categories and confluence of categories are specifically defined. The percentage of subjects in each group of subjects who qualified as three-factor successes, two-factor successes, single-factor successes, and nonsuccesses over Year 2 are shown in Figure 24. It was found that CD–E subjects had a significantly greater incidence of three-factor successes than CD–C subjects over Year 2 ($p < .01$). Nondrinker groups did not differ significantly from one another. This measure also demonstrates the distribution of individual subject success profiles within each experimental group.

PREDICTORS OF TREATMENT OUTCOME

Given that a multivariant approach suggests that treatments will be differentially effective for different types of subjects, then it is

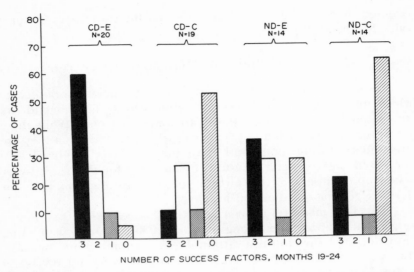

Figure 24. Percentage of subjects in each of the four IBT treatment conditions qualifying as 3-, 2-, 1-, and 0-Factor Successes during the final six months of follow-up.

crucial to determine how various subject and treatment characteristics in the IBT study related to treatment outcome. This section reports the results of a step-wise multiple regression analysis of the IBT outcome data—an analysis which investigated the predictive value of several variables. Since this is the first time these findings have been published, the analytic techniques are described in some detail. Readers who desire a more detailed explanation of these procedures are referred to several excellent reference sources (Kerlinger and Pedhazur, 1973; Nunnally, 1967; Tatsuoka, 1971).

METHOD

Multiple regression is a statistical method which can be used to relate two or more independent variables to the variation which occurs in a given dependent variable. The independent variables may be either continuous or categorical. Through the use of this technique, it is possible to estimate the independent contributions of each independent variable to the variance which exists for the given dependent variable (in this case, some measure of treatment outcome). The results reported here are derived from a statistical manipulation which examines covariation between several variables. Although it is a method which is invaluable for *suggesting* the relative importance of various factors, it is not a substitute for experimental design. However, the relationships suggested by the statistical analysis can help us choose which among several competing hypotheses should be given priority in experimental tests and thus can serve to aid in making clinical decisions until more empirical data has been compiled.

Other investigators, as discussed earlier, have concluded that a follow-up criterion interval of at least 12 months is required for stable group outcome data. On that basis, and because the studies they reviewed were not absolutely conclusive, we chose to restrict our dependent variables to outcome measures from the final quarter of follow-up (months 19–24). Additionally, since these measures represented the most recent interval of follow-up data, the selection of this interval also allowed investigation of the predictive relationship between earlier treatment outcome results and these later results (i.e., how well the earliest posttreatment functioning predicted later posttreatment functioning).

Finally, because of the time involved in performing multiple regression analyses, and because the probability of taking advantage of chance increases as the number of analyses performed on a single set of data increases, we restricted our outcome variables to those which were expected to allow the most meaningful and relevant interpretations. Four major outcome variables were selected from the follow-up data for months 19–24: (a) General Index of Outcome, (b) Percent of Days Functioning Well (Abstinent Days and Controlled Drinking Days), (c) Percent of Days Abstinent, and (d) Drinking Control Index. Separate regression equations were computed for each of these variables.

Further restrictions limited the number of independent variables chosen for investigation. Variables which were either of insufficient sample size or expected to have little explanatory power were excluded. Marital status is an example of the latter exclusion. In order to analyze these data so that significant relationships were likely to emerge, it would have been necessary to pool the categories of single, divorced, separated, annulled, and widower versus the category of married. The value of any finding derived by use of this variable would not, it was felt, have justified the degree to which it would lessen the sensitivity of the analysis. Pretreatment variables, therefore, included (a) indicants of prior severity of alcohol problems, (b) socioeconomic status, (c) age, and (d) education. The inclusion of education as a variable was deemed appropriate in that the experimental treatment involved a component possibly related to verbal skills (Problem Solving Skills Training).

Thus formulated, 13 independent variables were used in the regression equations:

Posttreatment variables

1. Percent of days subjects functioned well during follow-up months 13–18.

2. Percent of days subjects functioned well during follow-up months 7–12.

3. Percent of days subjects functioned well during follow-up months 1–6.

Within-treatment variables

1. Controlled drinking goal. (This variable was coded as a dummy variable, as were all categorical variables, with CD–E subjects coded as +1 and CD–C subjects coded as −1.)

2. Nondrinking goal. (This was also coded as a dummy variable, with ND–E subjects coded as +1 and ND–C subjects coded as −1.)

3. Order in study—subjects in each group were dichotomized according to whether they were treated either early or late in the course of the experiment (corresponding roughly to the first and second half of subjects in each experimental condition over time).

Pretreatment variables

1. Age in years.

2. Number of years of education.

3. Occupational status (categorized ordinally from 1 through 7 according to criteria established by Hollingshead and Redlich, 1958).

4. Self-reported number of years that drinking had been a problem.

5. Number of prior hospitalizations for alcohol-related problems.

6. Severity of previously experienced withdrawal symptoms, categorized as either (A) mild (tremors, agitation), (B) moderate (gastrointestinal upset, elevated blood pressure, sweating with tremors), or (C) severe (hallucinations, delirium tremens, seizures). Scores were based on the most severe symptoms a subject had ever experienced.

7. Total number of times arrested for alcohol-related reasons.

A step-wise multiple regression analysis, a relatively conservative procedure, was selected because, for the majority of independent variables, there was no *a priori* reason to expect a given variable to account for a greater amount of variance than any other variable.

FINDINGS

A summary of significant relationships obtained through the multiple regression analyses for all four dependent variables (outcome measures) appears in Table 9. Those readers who are unfamiliar with multiple regression analysis may find the following explanation more useful than Table 9.

When multiple regression equations were computed using all 13 independent (predictor) variables, the percentage of days that subjects functioned well during months 13–18 was found to be such a strong predictor of treatment outcome during months 19–24 (typically accounting for from half to three-fourths of the total variance) that the independent contributions of all other variables were overshadowed. That is, the percentage of days that subjects functioned well during months 13–18 explained such a high proportion of the variance in outcome that other variables were restricted and could account for only a very limited amount of variance. Therefore, acknowledging the strong predictive value of the percentage of days subjects functioned well during months 13–18, it was still of interest to determine how within-treatment or pretreatment variables related to outcome. Thus, multiple regression equations were recomputed for each dependent variable, entering as independent variables the three within-treatment variables and seven pretreatment variables. With the exception of the dependent variable of percentage of days abstinent during months 19–24, assignment to the controlled drinking goal (a within-treatment variable) was the primary independent contributor to outcome variance. Thus, a final set of regression equations was computed for each dependent variable, this time entering as independent variables only the seven pretreatment factors. Hence, three separate sets of multiple regression equations were computed for each of the four criterion dependent variables. The sets of independent variables included in each analysis are indicated by Xs in Table 9.

In Table 9, the symbol R indicates the overall multiple correlation of the combined independent variables with the dependent variable.

In order to legitimately interpret which independent (predictor) variables contribute significantly to the variance of the dependent variable (outcome measure), this overall correlation (R) *must* be statistically significant. The significance of the multiple correlation is tested using an F statistic, and levels of significance for significant Rs are included in Table 9. When the R is statistically significant, further interpretation is warranted. The squared value of the multiple correlation (R^2) represents the proportion of variance in the dependent variable scores which can be accounted for by the combined independent variables (predictors) in the equation. However, R tends to be systematically biased in a positive direction as a function of the ratio of the number of independent variables in an equation to the number of subjects contributing data. The higher this ratio, the greater the bias. In the present case, it was possible to calculate an unbiased estimate of the proportion of variance accounted for by the independent variables in any given equation by using a correction formula; these corrected values (Adj. R^2) are included in Table 9.

In the event of a significant multiple correlation, the relationship between outcome and predictor variables is indicated in Table 9 for each significant predictor variable by a standardization regression coefficient (β, usually interpreted as estimating the magnitude of the direct independent effect of a particular independent variable on a dependent variable, when the shared variance with other independent variables in the equation has been partialled out). The significance of each β value is then tested using an F statistic. The results of these analyses, for those occasions when significant relationships were found, are included in Table 9. If an independent variable (predictor) is found to be significantly related to outcome, these findings are usually stated in terms of the proportion of (outcome measure) variance (R^2) accounted for by the specific independent variable (predictor).

Several conclusions can be drawn from Table 9. First, it appears as though Gerard and Saenger's (1966) selection of 12–18 months as a criterion interval for stable follow-up is supported by the IBT data. That is, the outcome data for months 13 through 18 predicted a massive proportion of the variance in outcome results for months 19 through 24. In this regard, it is surprising that only a weak relationship was found between first-year outcome data and second-year data; however, contributions of the data for months 1 through 12 may have been overshadowed by the relationship of final outcome

Table 9

Summary Table of Significant Findings of Multiple Regression Analyses Conducted for Four Dependent (Predicted) Variables Using Thirteen Independent (Predictor) Variables, Significance Levels, Unadjusted (R^2) and Adjusted (Adj. R^2) Proportion of Variance Accounted for, and Standardized Regression Coefficients (β) for Significant Predictor Variables

Predicted variable (mos. 19–24)	Factors in equation (X)			Sig. level	R^2	Adj. R^2	Significant independent variables			
	Post-treatment (3)	Within-treatment (3)	Pre-treatment (7)				Predictor variables	Sig. level	R^2	β
General index of outcome	X		X	$p<.01$	.66	.57	% days functioning well mos. 13–18	$p<.01$	.61	.70
		X	X	$p<.05$	.25	.13	Controlled drinking goal	$p<.05$	.20	.46
			X	n.s.	–	–				
% days functioning well	X	X	X	$p<.01$	.80	.75	% days functioning well mos. 13–18	$p<.01$	.75	.78
							Controlled drinking goal	$p<.01$	.21	.48
			X	n.s.	–	–				
% Days abstinent	X		X	$p<.01$	.62	.53	% days functioning well mos. 13–18	$p<.01$	.56	.81
		X	X	n.s.	–	–				
			X	n.s.	–	–				
Drinking control index	X		X	$p<.01$	.70	.61	% days functioning well mos. 13–18	$p<.01$	.44	.36
							Alcohol hospitalizations	$p<.05$	.10	–.22
							Education	$p<.05$	.03	–.24
		X	X	$p<.01$	.56	.48	Controlled drinking goal	$p<.01$	.33	–.63
							Alcohol hospitalizations	$p<.05$	.16	–.30
			X	$p<.05$	.22	.13	Alcohol hospitalizations	$p<.01$	.17	–.44

results with data for follow-up months 13 through 18. In any event, it would certainly appear that the results for the dependent variables assessed were quite stable during the second year of follow-up.

Second, the relationship of assignment to a controlled drinking goal with successful outcome, derived mostly from the CD–E group (indicated by the positive beta weights, β), implies that the experimental treatment oriented toward controlled drinking was a significant determinant of treatment outcome, overshadowing all pretreatment variables for the CD–E group. A further indication that treatment had an effect is evident in the difference between variables related to the dependent variables of percentage of days abstinent and drinking control index. The controlled drinking goal dimension did not contribute significantly to the variance of percentage of days abstinent. In fact, it was subsidiary to the nondrinking goal as a predictor of outcome, although both were nonsignificant. For the outcome measure of drinking control index, however, assignment to a controlled drinking goal accounted for approximately 33% of the outcome variance when posttreatment variables were excluded from the multiple regression equations.

Finally, the pretreatment variable found to be most useful in predicting controlled drinking outcomes was prior hospitalizations for alcohol-related problems. *Subjects who had a greater number of previous hospitalizations were less likely to successfully engage in controlled drinking.* This is an important finding, as occasionally it has been suggested that a controlled drinking objective might be most appropriately used with individuals who have very chronic and serious drinking histories, presumably including several hospitalizations (Nathan and Briddell, 1977). The present findings clearly indicate that controlled drinking is less likely to be the outcome in such cases.

SUMMARY OF IBT RESULTS

WITHIN-SESSION FINDINGS

During treatment sessions, both groups of experimental subjects (ND–E and CD–E) drank in a manner so as to minimize the number of shocks they received. In early sessions, some shaping of ND–E drinking behavior was apparent. On the other hand, most CD–E subjects adopted an appropriate drinking pattern from the beginning of the treatment sessions.

TREATMENT OUTCOME FINDINGS

Treatment outcome data were obtained for 69 of the 70 IBT subjects over a two-year follow-up period. The results of statistical comparisons of major outcome variables are summarized in Table 10. Briefly, these analyses indicated that:

1. CD–E subjects functioned well (were abstinent or drinking in a controlled fashion) for a significantly greater proportion of the follow-up interval than CD–C subjects.

2. While ND–E subjects functioned significantly better than ND–C subjects during the first year of follow-up in terms of drinking behavior, this difference was not significant during the second year of follow-up.

3. Only CD–E subjects engaged in a substantial number of controlled drinking days over the entire follow-up interval, although

Table 10. Summary of Results of Statistical Analyses Performed between Respective Controlled Drinker and Nondrinker Experimental and Control Groups for Major Treatment Outcome Measures

	Groups compared	
Outcome variable	CD–E vs. CD–C	ND–E vs. ND–C
% days functioning well, Year 1	$p < .005$	$p < .005$
% days functioning well, Year 2	$p < .001$	$.10 < p < .05$
Drinking control index, Year 2	$p < .001$	n.s.
CIS evaluations of subjects':		
General adjustment, Year 1	$p < .05$	$p < .05$
General adjustment, Year 2	$p < .05$	n.s.
Occupational status, Year 1	n.s.	n.s.
Occupational status, Year 2	$.09 < p < .01$	n.s.
Vocational status, Year 1	n.s.	n.s.
Vocational status, Year 2	$.02 < p < .01$	n.s.
Residential stability and status, Year 1	n.s.	n.s.
Residential stability and status, Year 2	$p < .09$	n.s.
Driver's license status, Year 2	n.s.	n.s.
Physical health status, Year 2	$p < .08$	n.s.

some subjects in each of the other groups engaged in controlled drinking. During the final quarter of follow-up, CD–E subjects also had substantially more abstinent days than the other three groups of subjects.

4. Statistical analyses and individual subject drinking profiles demonstrated that when CD–E subjects drank in a controlled manner, their controlled drinking typically did not precipitate excessive drinking.

5. At the conclusion of follow-up, CD–E subjects also had significantly or near significantly better outcomes than CD–C subjects for several of the adjunctive treatment outcome measures (General Adjustment, $p < .05$; Occupational Status, $p < .09$; Vocational Status, $p < .02$; Residential Status and Stability, $p < .09$; Physical Health Status, $p < .08$). Nondrinker groups did not differ significantly on any of the adjunctive outcome measures.

PREDICTORS OF SUCCESSFUL OUTCOME

The pretreatment variable which best predicted a controlled drinking outcome was fewer prior alcohol-related hospitalizations. Assignment to the controlled drinking treatment goal was the best overall within-treatment predictor of outcome.

CHAPTER 8

IBT: Interpretation of Results

Based on drinking behavior and adjunctive outcome measures, it is clear that subjects who received the program of Individualized Behavior Therapy (IBT) with a treatment goal of controlled drinking (CD–E subjects) functioned significantly better throughout the two-year follow-up period than did their respective control subjects (CD–C subjects), who received conventional abstinence-oriented treatment. Moreover, the findings indicated that many of the CD–E subjects engaged in limited, nonproblem drinking throughout the follow-up period.

During the first year of follow-up, significant differences were found between Nondrinker Experimental (ND–E) and Nondrinker Control (ND–C) subjects for the variable of drinking behavior. While substantial differences continued in the second year of follow-up, they were not statistically significant. As might be expected, no significant differences were obtained between nondrinker groups during the second year of follow-up for any adjunctive outcome measures.

Given these results, one might conclude that the treatment goal of controlled drinking contributed more to successful outcomes than did the method of Individualized Behavior Therapy. However, *such a conclusion cannot be adduced from the present data.* The results of the IBT study are not only complex but unique, making interpretation and comparison of those data similarly complex, especially with respect to drinking outcomes.

FOLLOW-UP PROCEDURES AND THE INTERPRETATION OF
OUTCOME VARIABLES

In the IBT study, a great deal of effort went into obtaining official records of subjects' dysfunctioning and corroborating subjects' self-reports using multiple collateral information sources. However, despite the frequent and extensive use of alcoholics' self-reports in the alcoholism field, very few studies have investigated the reliability and validity of such reports. As mentioned in Chapter 6, comparison of IBT subjects' official arrest records with their self-reports of prior alcohol-related arrests found that their self-reports were surprisingly accurate and acceptable for use as a primary information source (Sobell, Sobell, and Samuels, 1974). Subsequent reports using other alcoholic populations (L. C. Sobell, 1976; Sobell and Sobell, 1975c; Sobell, Sobell, and VanderSpek, 1976) have also found that alcoholics' self-reports tend to be accurate sources of data, with the caveat that subjects should not be interviewed when they are drinking. At the present time, however, given the state of the art, it would be unwise to depend totally upon any single source of data for outcome evaluation.

The follow-up component of the IBT study was specifically designed to gather data from multiple sources: subjects' self-reports, the reports of multiple collateral information sources, and official records. Furthermore, data were collected on a monthly basis. Heretofore, follow-up of this magnitude has been lacking in the alcohol field. Therefore, the results reported here should be, at least, as valid as those of other well-designed alcoholism treatment outcome studies and probably more valid than the majority of other outcome studies in the literature.

Because of limited personnel and financial resources, the follow-up interviewer (L. C. Sobell) in the IBT study was not blind to the subjects' assigned treatment groups. Hence, one possible interpretation is that the results reflect a bias in favor of the experimental hypotheses due either to experimenter bias effects (Rosenthal, 1969) or to subjects' responding to subtle demand characteristics (Orne, 1969) in the follow-up interviews. While steps have already been taken to provide data regarding whether or not such bias may have occurred, the question of whether follow-up interviewers should or should not be knowledgeable about the nature of treatment will have critical import for the design of future treatment outcome evaluation studies. However, for the present, to suggest that follow-up interviewers be naive to all aspects of a study would disregard several important considerations: (a) subjects and their significant others are often interviewed about socially deviant behaviors; consequently, they might be reluctant to cast themselves in an unfavorable light with an unfamiliar interviewer; (b) subjects and/or collaterals might be distrustful of a naive interviewer, even if that person is obligated to protect the confidentiality of the data; (c) in order to assure that subjects are contacted frequently by naive interviewers, several interviewers would be needed, thereby incurring additional and possibly prohibitive costs; and (d) an unknowledgeable interviewer might not recognize or probe for important outcome information.

Conversely, there are several reasons why it might be preferable for follow-up interviewers to be knowledgeable about a study and familiar with the subject population. Certainly, interviewers who gather data for public opinion polls are to some extent knowledgeable about the studies being conducted (i.e., in polls of voter preferences) and apparently do not unduly influence their respondents. Furthermore, the whole question of subtle experimenter effects (Rosenthal, 1969)—whether conscientious experimenters will subtly and unintentionally bias their results if they are expecting a particular outcome—has been seriously challenged (Barber, 1976; Barber and Silver, 1968a, 1968b; Silver, 1973). There is little evidence in the experimental literature to document the presence or absence of such effects either in the natural environment or when experimenters conscientiously attempt to be objective. Even in situations conducted in the laboratory and using totally unskilled experimenters, experimenter effects have been difficult to produce. Typically, those studies which have found evidence of experimenter effects have (a) used experimenters naive to research studies (e.g., college freshmen, school teachers, etc.), (b) gathered data from subjects engaged in highly ambiguous tasks (e.g., viewing a portrait and judging how "successful" the pictured person has been), and (c) provided experimenters with special incentives (i.e., financial rewards) for finding results favorable to a stated experimental hypothesis. Most of the experimenter effects which have been found can be attributed to either overt persuasion by the experimenter or fraudulent gathering or reporting of data, rather than subtle communication from experimenter to subject.

Even if naive follow-up interviewers are used, it is expected that over time (e.g., two years) a sophisticated interviewer would become aware of the experimental hypotheses, even if never explicitly informed of them (Beatty, 1972). In a study such as the IBT experiment, which used procedures so clearly different from conventional treatment, it is very probable that differences between subjects would have been apparent to a sophisticated interviewer within the space of a single interview with the subject and his collaterals. When we consider that the IBT follow-up procedures involved multiple contacts with both subjects and their collateral information sources, as well as frequent exposures to subjects' behaviors, the possibility of a sophisticated observer having remained naive is highly unlikely.

Another aspect of this same problem involves establishing and maintaining rapport with subjects and their collaterals in order to follow and evaluate them over an extended period of time. Recent evidence suggests that unless outcome data are gathered for a large portion of subjects in any given study, the results might be biased in a positive direction. Often studies in the alcoholism literature fail to obtain outcome data for a sizable proportion of subjects. As mentioned in Chapter 6, several studies have now found that subjects who are more difficult to locate for follow-up are also typically functioning worse than other subjects in the same study. Data from the IBT study also supported this conclusion. Of the 69 subjects, 5 were extremely difficult to locate for follow-up. In some cases, final data for those subjects were only collected several months after their designated follow-up intervals had expired. Of those subjects, 2 were found to have functioned worse than all other subjects in their respective groups during the second year of follow-up (Z. N., CD–E, 0.81% days functioned well; B. D., ND–E, 0.00% days functioned well); 2 functioned considerably below their respective group averages (R. V., CD–C, 7.92% days functioned well; C. B., CD–C, 28.42% days functioned well); and the remaining 1 subject functioned slightly below the average for his group (R. H., ND–E, 58.20% days functioned well). Given the apparent necessity of gathering complete follow-up information for as many subjects as possible in a given study, it would seem that for the time being the preferred procedure for gathering follow-up information will be to use interviewers who are both knowledgeable and objective.

An independent, double-blind, third-year follow-up investigation of the IBT study has been completed by two investigators (Caddy and Perkins, in preparation) and is expected to be of value in answering questions about whether the interviewer's knowledge about the study and rapport influenced the results of the study. In the third-year, independent investigation, interviewers were totally blind regarding the original experiment, the experimental hypotheses, and assigned groups. Furthermore, they were academically naive to traditional or radical beliefs about the syndrome known as "alcoholism." Subjects were interviewed on or about the date of the conclusion of their third year following discharge from the hospital. Interviews with subjects and their respective collateral information sources were tape-recorded, and the recordings were then scored by other independent judges, equally blind to the hypotheses. That study had four basic objectives: (a) to determine how subjects functioned during their third year of follow-up; (b) to assess whether there were any indications from the third-year follow-up data that the previous monthly follow-up contacts may have functioned as a "continuing care" process; (c) to determine the validity of the two-year follow-up results already reported; and (d) to determine in what manner conclusions about alcoholism treatment outcome are significantly influenced by the nature of outcome measures used—the third-year project assessed treatment outcome using many of the measures used in the present study, along with some new evaluation measures.

Lastly, the third-year outcome study will provide additional information regarding an adequate criterion interval for the gathering of follow-up information. It will be recalled from our earlier discussion that a 12- to 18-month follow-up interval has been evaluated as adequate for obtaining relatively stable group results, although individual subject data may continue to fluctuate for a number of years. To some extent, the third-year outcome study will also indicate whether subjects' functioning remained relatively stable after the monthly follow-up contacts were discontinued.

THE VALUE OF MULTIPLE MEASURES OF OUTCOME

A popular and long-standing assumption in the alcoholism field has been that if an individual is abstinent, then treatment was "successful." However, several studies have provided cogent evidence that a change in drinking behavior (i.e., becoming abstinent) does not necessarily mean that individuals have improved their life functioning in other areas (Belasco, 1971; Emrick, 1974; Gerard and Saenger, 1966; Gerard, Saenger, and Wile, 1962; Pattison, Headley, Gleser, and Gottschalk, 1968). Still, there is often a high correlation between these variables, especially when group data are considered.

In terms of overall results, the IBT study clearly demonstrates the utility of multiple measures of treatment outcome. For instance, if we had restricted our outcome evaluation solely to drinking behavior, results for the nondrinker groups might have been interpreted as reflecting a significant difference, especially considering the small number of subjects in each group. However, in view of the lack of significant differences on other adjunctive outcome measures, such an interpretation was untenable. Thus, multiple measures were clearly of value in interpreting both results of drinking behavior and overall life health functioning.

The following case examples of IBT subjects lend further support to the premise that drinking behavior outcomes do not always relate positively to a subject's overall life health outcome.

CASE EXAMPLE: CD-E SUBJECT J. L.

If drinking behavior data were the only parameter by which subject J. L. had been evaluated, then he would have been considered to have functioned well for 96.4% of the days comprising Year 2, and 90.2% of all days during the entire two-year evaluation period. However, when other outcome measures were considered, it was found that the subject had (a) repeatedly moved from city to city leaving a trail of unpaid bills, (b) obtained welfare and funds for the indigent while working full-time, and (c) fraudulently staged a marriage in order to obtain funds and material goods from his friends and relatives. During the period immediately prior to the IBT study, this subject had engaged in similar types of "antisocial" behavior, even though drunk most of the time. This example points out that while the subject's drinking behavior had improved to the point where drinking interfered very little with the rest of his life, his total adjustment can be described in terms of his having become a "sober sociopath." In this regard, some of his friends felt that since he had stopped having drinking problems, he actually had more time to engage in antisocial and manipulative ventures.

CASE EXAMPLE: CD-C SUBJECT E. M.

The data for subject E. M. indicated that he was drunk 95.4% of follow-up Year 1 and 95.6% of Year 2. Essentially, this subject had 699 days when he drank anywhere from 12 to 16 oz. of 86-proof hard liquor, and only 33 days when he was abstinent. It must be noted that these two years of posttreatment drinking behavior did not differ markedly from the subject's self-reported drinking behavior during the two years prior to treatment. Interestingly, throughout the entire follow-up period, he was employed full-time, never missed a day of work, had a valid driver's license, was not incarcerated in any hospital or jail for alcohol-related reasons, did not stay in a halfway house, paid all his bills, and supported his family. In this case, it was obvious that the subject isolated his drinking so that it caused him minimal problems. For instance, although he was a cabdriver, he never drank on the job. Instead, he would get up in the morning, go to work, get off work, come home and ritualistically drink 12 to 16 oz. of hard liquor, eat dinner, and go to bed. While his family evaluated his follow-up adjustment as "worse" than the year or two preceding treatment, they were also careful to point out that he had adequately supported them and that there were few family arguments. Thus, whereas the subject's drinking behavior was almost totally dysfunctional, especially as relates to physical health, little impairment was found for other measures of treatment outcome.

CASE EXAMPLE: ND-C SUBJECT R. N.

In the first year of follow-up, subject R. N. worked full-time while being drunk 41% of all days. During his second year of follow-up, he failed to negotiate a curve while driving drunk, plunged his car over a steep cliff, and seriously injured himself. As a result of the accident, he was hospitalized in a full body cast for four and one-half months, is permanently disabled, and cannot return to his former vocation as a construction worker. During the second follow-up year he was drunk only 14.5% of the time, as he was hospitalized for a total of six months. For a time after his discharge from the hospital, he remained at home in bed in a full body cast and did not have free access to alcohol; consequently, he was abstinent most of the time. Interestingly, the subject's collateral, his wife, evaluated his general adjustment as "improved." Her evaluation was based on the fact that since he was not drinking, he could not further damage his physical health, even though he was hospitalized in a full body cast and had lost 60 pounds. Further, both the subject and his wife felt that his hospitalization constituted one of the first times that they had been able to sit down and talk when he was not drunk.

These three case examples serve to illustrate that changes in drinking behavior do not necessarily indicate that an individual has therefore improved his functioning in other areas of life health. In fact, in the last case example, while the subject was abstinent more during the second year of follow-up than the first, he had also experienced marked deterioration in both his physical and vocational life health. While most IBT subjects who demonstrated increased functioning in drinking behavior also demonstrated improved functioning in other areas of life health, these examples are sufficient to demonstrate the importance of using multiple measures in treatment outcome evaluation.

CONTROLLED DRINKING AS AN OUTCOME

Until quite recently, the use of a treatment goal of controlled drinking has been rare. It therefore creates certain problems for interpreting outcome data. For instance, daily drinking baseline data are not available for normal drinkers in the general population; thus, it is difficult to determine how well the IBT subjects approximated societal drinking norms. However, if a longitudinal baseline study were conducted using daily drinking dispostion measures, it is probable that normal drinking patterns would be found to consist of large proportions of both abstinent and controlled drinking days, accompanied in most cases by a few drunk days (e.g., greater than 6 oz. of 86-proof liquor or its equivalent in alcohol content).

As demonstrated by numerous studies, categorizing an alcoholic's drinking behavior as either "drunk" or "abstinent" constitutes an oversimplification and is unrepresentative of the actual drinking behavior of most alcoholics. It would be similarly naive to consider a controlled drinking outcome as stereotypically involving either daily drinking or *never* drinking to excess. For purposes of data collection and maintaining consistency of measures over the follow-up period, we arbitrarily defined "controlled drinking" in the IBT study. In terms of interpreting treatment outcome results, however, questions about whether, and to what extent, drinking may have interferred with subjects' life functioning are more important than quantity–frequency nomenclatures. In fact, since the completion of the IBT study, we now prefer to focus on the consequences and potential consequences of drinking, rather than attempting to assess a putative process of "self-control."

Given the foregoing, we prefer to interpret the outcome data contained in individual subject profiles in a manner similar to that suggested by Orford (1973). The individual profile data for subjects' drinking during the follow-up interval, taken in conjunction with their functioning in other areas of life health, suggest that, regardless of treatment goal, subjects manifested a range of treatment outcomes, from totally nonproblem drinking (including nondrinking) through various degrees of drinking problems, to a life-style dominated by drinking problems.

The relatively low rate of complete abstinence reported for subjects in the IBT study is of interest (Emrick, 1974). Before proceeding, however, the reader must recognize that the follow-up procedures and measures used in this study substantially differed from traditional techniques. Even using traditional evaluation procedures, the alcoholism treatment literature clearly indicates that long-term abstinence is difficult to achieve. Paredes, Hood, Seymour, and Gollob (1973), for instance, reviewed studies indicating that approximately 86% of treated alcoholics return to some type of drinking within one year of discharge from a treatment program. Gillies, Laverty, Smart, and Aharan (1974) also reported that of alcoholics admitted to any of six alcoholism treatment units, an average of only 12.7% "became abstinent during the one year after treatment begins" (p. 133). Orford (1973) similarly found that only 10% of 100 subjects had maintained total abstinence for a full year following a conventional treatment program.

A study we performed at the Orange County (CA) Alcoholism Services suggests that the outcome results of the IBT control groups were not atypical (Maisto, Sobell, and Sobell, unpublished manuscript, 1977). The Orange County study involved a six-month postdischarge evaluation of 52 alcoholics who had been treated in rehabilitation programs at three nearby private alcoholism hospitals. While almost all of the subjects were seriously debilitated from their drinking, they were generally not as physically and socially deteriorated as the IBT subjects. Complete six-month follow-up data were obtained from 88% of the subjects and from collateral information sources for 98% of the subjects. Drinking disposition questions were phrased similarly to the questions in the IBT study (i.e., "How many days during the past 180 days have you consumed any alcoholic beverages?"). In cases where both the subject and a collateral were interviewed (88%), only 15% of the subjects had been totally free of alcohol over the six months following their hospital discharge, even though all of the hospital programs were oriented toward total abstinence. Moreover, not all subjects who had consumed alcohol during the six-month follow-up interval drank to the point of drunkenness.

In Chapter 2 it was mentioned that 80 studies have been published demonstrating that controlled or nonproblem drinking is a documented treatment outcome finding for some persons who had alcohol problems, even problems of considerable severity. In the majority of cases to date, these outcomes have occurred for individuals who have participated in conventional programs whose sole treatment objective has been complete and total abstinence. Therefore, we believe the evidence is now clear and sufficient to justify the statement that *some* "alcoholics" (including some who have manifested physical dependence on alcohol) can successfully engage in nonproblem drinking. Similarly, there is little evidence to suggest that such behavior might precipitate a return to more serious drinking problems. Currently, there is no empirical data to suggest which behavior pattern—abstinence or nonproblem drinking—might be easier to maintain over time. In this regard, when nonproblem drinking is used as a treatment objective, it would seem prudent to recognize that individuals treated with nonproblem drinking objectives may at times acquire problem drinking patterns. This is no different from recognizing that individuals seldom become permanently abstinent simply as a result of entering treatment. In both cases, if a subject who has demonstrated an ability to abstain or moderate his drinking experiences a "slip," such an event does not necessarily indicate a need to change treatment goals.

Currently, it is not known what proportion of individuals, under appropriate low-risk conditions and as a result of a specifically designed treatment program, could engage in limited, nonproblem drinking. Using the IBT outcome data, we had hoped to derive (through multiple regression analyses) subject characteristics which predicted nonproblem drinking outcomes. The results of those analyses were not particularly helpful in this regard. The only pretreatment variable significantly related to the controlled drinking outcome was number of prior alcohol-related hospitalizations. While this finding is of some value, since it suggests that persons with more severe histories may be less able to pursue a nonproblem drinking objective, it is of little use when dealing with individuals who do not have a history of multiple prior alcohol-related hospitalizations. Thus, the determination of which types of clients might be best suited for nonabstinence-treatment objectives remains an incomplete task.

Another problem in interpreting the IBT results relates to the use of controlled drinking as a treatment goal for some subjects. While this treatment was specifically intended for use only with certain subjects, it was inevitable that other alcoholic patients in the hospital, including control subjects, were fully aware that controlled drinking was being experimentally investigated as a potential treatment outcome. Despite the fact that all control subjects were strongly and explicitly cautioned that without intensive participation in a special treatment program they should not attempt to perform limited drinking on their own, there was no way of assuring that they would heed this caution. Therefore, it is conceivable that some subjects, other than CD–E subjects, may have attempted to drink in a controlled manner after their discharge from the hospital. If this did happen, we have no way of determining whether such instances were a direct result of exposure to the controlled drinking concept. However, it should be recalled that one reason CD–C subjects were assigned to this treatment goal was because they did not accept traditional dogma about the nature or treatment of alcoholism. One indication of the appropriateness of this treatment goal assignment is reflected in the CD–C subjects' use of therapeutic supports during the follow-up interval. These subjects rarely used traditional therapeutic supports such as Alcoholics Anonymous.

It will be recalled that subjects who were able to engage in controlled drinking for a significant (greater than or equal to 5%) portion of the follow-up interval typically functioned considerably better throughout that interval than subjects who engaged in no controlled drinking at all. Thus, while some subjects may have attempted to perform controlled drinking, failed, and gone on to drink to excess, it does not directly follow that those subjects would have functioned better if they had attempted no controlled drinking at all.

OTHER CONSIDERATIONS

Beyond the major treatment procedures, several other characteristics of the IBT study may also have had a significant impact on the outcome results. For example, rotating therapists were used to conduct treatment sessions. This procedure was instituted because most of the staff were part-time employees, and sessions had to be scheduled to accommodate conventional hospital functions. Further, while the use of videotape self-confrontation of drunken behavior was designed to have a motivating function, this plan was an inference based on our previous work with this technique; to date, the motivating influence of videotape replay has not been empirically demonstrated. Additionally, staff members were fairly young and enthusiastic about their work. Their enthusiasm and lack of substantial exposure to traditional treatment methods may have played a subtle and important role in the use of a novel treatment modality. Also, subjects were allowed to engage in limited drinking within the experimental context, and during the study several subjects remarked about the value of being able to experiment "safely" (in a hospital) with drinking.

Finally, we must remember that whatever components were effective, their influence may have been limited to this subject population and this situation. Thus, whether these results will generalize to other subject populations needs to be evaluated. For example, IBT subjects may have been more deficient in a knowledge of appropriate behavioral alternatives to drinking than subjects with greater education, higher socioeconomic status, or less severe drinking histories. From our subsequent clinical experience, we feel it is reasonable to expect that extrapolation of the IBT methods to middle- and upper-class individuals will require different treatment strategies and activities than were necessary for state hospitalized alcoholics.

A FINAL ANALYSIS

In preparing this book, we went to considerable lengths to insure that the treatment of alcohol problems is perceived by the reader as a complex and multifaceted undertaking. This emphasis resulted, in part, from having conducted the IBT study. The fact remains, however, that a quite radical and intensive experiment was performed to test a specific broad-spectrum approach to the behavioral treatment of alcohol problems, and *the experiment was successful*. In particular, *only subjects treated by IBT with a goal of controlled drinking successfully engaged in a substantial amount of limited, nonproblem drinking during the two years of follow-up, and those subjects also had more abstinent days than subjects in any other group.* These findings remain the single most important result of the IBT study.

CHAPTER 9

IBT in Retrospect

A wealth of data has amassed since the IBT study was completed. Some of the data from that study have forced a reconsideration of traditional concepts of alcoholism. While the IBT study will probably be remembered for its controlled drinking treatment goal, several other findings emerged which also merit discussion. Although questions about the value of particular IBT components can be answered only by future studies designed to compare and contrast various aspects of the IBT procedures, we can provide some insight into the effectiveness of these various components as seen through the eyes of the subjects themselves.

As part of the IBT follow-up, subjects were asked to consent to a tape-recorded interview at the end of their two-year follow-up interval. The interview was intended to gather information about the subjects' impressions of the study. In particular, the interviews were intended (a) to have experimental (CD–E and ND–E) subjects evaluate various aspects of the IBT treatment program, (b) to provide information about the types of problems encountered by subjects who had a treatment goal of controlled drinking, (c) to evaluate whether subjects considered the follow-up contacts to be therapeutic, (d) to assess whether subjects understood why intensive monthly follow-up interviews were conducted for two years, and (e) to evaluate how all control subjects—Nondrinker Control (ND–C) and Controlled Drinker Control (CD–C)—felt about being assigned to a control condition (i.e., having been accepted for but not allowed to participate in the IBT treatment program). While some might suggest that subjects' comments are irrelevant, we found their reflections an important source of data—a source that all too often goes untapped.

For instance, experimental subjects' evaluative comments about various aspects of the IBT study allow one to speculate about the significance and importance of those factors, and the study as a whole, in a way that the outcome data preclude.

While complete two-year data were gathered on 69 of the 70 subjects, two of the subjects—one experimental and one control—died during the follow-up interval. Therefore, only 68 subjects could have been interviewed; interviews were conducted with 67 of these 68 subjects. The only interview not completed was with subject J. L. (CD–C), the subject who had never been found since the first six weeks after his discharge from the hospital.

Tape-recorded interviews were conducted with subjects either in person or by telephone, and permission to audio-record the interview was obtained from each subject prior to the interview. To preserve subjects' confidentiality, no names were used in the interviews. Three-fourths (76%) of the tape-recorded interviews were conducted by telephone, including one subject interviewed at the Salvation Army in Hawaii. The remaining subjects (24%, $N = 16$) were interviewed in person. The interviews were taped in a variety of settings—subjects' homes, relatives' homes, halfway houses, detoxification centers, jails, state hospitals, and even at a jail honor farm. Initially, we had decided not to interview subjects who were obviously intoxicated. However, some months after the end of their two-year follow-up interval, a small number of subjects were still being sought for the purpose of completing their follow-up data. These subjects were all known to be highly transient and difficult to locate, and interviews were therefore immediately obtained when these subjects were located. To our knowledge, 6 (9%) of the 67 subjects either had been admitted to an alcohol detoxification facility within the 24 hours preceding their interview or were intoxicated when their interview was tape-recorded.

Throughout this book we have repeatedly suggested that frequent follow-up contacts probably helped us maintain contact with subjects and their collaterals over the two-year follow-up period. Some support for this assertion derives from a comparison of the dates when two-year interviews were conducted with subjects' actual two-year post-hospital discharge dates. Of the 67 subjects interviewed, 51 (76%) were interviewed within two weeks of their exact two-year anniversary of hospital discharge. An additional 6 (9%) subjects were interviewed within two to four weeks of their two-year discharge date. Thus, the use of frequent and continued follow-up contacts with these subjects may have enabled us, in most cases, to contact them with relative ease.

SPECIFIC TREATMENT COMPONENTS

The tape-recorded interviews ranged in length from 25 to 45 minutes. Since the subjects gave a wide range of answers to the interview questions, their answers were coded for ease of analysis. Subjects were asked to evaluate four major components of the IBT treatment program. For obvious reasons, these questions were asked only of experimental subjects [Nondrinker Experimental (ND–E) and Controlled Drinker Experimental (CD–E)]. All experimental subjects were asked to describe in positive and/or negative terms the value of four major treatment components: (a) shock avoidance procedures, (b) videotape self-confrontation with drunken behavior, (c) availability of alcohol—drinking as part of the treatment program, and (d) individualized talk therapy sessions—the one-to-one (Problem Solving Skills Training) sessions. All experimental subjects [CD–E, $N = 20$; ND–E, $N = 14$ (one ND–E subject died during Year 2)] evaluated the four treatment components. While some subjects elaborately evaluated the various treatment components, other subjects merely gave a positive or negative comment for each component. Therefore, subjects' overall responses were coded for comparability as either "positive" or "negative" for each component.

Table 11 displays the mean percentage of the experimental subjects (CD–E, ND–E, and both groups combined) who evaluated each of four different IBT treatment components as either positive or negative. For all subjects combined, the only treatment component primarily evaluated as negative was the use of shock avoidance schedules. Furthermore, this was the only component for which CD–E subjects and ND–E subjects differed regarding the direction of their evaluation. While 55% of the CD–E subjects regarded the use of electric shock as positive, only 14% of the ND–E subjects said the shocks had positive value. In all fairness, it must be pointed out that the shock avoidance contingencies differed for the two groups. For CD–E subjects, shocks were used to shape appropriate nonproblem drinking behavior, whereas for the ND–E subjects they served to punish all drinking behavior.

Both groups of subjects evaluated the individual therapy sessions very positively. In fact, this component received the highest combined

Table 11. Number and Percentage of Experimental Subjects Who Evaluated the Value of Four Different IBT Treatment Components as Either Positive or Negative

Treatment component	Subjects' evaluation	Experimental condition[a]					
		CD–E		ND–E		CD–E + ND–E	
		%	N	%	N	%	N
Shock avoidance	Positive	55	11	14	2	38	13
	Negative	45	9	86	12	62	21
Videotape replay	Positive	95	19	79	11	88	30
	Negative	5	1	21	3	12	4
Consumption of	Positive	75	15	93	13	82	28
alcohol	Negative	26	5	7	1	18	6
Individual therapy	Positive	90	18	93	13	91	31
sessions	Negative	10	2	7	1	9	3

[a]Experimental conditions were Controlled Drinker Experimental (CD–E), $N = 20$, and Nondrinker Experimental (ND–E), $N = 14$.

positive evaluation—91% of the subjects evaluated the sessions as beneficial. While the use of videotape replay and the actual consumption of alcohol both received favorable evaluations of 88%and 82%, respectively, the CD–E subjects evaluated the videotape replay more positively than ND–E subjects. Conversely, ND–E subjects evaluated the actual consumption of alcohol more favorably than CD–E subjects.

As mentioned earlier, some of the subjects gave more extensive evaluations of various treatment components. The following are selected comments from the subjects' comments regarding their evaluations of the four treatment components.

SHOCK-AVOIDANCE SCHEDULES

ND–E: The electric shocks were frightening, but it didn't seem to have the lasting impression as far as drinking or not drinking, asking for a drink, or refusing one.

ND–E: To me it was nil; I don't think it had any value for me.

ND–E: I really wasn't shocked that much; I don't remember being in that type of program.

ND–E: For me the electric shock didn't really carry over; you know, it was something I was doing while I was there. I knew that if I reached for the drink that I would be shocked . . . and I don't think it really helped me that much.

ND–E: Oh, the electric shocks? Things on the board? I already told you before I worked in electronics a long time ago and those shocks don't bother me.

ND–E: The electric shocks to me didn't keep me from drinking or taking a drink when I had it on, or influence me in any way whatsoever.

ND–E: I did not definitely see that it had too much value, because you could refuse to drink on the day of the shock. Therefore, it didn't have any value to you one way or the other.

CD–E: Well, the value of the electric shocks is more or less to me that they put me in line and made me go by the set-down rules, just to take a sip instead of a gulp. Even after I got out of the hospital, I was drinking in some bars, and sometimes I consciously chug-a-lugged about the last two ounces and sort of expected it [a shock]. And that was a year after, and I've . . . it sort of went through my mind.

CD–E: All it really did, the shock wasn't really that great. If I wanted the drink, I would have gone ahead and drank it anyway. It just sort of helped me find the limitations of what a sip should be in my mouth.

CD–E: I don't think it's too hot. Frankly, I think it . . . you know, a human being is not exactly like an animal. Now an animal you can train by this, but a human being, . . . he doesn't respond the same way as an animal. He'll respond the same way right at the instance, but he has too much sagacity . . . to think this is going to be a permanent thing.

CD–E: At the very beginning, it was a matter of pride not to get one. And this remained with me. When I take a drink I can still feel the electrode on my finger. Not the fear of the shock, but just the matter of pride that I should not gulp this.

CD–E: I never had one.

CD–E: The drink didn't mean enough to me that I wanted to get shocked for it. I'll guarantee you that.

VIDEOTAPE REPLAY OF DRUNKEN BEHAVIOR

ND–E: Well, I think it's good for one thing—it said that you are two people.

ND–E: I think those were very good, for me to see myself when I was becoming intoxicated.

ND–E: It gave you a chance to observe yourself and maybe find out at which point in your drinking you start to lose control of yourself and the situation.

ND–E: Well, I think that is real important because none of us realized what an ass they make of themselves when they are drinking and this certainly emphasized it.

CD–E: Repulsive. When I saw myself as other people—I know that they have to see me the same way if they are sober. It was kind of repulsive, kind of sickening. I think it was positive.

CD–E: I think that it was really good, because I was able to see myself in a drunken stage and hear some things I've said to people that I wouldn't have normally said when I was sober.

CD–E: I think it is fantastic—it shows you just like you are, and a person doesn't realize what they are like. They think they are the greatest thing since life's bread, and yet when you're slopping all over a bar or something like that, you think, that's it! Oh, is that me?

CD–E: I think that it held a certain value, because I know at least in my case when I drink to the point that I did, I black out every time, and I have no recall of what I've done or what I've said.

CONSUMPTION OF ALCOHOL

ND–E: It did prove a point, that I still can't or couldn't drink and control it. That's why I more or less decided to be abstinent.

ND–E: I feel mixed about it. I think that the positive thing was that it was there and that's the problem and you're working with it. I think that it had value for me, in having the booze sitting there, and having the type of questions thrown at me. They got me upset, and not latching on to the booze was something I did not think I was able to do.

CD–E: Positive, in the sense that it might have opened up some avenues of talk and rapport with the workers.

CD–E: Well, I proved to myself I could drink socially, that's the best part of it.

CD–E: I think that it was very valuable, because it was the first time I had been able to sit down in ten years and have a few drinks. It made me realize that it was possible to have a few drinks, then stop.

CD–E: Well, I don't think you could do it any other way. There is no possible way to run an alcoholic test treatment without using alcohol.

CD–E: I thought it had tremendous value. Because I don't believe that "one drink and then drunk." I feel that this is something you're going to have to deal with, and you just can't lock up all the liquor. It has tremendous value, because it taught you that you can go on and deal with it. It's here, there's nothing you can do. But you can't lock up all the liquor, so you have to learn how to cope with it and learn how to drink.

INDIVIDUAL THERAPY SESSIONS

ND–E: I think that was very important. Here again, the staff was very thorough in that phase of it and drew the patients out and established certain facts that were necessary.

ND–E: I found out more about myself that way. Ways to go about life. Learning to understand myself better.

CD–E: This I'm for. I hate group therapy.

CD–E: I think that's one of the best parts of the program too. It's because in the bar . . . maybe the few drinks make you feel just enough at ease so you can talk about your problems more than you would in a group, and you know that it's on a one-to-one basis. I felt that I could talk about things to the researchers on a one-to-one basis in a bar that I really didn't care to bring out at other times.

CD–E: Well, I think that's the best part of the whole thing. That one-to-one session, just sitting there and you and me and whoever's serving the drinks would talk.

CD–E: Well, I guess they kind of bring things out in the open that you might not discuss or didn't want to.

CD–E: I think it's very good because I imagine the different people performing the different one-to-one sessions had to do a lot of studying from previous notes and things like that to take up and come up with the questions they felt would be best to take and open up one's hang-ups and kick around or interject a thought or alternatives.

These selected comments demonstrate the diversity of subjects' interview responses and seem to indicate that they gave some thought to how they were affected by each treatment component. It would appear from their comments that both groups of subjects unequivocally agreed that the videotape replay, while "shocking and embarrassing," showed them what they were like when they were drunk—something they had frequently been told but had never seen. Taken collectively, the subjects' comments also suggested that the individual therapy sessions allowed them to discuss problems they had not had an opportunity to discuss before. Subjects' comments on the use of alcohol in treatment sessions ranged from statements that it should be a necessary component of alcohol treatment programs because it showed them that they had control over their drinking to assertions that it demonstrated to them that they could not control their drinking. Lastly, the use of electric shocks elicited the most provocative comments. At present, we believe that electric shock avoidance contingencies are not necessary for training moderate, nonproblem drinking because (a) very few subjects in the CD–E group actually received shocks for inappropriate drinking, (b) subjects evaluated the shocks equivocally, and (c) generalizability (from research setting to extratreatment environment) of this treatment component is questionable. Within the treatment context, a suggested alternative procedure would be to use verbal feedback to inform subjects when they are drinking inappropriately. In an outpatient setting, verbal feedback from the therapist, coupled with the subject's self-monitoring of his or her drinking behavior, would seem potentially more effective for maintaining a long-term nonproblem drinking pattern.

CONTROL GROUP ASSIGNMENTS

As in most research studies, we used control groups for the reason that we had no basis for making a priori assumptions about the effectiveness of the various treatment programs. While we randomly assigned subjects within each treatment goal to either an experimental or control group, we encountered expected difficulties when explaining the results of the random assignments to subjects. Prior to their acceptance into the treatment program, all subjects were given a thorough and detailed explanation of how treatment goals would be selected and informed that they would be randomly assigned to either an experimental or control group. Still, a few subjects had considerable difficulty accepting the results of those procedures. As will be seen in the comments to follow, this confusion continued to exist two years later.

In an effort to assess how control subjects felt about having been selected for the study, but not allowed to participate in the experimental treatment program, we asked all control subjects at the time of the tape-recorded interview how they felt about their assignment to control group. We first reminded these subjects that the random assignment had actually kept them out of the research program and then asked them how they felt (at two years after discharge) about that decision. Since the subjects gave a wide variety of responses, their answers were coded into the categories shown in Table 12. Table 12 indicates that slightly over one-third of the CD–C subjects did not

Table 12. Number and Percentage of Control Subjects' Answers to the Question Asking How They Felt about Being Randomly Assigned to a Control Group Rather Than an Experimental Group

Types of comments categorized	Experimental group[a]			
	CD–C		ND–C	
	%	N	%	N
Did not bother me; no complaints; not resentful.	37	7	14	2
Regretted not going through the program, felt rejected.	21	4	29	4
Glad did not participate; wanted to participate at first; initially was resentful.	21	4	14	2
It was a set-up; did not understand random selection process.	11	2	0	0
Was better off as a result of not going through the program.	5	1	29	4
Answers not codable/interpretable.	5	1	14	2

[a] Experimental groups were Controlled Drinker Control (CD–C), $N = 19$, and Nondrinker Control (ND–C), $N = 14$.

appear to be particularly resentful of their assignment. However, approximately 42% of the CD–C subjects responded that at one time or another they felt somewhat rejected, or resentful about not participating in the experimental treatment program. Similarly, 43% of the ND–C subjects indicated that they had at one time or another wanted to go through the IBT program, or that they had felt rejected as a result of not being allowed to participate. Interestingly, while four (29%) ND–C subjects indicated two years after discharge that they felt better off as a result of not going through the IBT program, only one (5%) CD–C subject made such a statement.

The following selected interview excerpts give the reader an understanding of how subjects felt about being told (as required by principles of informed consent) that they were control subjects. These comments also reflect the subjects' comprehension of the nature of random assignment.

ND–C: Well, I felt mad at the time because I wanted to try it. I was wondering why I wasn't accepted.

ND–C: Now, actually I haven't given it much thought, but at that time I felt like I had missed out on something. It sort of bummed me, but in a way, now that I think about it, maybe I was just lucky because things worked out better than if I had gone to that treatment.

CD–C: Well, I regret it very much, and I think about this once in a while that as you know I tripped off here a few weeks ago. And I think about this every so often and wonder in my mind if it was a toss of the coin or not. And I've questioned myself and said, well did you make a bad presentation to those people, did they reject you because you're somewhat of an intellectual, did they want a different type, was it truly a toss of the coin, and were you a victim of fate there?

CD–C: Oh, it didn't bother me that much. I mean I wasn't there just for a particular program. I didn't even go there with the idea they had certain programs. I just wanted help and I went there.

CD–C: I thought it was a set-up.

CD–C: I resented it. I really felt like, then I could be a social drinker. And today, I just feel this way, that it would have helped me become better adjusted controlling myself and being a social drinker.

CD–C: I never could understand why you flipped coins. I felt that you should have taken people on the basis of perhaps personality and not a coin flip.

CD–C: When it happended, I was mad. But I think you were correct. I couldn't be a social drinker.

CD–C: I don't miss it at all. It may have been quite an experience. It might have proved something to me and it might have not. I don't know. I'm not resentful of the fact that I couldn't have gone through with the whole program.

The last subject's response generally characterizes the comments of a number of other subjects. They were not resentful of the control group assignment, but they wondered how they would have done if they had participated in the experimental program.

The responses of subjects who initially said they felt rejected but later they were glad to have been assigned to the control group seemed related to their environment and functioning at the time of the interview. That is, those control subjects who were functioning well tended to make such comments, and subjects who were experiencing many drinking-related problems often felt resentful and speculated that the IBT program might have been helpful to them.

Some subjects demonstrated considerable lack of understanding about the random assignment process, the nature of a control group assignment, and even about the treatment group to which they were assigned. This is best demonstrated by the comments of two ND–C subjects.:

ND–C: I think that it's just as well that I didn't go through the program, because I know there's no way of making a social drinker out of me. I could never drink with control; I know I couldn't.

ND–C: Well, I don't know. I wanted to try the controlled drinking because I think I could have done it and all that. That's all. Well, I was kind of unhappy because I wasn't accepted that way.

This confusion might have resulted because some subjects mistakenly thought the controlled drinking treatment goal constituted the entire program, even though all subjects were informed that this was not the case.

CONTROLLED DRINKING FROM THE SUBJECTS' VIEWPOINT

When we decided to use a controlled drinking treatment goal in the IBT study, we recognized that "alcoholics" who attempted to drink in a nonproblem manner might be confronted with serious social pressure and skepticism about such drinking. At times during the two-year follow-up period, several CD–E subjects related various incidents they encountered when engaging in nonproblem drinking. To systematically evaluate the types of problems CD–E subjects experienced about a controlled drinking goal after the IBT treatment, and their views about the value of such a goal for some subjects, they were asked various questions about these issues.

While complete interviews were conducted with all 20 CD–E subjects, questions related to controlled drinking were asked only of subjects who had engaged in any successful controlled drinking during the two years of follow-up. The two sets of questions which concerned controlled drinking were as follows: (a) "You have been doing some controlled drinking for the last two years; what kind of trouble did you have convincing others who knew you that it was OK to drink in a controlled manner and that you had the ability to control your drinking? How did you convince others who knew you, your friends and relatives, that you were able to control your drinking? Did you have to give up any of these friends or previous treatment supports because you did controlled drinking?" and (b) "What value do you think a treatment goal of controlled drinking has to others with problems of excessive abuse of alcohol, similar to yours (when you entered Patton)? That is, what value is the goal of controlled drinking?"

The number of subjects, who responded to the first question was 16. Surprisingly, 9 (56.25%) of the 16 reported having few, if any, problems convincing friends and relatives of their ability to control their drinking. Of those 9 subjects, 3 frankly stated that they did not try to convince others. The remaining 7 subjects all reported having immediately encountered some problems and skepticism from friends and relatives regarding recognition of their (the subjects') ability to drink in a controlled fashion. However, these subjects also mentioned that this initial skepticism dissipated over time, as they were able to demonstrate that they were able to control their drinking. The following interview comments by CD–E subjects should help the reader understand some of the problems these subjects encountered and how they resolved those problems.

> CD–E: Well, I'll tell you now. One of my ex-bosses was pretty dubious about it because, well, naturally, like most people— once a drunk, always a drunk. But, oh, it was a matter I would say of about three months, four months, after I returned from the program and was over to their home and was watching a football game or some doggone thing; I was very dubiously offered a drink and accepted that and, oh, it was about an hour and a half later at the halftime, and when I had another drink, and that's all I really wanted that particular day. I wasn't trying to snow [them] or anything. And so they tried to offer me more drinks which I really didn't want. And so now if I'm over to the house, they think nothing of saying "do you care for a drink?" and if I do, I do, and if I don't, I don't.

> CD–E: I haven't had any [problems].

> CD–E: I think at first everyone was skeptical, maybe even me. I was convinced I could drink socially, but then I could see the doubt in other people, and I began to doubt it myself. But then I'd go out like dancing for an evening, and I'd have five or six drinks from say eight or nine in the evening until two A.M. It didn't bother me. I'd come home and go to bed and no problems. So then I found that there's something to it after all. You have to show them. They have to see you, be out with you, see you, and know you as you was [sic] before and see the change in you.

> CD–E: No, I haven't tried to. I know myself and I know at the time what I want to do, so I just go ahead and do it.

CD–E: I had a lot of opposition from my family. They still don't
believe it. Even though I've proved it, they still don't believe
it. My mother doesn't believe in liquor. I've convinced my
wife. She's been with me, drank with me, and she's seen it.

CD–E: Oh, very little. I just told them I knew what I was doing.

CD–E: The majority of people that I have come in contact with
believe the commercialism of the AA of "one drink, then
drunk," and they believe this is another con-job by a con-
artist. It's very hard for those people to admit, even though
they have seen the proof that it can be done. Yes, I have given
up AA and several of my old friends who have convinced
themselves they cannot take a drink. It's not good for them
and myself to be around them.

CD–E: You know, I don't even try. Cause most people have got their
minds set that you're a drunk, and they figure before you
even come in. I've gone into a bar and sat down and drinking
cokes and have guys walk in and say, "Well, drunk again." So
I don't even try to convince some of these bastards. I've got
relatives who say, "Hey, how's your drinking problem?" I'll
say, "How is yours? Mine's pretty good," and let it go at that.
It's kind of a flippant attitude, I know, but I've gotten so tired
of people bugging me about my drinking, because I haven't
actually affected their lives. Now if my wife was one of those
type people then it would be different. But it isn't my wife, it's
those other people . . ..

CD–E: I haven't really had any problems.

It would appear from some of the subjects' comments that successful
early posttreatment drinking experiences may be very important with
respect to how significant others will respond to controlled drinking
by individuals who have had drinking problems.

Of the 13 CD–E subjects who answered the question about the
value of a controlled drinking goal for others with drinking problems,
4 felt that while a controlled drinking treatment goal was good for
some individuals, its value was really dependent on the particular
person. While most of the subjects' answers to this question varied,
collectively, their comments are reflected in a statement made by one
subject: "It allows a person to retain his dignity; one can escape the
effects of labeling; one learns to deal with problems; and it takes the
fear away from the bottle."

All IBT subjects were asked the following question about controlled drinking: "Do you think any person, not necessarily yourself, but
it could be yourself, who's drunk excessively before and has been
labeled an alcoholic can ever return to successful normal drinking,

otherwise called social or controlled drinking?" Of the CD–E subjects, 80% (16 of 20) felt that alcoholics could return to moderate drinking. However, only 59.52% (25) of the 42 subjects in the remaining three treatment groups (CD–C, ND–E, ND–C) who answered this question felt that an alcoholic could return to some form of nonproblem drinking. Given the results of the IBT study, the interviews with the CD–E subjects, and similar work we have done with other clinical populations, we believe that controlled drinking treatment goals may be more feasible with higher resource, and more stable clients, in contrast to state hospitalized *gamma* alcoholics.

From the evidence and comments of the CD–E subjects who engaged in nonproblem drinking, it appears that successful practice of such drinking by former "alcoholics" largely depends on the supportive nature of the individual's environment. In this regard, we suggest that any treatment program using nonproblem drinking goals explicitly make clients aware of the opinions inherent in the general population about alcoholics who return to some form of limited, nonproblem drinking. That is, clients should be aware of possible resistance to their limited, nonproblem drinking from friends, relatives, and unexpected sources like physicians and judges.

FOLLOW-UP AS CONTINUED CARE

Usually, follow-up is conceptualized as simply a data-collection procedure. In fact, the follow-up component in the IBT study was explicitly designed to gather data to evaluate treatment effectiveness. As will be recalled from Chapter 6, the IBT study differed from other alcoholic follow-up studies in that subjects and their collaterals were contacted monthly as opposed to longer time intervals (e.g., 6 months, 2 years, etc.). The initial rationale for frequent and continued follow-up contacts was to maximize the opportunity to gather specific and valid data on subjects' drinking behavior.

Several findings which were totally unexpected emerged from the follow-up. First, it became apparent early in conducting follow-up that the frequent interviews not only furnished opportunities to gather data but also seemed to provide some type of "continuing care" for many of the subjects. This "continuing care" aspect became apparent during the follow-up interviews when some subjects wanted to discuss personal problems, talk about current emotional crises, talk about what they perceived as their "good prolonged functioning," or request help for their self-damaging drinking. In the latter instances, arrangements were always made to help subjects enter a detoxifica-tion facility if they so desired. Ethical considerations demanded that we consider the needs of all subjects, regardless of treatment group. As it turned out, intervention occurred more frequently for control subjects than experimental subjects. Thus, it appeared that the IBT follow-up interviews were serving a dual function—gathering out-come data *and* providing "continuing care" for subjects.

This alternative conceptualization of follow-up as "continued care" is not novel; it simply has been labeled differently—"aftercare," "therapeutic support," or "continuity of treatment." Unfortunately, while several persons have suggested that follow-up interviews supply a kind of aftercare function (e.g., Blake, 1965; Plaut, 1967; Pokorny, Miller, Kanas, and Valles, 1973), few have actually documented or examined the effects of follow-up contacts.

Gallen (1974) has published one of the few studies which clearly documents the therapeutic effects of frequent follow-up contacts with alcoholics. He found that over half of his subjects explicitly acknowl-edged that follow-up contacts played an important role in their post-hospital discharge functioning. Additionally, the collateral in-formants in this study also felt that the continued contacts contributed significantly to the subjects' adjustment.

In order to investigate further the clinical value of follow-up, all IBT subjects were asked three questions about the follow-up contacts as part of the tape-recorded interview. The three questions that related to the follow-up procedures were stated as follows: "The next few questions are about the follow-up that we've conducted for the last two years. First of all, what do you like about the continuous monthly two-year follow-up that we have conducted? Second, what do you dislike about it? Third, if you had your choice now, would you like us to continue doing follow-up?"

Again, as with the other interview questions, the questions about follow-up contacts were open-ended. Thus, subjects' responses to the first two questions were coded for ease of analysis. Seven categories were used to code subjects' answers to the question about what they liked about the follow-up contacts. Those categories were: (a) Care, Interest, Concern, Help; (b) Someone to Talk to; (c) Awareness, Reminder of Past or Present; (d) It Might Be Helping Others; (e) Research Element; (f) General Unspecified Like; and (g) No Stated Like. These coding categories and subjects' answers are displayed in Table 13 for experimental subjects (CD–E and ND–E), for control subjects (CD–C and ND–C), and for all subjects combined. So that

**Table 13. Number and Percentage of Subjects' Responses Describing
What They Liked about the Frequent Follow-Up Contacts**

	Experimental condition[a]					
	EG		CG		EG + CG	
Types of categorized likes	N	%	N	%	N	%
Care, interest, concern, help	20	59	16	49	37	53.7
Someone to talk to	4	11	4	12	8	12.0
Awareness, reminder	3	9	2	6	5	7.4
It will help others	2	6	1	3	3	4.5
Research element	1	3	1	3	2	3.0
General unspecified like	1	3	3	9	4	6.0
No stated like	3	9	6	18	9	13.4

[a] Experimental conditions were experimental groups (EG: CD–E and ND–E),
control groups (CG: CD–C and ND–C) and all groups combined (EG and CG).

the reader can better understand these categories, comments representative of each category will follow shortly. As seen in Table 13, the category which both experimental and control subjects used most often to describe what they liked about the frequent follow-up contacts was "care, interest, concern, help." While almost half of all subjects used this category, more experimental subjects described the follow-up contacts in this manner than did control subjects. For subjects' answers to be coded into this category, the subjects had to explicitly use one or more words in this category in their answer. Equal numbers of experimental and control subjects indicated that they like having "someone to talk to," while twice as many control subjects (18%) as experimental subjects had no specific stated likes about the follow-up. Overall, 73.1% of all subjects indicated that the follow-up served some type of continuing care function for them, ranging from someone to talk to, to an interest in them, or as a reminder of their past or present.

Representative answers for each of the coding categories are listed below:

CARE, INTEREST, CONCERN, HELP

CD–E: Well, I liked the fact that someone was interested in me as a person.

CD–E: Well, it still shows that somebody does care about people in my condition.

CD–E: Anything that has anything to do with trying to help the alcoholic, I'm for. If this will help anyone, fine.

CD–E: Although I knew that it was research, I also knew that you personally were interested, too, and it made me feel good to realize that people did care. I think that it was a good idea and it was done regularly.

CD–E: I appreciated that you kept in touch and somewhat cared.

CD–E: Well, it sort of gives me the feeling that around the middle of the month somebody is going to call me and not personally involved, but involved in some way that . . . I got one person maybe worried about me, not worried about me but concerned, even if it's not personal or something.

CD–C: To me, this is beautiful because it shows that someone has an interest in me and what's happening.

CD–C: What I like about it, and have been thinking about these last few days about losing it, is just that I have a contact with someone who is concerned. And I don't mean on a program basis, but I've always felt a personal relationship.

CD–C: Well, I think personally, it's the interest that some other person has in you.

CD–C: Well, it gave me the feeling of somebody caring . . . you know I've heard a lot of deals that you're going to have this follow-up, people care about you, and all of this. This is the first program with all sincerity and all honesty that . . . it's a personal thing and it's a darn nice thing. When I call my mother and she says you want me to call you right away, it gives you a real belonging feeling.

CD–C: Oh, I think the interest. Once you leave the place, you're not gone and forgotten and the only time they consider you is if you come back and say, "Aha, I knew you'd be back!"

ND–E: I think it was great because I figure that although I realized it was a clinical study, I personally felt that there was somebody in the state of California other than my so-called friends—I wasn't married at the time—that was really interested in trying to follow-up and find out how I was doing and was willing to offer or suggest methods of assistance.

ND–E: I liked it for two reasons, that it shows me that somebody is interested in me . . . .

ND–C: I like it very much, because it helps me every time I get a call. Why, if I'm on a binge or have been on a binge, it puts me back in a sobriety [sic] for at least a week or better.

ND–C: It seems like somebody cares at least, you know.

SOMEONE TO TALK TO

CD-E: I think it's valuable, like a relative or something talking to you.

CD-C: The contact is being able to talk to somebody that understands that I do have a problem. And being able to tell somebody that I do have a problem.

CD-C: Somebody I could talk to in absolute confidence and understanding, that's the main thing I think.

CD-C: Well, it gives you a little opportunity to blow off a little steam.

ND-E: Well, for one thing, if something were bothering me that I could come in and talk to you about it.

ND-E: Mainly I like hearing from you. I think you're able to talk. It's enjoyable to sit back and when the calls come, I can give myself a stroke, that I've worked on my own problems and I'm handling it.

ND-E: Oh, I look forward to it really. Knowing that I can tell my personal problems, if I have any, or just talking to someone who understands me.

AWARENESS, REMINDER

CD-E: Well, I'd like to have that continued because it makes me a little bit more aware. At times, I work under quite a bit of pressure and sometimes I get a lapse, I mean not a lapse in the sense that you think of as far as drinking is concerned. I get a lapse to the point that I forget where the pressure point is—you know what I mean? When you call, then all of a sudden it brings it back to me and it says, OK, now remember, and then I remember.

CD-E: It . . . refreshes my memory that what I once was I could become again if I'm not careful. It's a reminder, a very friendly reminder.

CD-E: It's a little reminder to me that I do have a problem and I have to stay on top of it. For this reason your follow-up has been great.

CD-C: I appreciate them, because it makes me dig into myself, which I don't do very often. As often as I should.

ND-E: I enjoy it. It keeps me on guard looking to answer, being ready to answer your questions.

ND-C: The fact that you call me. The fact that you check on me. I get a great deal of thoughts . . . I don't know whether it's going to do me any good or not but I'm going to do a lot of thinking.

IT WILL HELP OTHERS AND RESEARCH ELEMENT

CD-E: It's nice that maybe by me going through the series of tests, it might be helping other people out too, later on.

CD-E: Anything that has anything to do with helping the alcoholic, I'm for. If this will help anyone, fine.

CD-C: I feel this way about it. I've been under the national research program and I feel like the only way I can repay for the help I got was maybe in some little way I could help somebody else by these interviews.

CD-C: I'm impressed with the fact that there are those such as yourself that are empathetic enough for the situation to want to compile information and learn about people such as myself, have the desire to be helpful in the field. I like your interest, in other words. I'm most impressed by that, your enthusiasm.

CD-C: That perhaps something is being done by it that may help someone out.

ND-E: I think the main thing is that possibly the survey will help research to the point that it will help those in the future.

GENERAL LIKES AND/OR DISLIKES

CD-E: Well, I don't particularly like them. I figured with my problem I didn't need it.

CD-E: I think that it was a good idea, and it was done regularly.

CD-E: There's nothing that I didn't like about it. Just, it would have been better person-to-person rather than on the phone.

CD-E: Well, I, anybody that's gone out and has failed again kinda resents having to write down or tell somebody over the phone, but that's something you have to accept if you want to do the research or come out valid in the program to help other people. So on a personal basis, I can't say I have had any personal resentment about it whatsoever.

CD-E: I would like some closeness. I would have liked to see you people.

CD-E: I can't say as I dislike anything about it, other than the fact that every time I'm down like this, it embarrasses the hell out of me to see you.

CD-C: Trying to remember. Remember just what I've been drinking and that stuff. 'Cause a lot of times I don't put it to my mind of remembering how much I drink.

CD-C: The only thing that I can honestly say that I disliked is that it's brief and not very inclusive: In other words, it's like, "Hi, how are you?" "How do you feel?" and I think I probably could have suggested it myself, but that a visit I'll say every six months or so, and going into a little more depth and not only, "Hi, how are you?" "Fine." "How do you feel?" "Good." but why. A little more information gained would be more beneficial for you perhaps and even satisfactory for me in just giving me the opportunity to talk to somebody about it.

CD–C: Your continual attempts to contact me. What bothered me was that you contacted my sister and my daughter and that irritated me.

CD–C: I don't like anything about it, because I don't like being spied on, followed, or having tabs kept on me. In fact, I've been rather resentful about it as you may know. That was keeping the research on me. Calling up people and asking where I'd been.

ND–E: In my opinion, I conditioned myself into a life where I live today. In other words my past times are completely obsolete. Therefore, any time I get a phone call, or like I would go to AA and where it says "I am an alcoholic" or "Did you drink?" or whatsoever, I remembered [sic] of my past. And my past life is obsolete for me.

ND–E: Sometimes I'm busy or on the other side, usually it's when I'm weak or closer to a drink, being reminded that I do drink alcohol when I drink, and when I'm drunk it's been alcoholically, and brings back bad memories.

ND–E: I appreciate it.

ND–C: I liked everything about it.

When subjects were asked to describe what they disliked about the frequent follow-up contacts, for the second interview question, most subjects did not have any stated dislikes. Those subjects who explicitly stated that there was nothing they disliked about the follow-up were 26 of the experimental subjects and 24 of the control subjects. Thus, of all subjects combined, 74.6% had no stated dislikes about the follow-up contacts. Only 15 of the total 67 subjects interviewed had any specific dislikes about the follow-up. Of these, 8 were experimental subjects, and 7 were control subjects. There were 2 subjects who gave no answer to this question.

As can be seen from most of the comments, the control and experimental subjects who disliked follow-up did so for clearly different reasons. Of the 8 experimental subjects who mentioned dislikes about the follow-up contacts, 6 stated that it reminded them of their past and/or present drinking behavior. It should be noted that some of these subjects voiced this dislike not because they were doing poorly but because they were functioning well and did not wish to be reminded of their former problems. Of the control subjects who indicated dislikes about follow-up, 5 of the 7 either did not like being contacted at all or did not like the fact that the follow-up was a research venture. Surprisingly, 3 subjects expressed their dislikes as not only wanting more follow-up visits but wanting more personal contacts rather than telephone or letter contacts.

Answers to the third interview question, which asked all subjects if they would like follow-up continued beyond the two-year period, indicated that 80% of all subjects expressed a desire to have the follow-up contacts continued. The only subjects who did not want the contacts to be continued were 3 control subjects. Interestingly, 4 experimental subjects indicated that the follow-up contacts were no longer necessary, as they felt they were functioning quite well on their own.

The IBT subjects' interview responses to questions about the frequent follow-up contacts indicated that they felt such contacts functioned as a "continuing care" process, having beneficial and desirable consequences. However, these results may be restricted to this particular population—state hospitalized chronic alcoholics. These kinds of alcoholics often have very few intact social and familial relationships and, thus, may be considered as somewhat socially deprived. Consequently, frequent, intensive follow-up contacts may be more rewarding for this population of alcoholics, as opposed to other clinical populations (e.g., higher resource clients, outpatient alcoholics, etc.).

Given the foregoing, it is possible that the follow-up conducted in the IBT study may have enhanced the outcome of all subjects, experimentals and controls. Specifically, all groups of subjects improved somewhat over the course of the two-year follow-up period. It could be hypothesized that the follow-up process consolidated and increased the gains made in treatment by providing "continuing care" for all subjects. If frequent follow-up contacts do, in fact, serve a "continuing care" function for some subjects, then the manner by which this type of therapeutic contact or support is terminated should be considered with great care. An important question concerns what might happen to subjects if contacts are abruptly terminated. In this regard, all IBT subjects had been followed for two years. At the end of the two-year period, we informed them that we would have to discontinue follow-up. Subjects were, however, encouraged to continue to call or write us if they wished. Nevertheless, it is possible that the abrupt termination of follow-up contacts may have been detrimental to some subjects' immediate functioning. We base this view on the fact that some of the control subjects contacted us within six months following the termination of follow-up, indicated that they had relapsed to drinking, and said they felt that continued follow-up might have prevented or minimized their drinking. Consequently, it is suggested that until further evidence is available, frequent follow-up contacts should be terminated in a graduated manner (e.g., a decreasing frequency of contacts, rather than an abrupt cessation).

REFLECTIONS ON A LARGE-SCALE
CLINICAL RESEARCH PROJECT

Even though we were fully aware of the need to collect intensive follow-up data on all clients, we initially underestimated the amount of time and effort needed to conduct follow-up. This occurred partly because at that time no one had ever before conducted such an intensive and comprehensive follow-up study with alcoholics. Fortunately, even though we initially underestimated the scope and complexity of the follow-up, we were able to devote the necessary time and effort to the project so that the collection of data was not affected.

Given our experiences, we suggest that follow-up treatment-outcome evaluation is essential for determining the effectiveness of *all* alcohol treatment programs and that the amount of time, energy, and personnel involved in such a project cannot be taken lightly. Problems encountered in conducting follow-up can be minimized, if not avoided, by carefully planning and designing the follow-up component in advance of the alcohol study.

Originally, the collateral information sources—friends, relatives, employers—were included in the IBT follow-up study to verify subjects' self-reports. Much to our surprise, the use of multiple collateral information sources served some additional but unanticipated functions: (a) they provided information about subjects' whereabouts, (b) they were supportive of the subjects' functioning, (c) when we were unable to contact subjects directly, collaterals often asked the subjects to contact us, and (d) frequently collaterals contacted us on their own if they had concerns about a subject's drinking. Our experiences with collaterals in the IBT study were extremely favorable; at no time were any of the collaterals uncooperative.

Lastly, the cooperation and support of the clinical alcohol treatment staff at Patton State Hospital (e.g., unit psychiatrist, hospital administrator, nurses, technicians, etc.) were invaluable. In this and in any clinical research study, the regular clinical or hospital treatment staff have abundant opportunities to sabotage or undermine a research study. However, all the alcohol treatment staff at Patton were supportive of the IBT project.

CHAPTER 10

IBT in Private Practice and Outpatient Programs

Until now, this book focused primarily on research and treatment with inpatient alcoholics in a state hospital setting. That population and setting, however, contrasts markedly with other clinical treatment settings (e.g., outpatient treatment and private practice). Obviously, each clinical setting presents different challenges, constraints, and opportunities. In this chapter, we consider how individualized behavioral treatment (IBT) of alcohol problems can be used in outpatient and private practice settings.

DIFFERENCES BETWEEN INPATIENT AND OUTPATIENT TREATMENT

To better understand the differences between inpatient and outpatient techniques, it is important to recognize the general differences between these two clinical settings. Each setting can be described in terms of a set of concurrent advantages and limitations.

In an inpatient setting, the client is removed from many environmental circumstances which may be directly related to his or her drinking. The primary advantage of an inpatient setting is that the client is sheltered from daily problems and is largely free of immediate crises. This allows both client and therapist more time to examine and deal with factors associated with the client's drinking. Moreover, more radical treatment procedures may be initiated in the protected inpatient environment, as safeguards are available should adverse reactions occur. Therefore, in an inpatient setting, the therapist and client are often freer to engage in stress-inducing activities, and compliance with the treatment regimen can be closely monitored by staff.

Conversely, several factors limit the value of inpatient settings. The most notable of these is that treatment effects sometimes fail to generalize to the client's usual living environment. Safely secluded, a person may demonstrate rapid and remarkable behavior change, only to revert to familiar patterns shortly after discharge from the program. Another problem with inpatient treatment is that it involves greater personal and financial costs, as compared with outpatient treatment. These kinds of problems, coupled with the necessity for the client to take time off from work and removal from his or her usual environment, may well make many individuals reluctant to participate in inpatient treatment unless absolutely necessary. For these reasons, inpatients may often have more serious and pervasive alcohol problems than clients seen in outpatient settings.

Furthermore, an inpatient setting to some degree restricts the types of problems that can be dealt with in treatment. That is, the inpatient format sets restrictions upon both the ways in which topics can be addressed and the types of behavior changes which can occur in treatment. In contrast, clients' activities in outpatient treatment are usually not monitored or restricted. The opportunity to deal with actual situations when they occur is a major advantage of outpatient treatment. Since treatment concerns are related to immediately occurring life problems, generalizability of treatment to the extra-treatment environment is much less of a problem. Therefore, it would seem that outpatient treatment should be preferred to inpatient treatment, unless the client's circumstances are serious enough to warrant hospitalization.

To reiterate, the advantages of outpatient treatment are: (a) reduced financial costs, (b) little, if any, disruption of one's daily life patterns, and (c) more opportunities to deal with presenting life problems. We must not forget, too, that in outpatient settings clients are continually confronted with the environment in which they have experienced drinking problems. Consequently, outpatient treatment may be somewhat less intense and of longer duration than inpatient treatment, simply because there are more factors which can interfere with the course of treatment. Additionally, while most inpatients are likely to cooperate with their treatment plan, outpatients may often find compliance difficult (e.g., when it involves effecting changes in some part of their environment).

Lastly, one might speculate that individuals who have not yet suffered serious adverse consequences as a result of drinking, (i.e., disrupted social relationships, loss of jobs, increase in familial arguments, etc.) might be better candidates for outpatient behavioral treatment approaches. These individuals are more likely to have a greater number of behavioral options in which they can engage rather than drinking, they may be better able to change environmental contingencies related to their drinking, and more environmental rewards may be available contingent upon their behavior change (in contrast to individuals who have been chronically unemployed and have few intact interpersonal relationships).

In developing a preliminary format for conducting individualized behavioral treatment in an outpatient alcohol treatment setting, we have synthesized and extended information from: (a) various inpatient controlled research studies, (b) a limited number of outpatient research studies, (c) the published literature on behavioral approaches to outpatient treatment, and (d) our own clinical experience. As further research is conducted in this area, we recognize that extensive revisions of our clinical opinions may be needed.

GENERAL CONSIDERATIONS

COMPLIANCE AND PLANNING TREATMENT

It must be recognized that a client is subject to a host of environmental contingencies, of which treatment constitutes only one set. Therefore, behaviors encouraged by a particular treatment plan may, at times, conflict with other contingencies influencing the client. Ultimately, such a conflict may result in the client's leaving treatment. To minimize the chance of this happening, it is very important to perform a thorough analysis of the functions of each client's drinking and the major environmental contingencies relating to his or her life.

The problem of compliance is an important and often neglected topic. We suggest that the following approach can be used to minimize the problem of noncompliance. Treatment plans and strategies should be chosen not only because they are likely to be *effective* but also because they will be *efficient*. Earlier, it was mentioned that most treatment strategies involve some amount of personal cost for clients. These personal costs may range from the time spent attending treatment sessions to possibly instituting major changes in one's life style. In most cases, a *variety* of potentially effective treatment strategies can be developed. *An effective treatment strategy is one which results in desired behavior changes for the client.* Once potentially effective treatments have been indentified, however, issues of compliance become a vital concern. In this regard, we define *an efficient treatment strategy as one which achieves the desired behavior change while requiring the least personal cost from the client.* It is a reasonable assumption that the probability of a client's remaining in treatment and cooperating with a treatment plan is directly related to the demands the treatment plan places upon the client.

SHAPING

The principle of *shaping* refers to changing behavior gradually by reinforcing successive behavior changes which increasingly approximate a desired behavioral outcome. Shaping can also be viewed, therefore, as reinforcing incremental approximations to success. From a clinical perspective, shaping might be seen as necessitating the delineation of short-term as well as long-term treatment goals. Since clients may often receive little environmental reinforcement for working toward long-term behavior changes, it is helpful to break down the total desired behavior change into multiple components. This, in turn, creates numerous opportunities for rewarding the client within the therapeutic situation and increases the client's awareness of behavior changes. These same principles can be used to enhance gradually the client's involvement in the therapeutic process. In extreme cases, it may be necessary initially to reinforce a client for behaviors as minimally demanding as arriving on time for an appointment.

Shaping can be used in virtually all phases of the treatment process. However, with respect to the termination of treatment, we feel that shaping can serve a particularly vital and, to our knowledge, frequently neglected function. A cursory review of the literature describing treatment of persons with alcohol problems, including behavioral treatment approaches, reveals that outpatient treatment is typically terminated in one of two ways: (a) a negotiated or prescribed end of treatment, or (b) the client self-terminates treatment (i.e., drops out). Usually, these alternatives each involve an abrupt termination to treatment.

Several problems may ensue when treatment ends abruptly. First, in such cases there is often an inherent assumption that the client possesses satisfactory skills for continued successful functioning without further therapeutic contact. Clients sometimes recognize this assumption and, consequently, avoid seeking additional treatment if further problems are encountered. Clients who find themselves in such circumstances often speak of "not wanting to let the therapist down," or not wanting to let the therapist know that they have "failed." While it is unfortunate that such connotations develop, that does not dispel their reality. And although these difficulties are somewhat overcome by allowing the client to determine the termination of treatment, they are replaced by a collage of uncertainties. These uncertainties may then serve to hamper a needed resumption of treatment.

For the past several years, we have used a rather simple and straightforward shaping procedure to terminate outpatient treatment. This procedure is intended (a) to minimize the risk that the client will be too embarrassed to seek further treatment, and (b) to increase the opportunity for the therapist to provide the client with effective feedback. Specifically, the procedure is one of gradually lengthening the time interval between a client's appointments, while concurrently monitoring how well the client functions during these extended intervals. For example, appointments may be lengthened from weekly to biweekly, and subsequently to once every three weeks, six weeks, and so on, as necessary. If problems arise, appointments are then scheduled to occur more frequently until those problems are resolved, after which the intervals between appointments are once again gradually increased. Using this type of shaping procedure, we have found that treatment sessions can often be of shorter length (e.g., 30 minutes as opposed to an hour). Furthermore, at times the client may have little to discuss in terms of actual problems. However, when problems do occur, the client is aware that the discussion of ongoing problems is, indeed, appropriate. After a number of months of adequate functioning, a client may simply retain occasional telephone contact or personal contact with the therapist.

This shaping procedure may provide benefits for the therapist as well as the client. The primary advantage for the therapist is the opportunity to personally monitor the client's progress, rather than assuming that "no news is good news." Finally, information obtained by the therapist over this long-term shaping process can be considered as treatment outcome data. Therefore, the use of monitored shaping procedures to terminate treatment can provide therapists with valuable feedback concerning their own therapeutic effectiveness.

ADDRESSING IMMEDIATE TREATMENT NEEDS

The immediate needs of each client must be a paramount concern in all cases of outpatient treatment of alcohol problems, since it is often the case that immediate contingencies exert a stronger influence on behavior than long-term contingencies. Therefore, therapists must address a client's immediate life problems as a prerequisite to developing a long-term treatment plan. This is especially important in the treatment of alcohol problems, as the multiple life-health consequences of problem drinking can often influence the course of further treatment in a direct and catastrophic manner. For example, if a client is cited for driving under the influence of alcohol, the results of that conviction can have a resounding effect on his or her legal, financial, vocational, and interpersonal life-health. Thus, immediate difficulties usually need to be addressed promptly so they do not develop into serious long-term problems.

OUTPATIENT BEHAVIORAL TREATMENT METHODS

The remainder of this chapter focuses on the development of outpatient treatment strategies. The descriptions of behavioral treatment methods are neither exhaustive nor complete; however, the interested reader can find more detailed explanations of these methods in the behavioral treatment literature. In all cases, we suggest that treatment strategies be tailored or individualized to meet the needs of each client. Further, therapists should consider all available treatment techniques and methods when generating treatment plans, as this provides an array of alternative treatment strategies. Finally, although many of the treatment methods discussed were not initially developed for treating individuals with alcohol problems, they can be applied to that population.

While various behavioral treatment strategies can be conceptualized as dealing primarily with either the antecedents or consequences of behaviors, or directly with the behaviors themselves, it is seldom that a method deals exclusively with either antecedents or consequences of drinking or the drinking itself. Further, it is not uncommon for several methods to be used simultaneously to treat a given case.

METHODS WHICH PRIMARILY INVOLVE CHANGING THE ANTECEDENTS OR CORRELATES OF DRINKING

Self-monitoring and Recording of Drinking. While total abstinence is often viewed as desirable, it is highly unusual for individuals with alcohol problems to immediately cease drinking after entering treatment, especially in an outpatient setting. When drinking occurs, therapists can respond to those events in a variety of ways. Unfortunately, treatment providers often intentionally or inadvertently punish client disclosures about drinking. Although there are no systematic empirical investigations of how therapists' responses to clients' self-reports of drinking may influence the course of treatment, we believe that such reactions are frequently severe enough to cause clients to fail to report any further drinking during the course of treatment. In this regard, how can a therapist encourage client self-reports of drinking while at the same time not condoning self-damaging drinking (i.e., the client may drink *in order to report* that drinking to the therapist and to consequently receive praise and attention for reporting it)? Disclosure of drinking is important from a behavioral viewpoint, because the therapist can be relatively certain that the circumstances related to the drinking—its antecedents, its consequences, and the nature of the drinking itself—are likely to provide valuable information regarding environmental influences on the client's behavior. We found that the use of written logs of daily drinking behavior is an effective method for encouraging disclosure of drinking with outpatient clients (Sobell and Sobell, 1973c). The technique is rather simple. The client is asked to monitor and record his own daily alcohol consumption and the circumstances associated with that drinking. Two examples of such recording instruments appear in Figures 25 and 26.

Self-monitoring of drinking compels clients to continually be aware of their drinking and, it is hoped, to learn to identify situations which might lead to problem drinking. Further, the self-feedback provided by drinking logs legitimizes and encourages the discussion of situations in which drinking has occurred. Additionally, if a problem drinking pattern becomes evident, the use of drinking logs can facilitate an early treatment intervention. However, using drinking logs is a procedure where compliance with the treatment plan is critical. While a client may resist, for many reasons, the notion of recording his or her drinking behavior, the therapists' behavior can

DAILY DRINKING AWARENESS RECORD

Client's Name: _____

Date*	Type of Drink (Describe: Beer, Wine, Type of Mixed Drink, or Whiskey)	Time Drink First Ordered	Number of Sips Per Drink	Amount of Alcohol in Each Drink (Number of Ounces)	Where Drinking Occurred (Bar, Home, etc.)	Whom Were You With When you Drank	Did You Refuse Any Drinks You Were Offered? (YES/NO)

* Each drink consumed goes on a new line. If no alcohol was consumed on a day under type of drink write the word NONE.

Figure 25. Daily drinking awareness record.

help to minimize that resistance. It is important that the therapist neither punish nor ignore these disclosures but, rather, use these reports as a source of valuable information. While drinking is not necessarily encouraged, the client should be encouraged to accurately report whatever drinking does occur during treatment.

Although the use of drinking logs might appear relatively simple, in practice they must be skillfully integrated into an overall treatment plan. We have found the following procedure to be helpful when using drinking logs. Should drinking be reported, it is of importance to *first reinforce the client for accurately recording and reporting the drinking, whether or not the drinking resulted in damaging consequences. Then, the drinking should be analyzed in terms of the consequences which it incurred or could have incurred.* Such a procedure makes salient the fact that inappropriate drinking is likely to result in increased problems. Thus, rather than assuming that the client will readily recognize the long-term consequences of his or her drinking, the therapist can assure this association by making the functional analysis of drinking instances an explicit part of the treatment process. Using such a procedure, we have found that most clients will report drinking instances.

Since drinking is the *sine qua non* of alcohol problems, it is imperative that the therapist be aware of any drinking which occurs. Conversely, a record indicating no drinking over an extended time period can serve as a significant reward for the client. In this way, the drinking record may actually motivate the client to continue to refrain from problem drinking.

Measurement of Blood Alcohol Concentration. Blood alcohol concentration (BAC) is a direct indicant of alcohol intoxication. It is usually expressed in terms of milligrams of ethyl alcohol per 100 milliliters of blood volume, or as a percentage of blood volume. For example, a BAC of 0.10% is equivalent to 100 mg of ethyl alcohol per 100 ml of blood. There are numerous occasions when measurements of a client's BAC can aid in making therapeutic decisions. For instance, because of the phenomenon of *acquired tolerance*, direct observation of a client's behavior is sometimes not a valid indication of the client's actual level of alcohol intoxication (Sobell, Sobell and VanderSpek, 1976).

Acquired tolerance summarizes the observation that with frequent use of some drugs, including ethyl alcohol, the user over time is less sensitive to those drug effects. Put differently, with repeated exposure to alcohol, one requires a larger dose of alcohol to achieve

WEEKLY DRINKING AWARENESS RECORD

Name _____

Date	Total Number and Type of Standard Drinks[1]					Approximate Time Spent in Drinking Situation (e.g., if you spent 3½ hours at a party where you were drinking put "3½ hours").	Feelings While Drinking[2]		Drinking Context (Check One)				Total Number of Drinks Refused	Estimated Total Number of Drinks To Be Consumed Tomorrow
	Mixed Drinks						Emotional	Physical	Alone	With Others	Private Place	Public Place		
	Straight	Mixed Drinks	Beer	Wine	Total									
1														
2														
3														
4														
5														
6														
7														

[1] One (1) Standard Drink = 1 oz. of liquor, 4 oz. wine, or 12 oz. of beer.

[2] You may indicate more than one feeling at one time. If your feelings *change* during a drinking situation, indicate this by an arrow. For example, C,G → E means first you felt tense and angry, then you felt sad.

Feelings Code—Emotional

A = Happy   F = Depressed
B = Bored   G = Angry
C = Tense, Nervous H = Nostalgic
D = Calm, Serene   I = Lonely
E = Sad   J = Emotionally Drained

Feelings Code—Physical

A = Headache   E = Simple Cold
B = Felt Very Good F = Felt Ill, Very Sick
C = Felt OK   G = Tired, Sleepy
D = Exhausted   H = Weak but Not Ill

Figure 26. Weekly drinking awareness record.

the same degree of effect previously attained with a smaller dose (for a scientific discussion of acquired tolerance, see Kalant, LeBlanc, and Gibbins, 1971). When dealing with individuals who have an extensive history of drinking, therefore, clinical judgments of a person's degree of alcohol intoxication based solely on behavioral impairment may sometimes not be valid. Nevertheless, accurate assessment of a client's level of alcohol intoxication is vital, because, as a client demonstrates increased tolerance during a drinking episode, it becomes increasingly likely that he or she has developed physical dependence upon alcohol during that episode. After some experience, one finds that physiological assessment of a client's BAC, coupled with observations of the client's behavior, is invaluable for assessing the severity of a drinking episode (i.e., the combination of relatively few behavioral indications of intoxication along with a relatively high BAC [e.g., 0.21%] usually indicates a more serious episode than does the presence of many behavioral manifestations of intoxication combined with a lower BAC [e.g., 0.08%]).

Blood alcohol concentration is usually measured with commercially available devices. These devices were originally developed to assess the BAC of persons apprehended while driving under the influence of alcohol. Because of the need for legal evidence, these devices are typically sophisticated, nonportable and highly accurate, but costly. An example of such an instrument, the Alco-Analyzer Gas Chromatograph, appears in Figure 27. Although requiring a substantial investment, i.e., approximately $3,000, this type of tool can be of substantial value in a large-scale outpatient program (Feldman, Pattison, Sobell, Graham, and Sobell, 1975).

In clinical practice, however, there is usually no need to determine the client's BAC with great precision. Therefore, it is unlikely that most private therapists or alcohol programs could justify an expenditure of several thousand dollars for a breath–analysis instrument. Fortunately, a few inexpensive, portable devices are available for determining BACs with a degree of accuracy sufficient for clinical applications. We have used one such device, the Mobat (Mobile Breath Alcohol Test), for a wide variety of purposes. The Mobat is relatively inexpensive (the price per test is approximately 70 cents), self-contained, and simple to use.

The Mobat is purchased as a kit containing materials sufficient for five complete tests. The basic contents of the kit are shown in Figure 28. The chief component of the Mobat is a tube which contains dry silica gel treated with a reagent of chromate ions in sulfuric acid.

Figure 27. The Model 1000 Alco-Analyzer Gas Chromatograph. One of several highly accurate breath analyzers available for commercial purposes. Photograph courtesy of Luckey Laboratories, Inc.

The reagent is arranged in a series of three discrete yellow rings which turn green as a result of the interaction with alcohol contained in the breath. The three rings indicate BAC ranges from 0.00 to 0.10%, 0.10 to 0.20%, and 0.20 to 0.30% by blood volume, respectively. The yellow rings progressively turn green as a direct function of the concentration of alcohol in the breath. Thus, the tubes are read in a linear, thermometerlike fashion, with BAC estimates corresponding to the highest position reached by the color change. In the majority of states, a BAC of 0.10% is the legal criterion above which persons are considered legally intoxicated.

As with all breath tests for alcohol, the Mobat should not be administered within 15 minutes of drinking alcohol (e.g., whiskey, mouth wash, etc.) or the test will register a false positive reading due to alcohol residuals in the mouth. In order for a test to be administered, the device is first assembled as two units. The desiccant crystals, stored in each end of the glass reagent tube, are discarded, and the tube is then attached to a plastic volumetric bag. A balloon is then attached to a short plastic mouthpiece, and the subject is instructed to inflate the balloon to full volume. After the balloon has been fully inflated, (a) the end of the balloon is pinched so that the stored breath cannot escape, (b) the free end of the mouthpiece is attached to the free end of the reagent tube, and (c) the air in the balloon is then released to flow through the reagent and into the volumetric bag. The completed single unit appears as shown in the center of Figure 28. After the volumetric bag has fully expanded, the reagent tube is disconnected from the other apparatus and capped on both ends, thereby maintaining a closed system. The balloon and mouthpiece are discarded, while the volumetric bag is evacuated for reuse. As described earlier, the tube is then read in a thermometerlike fashion. The total time involved in administering a test is usually less than one minute.

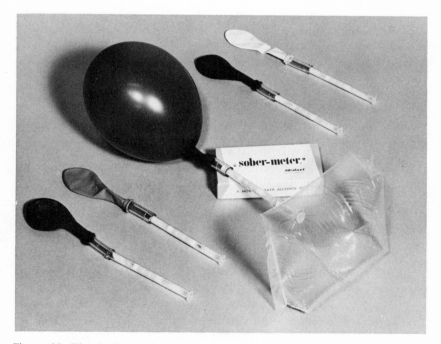

Figure 28. The Mobat, Sober-Meter Kit SM–6. Mobat is the trade name for Sober-Meter Kit SM–6, manufactured by Luckey Laboratories, Inc., 7252 Osbun Road, San Bernardino, CA 92404. Reprinted from Sobell, M. B. and Sobell, L. C. A brief technical report on the Mobat: An inexpensive portable test for determining blood alcohol concentration. *Journal of Applied Behavior Analysis,* 1975b, *8,* 117-120. Permission granted by the Society for Experimental Analysis of Behavior, Inc.

In a systematic evaluation of this device (Sobell and Sobell, 1975c), we found the Mobat to have an average deviation of $\pm 0.04\%$. Evaluation of BAC estimates is further aided by the knowledge that a reading of less than 0.10% is likely to be overestimated, a reading exceeding 0.10% will generally be underestimated, and a reading around the criterion of legal drunkenness (0.10%) will be relatively correct.

Breath testing for BAC can serve multiple purposes in treatment. For example, it can be used to validate clients' self-reports of recent drinking. Also, because of low cost and portability, clients can purchase Mobat kits to obtain immediate feedback regarding their own level of intoxication. For instance, should a client drink to legal intoxication, the Mobat can be used to provide a basis for deciding whether or not to risk driving. Breath testing also allows for rapid resolution of disagreements regarding drinking which has occurred and the amount of such drinking, if any. Thus, conflicts between clients and their relatives can be readily resolved, if the client is willing to "test." Using a similar but slightly more expensive device, Miller, Hersen, Eisler, and Watts (1974) effectively arranged for lessened drinking by a male chronic alcoholic in outpatient treatment, using contingent reinforcement of lowered BACs. Lastly, breath testing can be used by clients to gain experience in estimating their own BAC. This, in particular, is relevant to the following method.

Blood Alcohol Concentration Discrimination Training. Blood alcohol concentration discrimination training is a procedure developed by Lovibond and Caddy (1970) to train outpatient clients to judge subjectively their own level of intoxication. The technique was initially incorporated as part of a multiple-component treatment program. Basically, the method is intended to focus clients' attention upon the internal sensations which accompany various degrees of alcohol intoxication and the external or constant variables which affect their level of intoxication (e.g., amount of ethanol consumed, time period over which ethanol was consumed, presence or absence of food in the stomach, etc.). In training, individuals first estimate their own BAC and are then provided with feedback as determined by breath test. Under these conditions, clients are soon able to estimate their own BACs with some accuracy.

Considerable controversy presently surrounds the basis upon which subjects can make accurate BAC estimates (see Caddy, 1977; Nathan and Briddell, 1977). In fact, a recent study (Maisto and

Adesso, 1977) suggests that under properly controlled circumstances individuals cannot learn to make valid BAC estimates based solely on internal physical sensations generated by alcohol. This finding is not unexpected, when one considers the relative variability of such effects, as demonstrated by the phenomenon of acquired tolerance. From a clinical perspective, however, the utility of the technique of BAC discrimination training lies in the fact that subjects can learn to perform such estimates, given appropriate information. The fact that these estimates may be based on cues other than the client's physical state is not that important. What is important, though, is that clients can be trained to estimate their own degree of alcohol intoxication with some validity. This can be crucial in preparing a client, for instance, to avoid risking legal consequences when intoxicated (i.e., drunk driving).

Relaxation Training and Systematic Desensitization. The technique of deep muscle relaxation (Jacobson, 1938) is often used by behavior therapists to train clients to relax. When the antecedents or correlates of drinking have been identified as involving anxiety or nervous tension, especially if that tension seems to stem from unavoidable circumstances, one element of the treatment plan might include training the client to minimize the effects of that nervous tension. Relaxation training is also particularly useful when incorporated as part of a systematic desensitization treatment (Wolpe, 1969). Systematic densitization is a well-defined behavioral technique used to extinguish specific fears. In a graded manner, the client is repeatedly exposed to imagined or real aspects of the phobic situation under conditions which prevent or minimize the arousal of anxiety. One such condition is a deeply relaxed state. Not many studies have been published using systematic desensitization and relaxation training to treat alcoholics.

Cognitive Behavior Modification. Focusing on anticipatory thought processes as antecedents of behavior, Lazarus (1971) has discussed a clinical methodology he calls "cognitive restructuring." Basically, Lazarus's methods seem to involve verbal interactions between the client and therapist whereby the client's misperceptions are corrected and assumptions lacking an objective basis are identified. Meichenbaum and Cameron (1974) have developed similar techniques which deal with modifying clients' self-verbalizations. While use of these methods has not been reported in the treatment of alcohol problems, their applicability seems obvious.

METHODS WHICH PRIMARILY INVOLVE CHANGING
BEHAVIORAL REPERTOIRES

Training in Problem Solving Skills. This procedure was discussed at length in Chapter 5. Thus, we will not reiterate it here, other than to say that in outpatient treatment programs the problems most often addressed are actual and current. Problem solving skills are presumed to develop as the client learns to identify and deal with problem situations. Furthermore, as the client gains experience in identifying and resolving problems, this process should gradually become easier. Lastly, the therapist can play a critical role in providing short-term support for the client while the client is in treatment and is making functional long-term behavioral changes.

Establishing Behavioral Repertoires. When a client's drinking is functionally analyzed, it may be determined that the client lacks necessary skills to engage in appropriate alternative behaviors to drinking. The topic of establishing behavioral repertoires subsumes a variety of more specific techniques, where the client, with the help of the therapist, learns desired but heretofore lacking social or personal skills in either imaginary, analogue, or *in vivo* situations. For a discussion of specific behavioral techniques the reader is referred to Goldfried and Davison (1976).

The following behavioral techniques are frequently used to shape the acquisition of behavioral repertoires which the client lacks: role playing, modeling, social coaching, role reversal, and social rewards. As Goldfried and Davison (1976) point out, these procedures can also be used to help individuals deal with situations which can be identified but which they have not previously encountered. These types of behavioral techniques have been used to treat individuals with alcohol problems. For example, Eisler, Miller, Hersen, and Alford (1974) reported a case study which described the effective use of assertion training to teach alcoholics to effectively refuse drinks. Such methods were also used in the inpatient IBT program.

Aversive Conditioning. Aversive conditioning describes a variety of different procedures which attempt to abolish or reduce the strength of drinking behaviors by pairing a component of that class of behaviors, such as the sight, smell, thoughts, or taste of alcohol, with an aversive event. The aversive event can be an electric shock (set at painful but harmless levels), chemical stimulation (typically an emetic like Emetine or Apomorphine), or imaginary (generated as the result of a behavioral procedure called covert sensitization; see Cautela, 1970).

Recently, researchers have seriously questioned the efficacy of electrical aversion conditioning; specifically, it has been suggested that when positive effects do occur, they are not the result of a conditioned aversion (Rachman and Teasdale, 1969; Wilson, Leaf, and Nathan, 1975; Nathan and Briddell, 1977). Aversion conditioning by chemical and covert sensitization methods has been similarly suspect, but clear empirical tests of the efficacy of these procedures have not been reported. Given the questionable efficacy of aversive procedures, it would seem that they should not be the treatment of choice, except in exceptional circumstances.

METHODS WHICH PRIMARILY INVOLVE CHANGING THE CONSEQUENCES OF BEHAVIORS

Behavioral Commitment and Contracting. Earlier, we mentioned that behaviorally oriented therapists often work to develop a rewarding therapeutic relationship for the client. Once this has occurred, the client can be considered to have developed some degree of commitment to the therapeutic relationship. Oftentimes, however, a client's environment is not responsive to behavioral changes made by the client. In this regard, a rewarding therapeutic relationship allows the therapist to provide social reinforcement for such changes.

Occasionally, written agreements may be necessary for achieving behavioral change. While such a written agreement is seldom necessary between client and therapist, sometimes it is useful to formulate a written contractual agreement between the client and one or more significant others. This is particularly important when the significant others (e.g., spouse) do not trust the client and are reluctant to cooperate with the treatment plan. In such cases, behavioral contracting (DeRisi and Butz, 1975) can be valuable. The process usually involved defining explicitly a set of desired behaviors and their associated consequences. Often, such an agreement is negotiated as a set of reciprocal obligations (Azrin, Naster, and Jones, 1973).

Behavioral contracting assures that all parties agree to expected behaviors, appropriate reactions, and the ways by which behavior change will be recognized and rewarded. Miller (1972) successfully used behavioral contracting with an alcoholic and his wife to establish and maintain a controlled drinking pattern.

Contingency Management. Contingency management refers to a variety of procedures aimed at arranging a person's environment so that positive consequences will follow desired behaviors and negative consequences or no consequences will follow nondesired behaviors. This method uses basic behavior management techniques fundamental to token economies and generally requires a considerable amount of time and effort. Therefore, when considering contingency management procedures, one should carefully evaluate the degree of cooperation which can be expected from various elements of the client's environment.

Hunt and Azrin (1973) and Azrin (1976) have reported an extremely comprehensive contingency management approach to alcohol problems. They developed an individualized broad-spectrum "community reinforcement" network for chronic alcoholics whereby social, vocational, recreational, and familial rewards were made contingent upon continuing sobriety. These "community reinforcers" were also arranged so that drinking produced a time-out from the high density of reinforcement for clients. The "community reinforcement" group spent less time drinking, unemployed, away from home, or institutionalized during the six months following treatment, when compared to a matched control group of alcoholics who did not receive the behavioral intervention.

Bigelow, Liebson, and Lawrence (1973) used contingency management procedures as part of an occupational alcoholism program. Employees whose jobs were in jeopardy as a result of their drinking were given the opportunity to continue working contingent upon taking Antabuse (disulfiram) daily.

Miller (1975) recently used contingency management procedures with chronic skid-row alcoholics. In collaboration with community agencies (e.g., Salvation Army, Union Rescue Mission, etc.) he arranged for some randomly selected skid-row alcoholics to receive various goods and services (e.g., clothing, cigarettes, etc.) if and only if they were abstinent as determined by a breath test. When compared with a group of alcoholics not similarly accountable for their sobriety, the contingency management group showed a significant decrease in their level of intoxication and number of arrests over a two-month period. They also showed a significant increase in the number of hours they were employed for pay.

CONCLUDING COMMENTS

In summary, behavioral approaches to the treatment of alcohol problems are dynamic in that they involve *continued assessment and evaluation* of problems and treatment effects. Further, since individuals have idiosyncratic learning histories, it seems appropriate that treatment strategies be tailored to the characteristics of each individual client. While *individual treatment plans* are certainly not novel, they have been the exception rather than the rule in the area of alcohol treatment.

This chapter has clearly emphasized the need to select individual treatment strategies that are *efficient* in terms of *minimizing the client's personal cost while still achieving a given set of objectives*. Davison and Stuart (1975) have conceptualized this orientation as a "principle of least severity." Stuart (1975) has discussed this principle as stressing that "intervention should be the least drastic method which is likely to achieve the stated goals" (p. 169). Our approach to the treatment of alcohol problems has been to emphasize consistently that, in most cases, *there are a variety of potentially effective treatment strategies which can be used*. Only an individual case analysis, however, can suggest which strategy is best suited to a given client.

References and Selected Readings

REFERENCES

Alcoholism Report, The. Alexandria, Virginia: JSL Reports.

American Psychological Association. *Diagnostic and statistical manual of mental disorders (2nd ed.).* Washington, D.C.: American Psychiatric Association, 1968.

Anonymous, *Alcoholics Anonymous.* New York: Works Publishing, Inc., 1939.

Armor, D. J., Polich, J. M., and Stambul, H. B. *Alcoholism and treatment.* Report R–1739–NIAAA. Santa Monica, CA: Rand Corporation, 1976.

Azrin, N. H. Improvements in the community-reinforcement approach to alcoholism. *Behaviour Research and Therapy*, 1976, *14*, 339–348.

Azrin, N. H., Naster, B. J., and Jones, R. Reciprocity counseling: A rapid learning-based procedure for marital counseling. *Behaviour Research and Therapy*, 1973, *11*, 365–382.

Bailey, K. G., and Sowder, W. T., Jr. Audiotape and videotape self-confrontation in psychotherapy. *Psychological Bulletin,* 1970, *74,* 127–137.

Bandura, A. *Principles of behavior modification.* New York: Holt, Rinehart & Winston, 1969.

Barber, T. X. *Pitfalls in human research.* New York: Pergamon Press, 1976.

Barber, T. X., and Silver, M. J. Fact, fiction, and the experimenter bias effect. *Psychological Bulletin Monograph*, Part 2, 1968a, *70*, 1–29.

Barber, T. X., and Silver, M. J. Pitfalls in data analysis and interpretation: A reply to Rosenthal. *Psychological Bulletin Monograph*, Part 2, 1968b, *70*, 48–62.

Barr, H. L., Rosen, A., Antes, D. E., and Ottenberg, D. J. Two year follow-up study of 724 drug and alcohol addicts treated together in an abstinence therapeutic community. Paper presented at the 81st Annual Convention of the American Psychological Association, Montreal, August, 1973.

Barry, H. B., III. Psychological factors in alcoholism. In B. Kissin and H. Begleiter (Eds.), *The biology of alcoholism, Volume 3: Clinical pathology.* New York: Plenum Press, Inc., 1974.

Beatty, W. W. How blind is blind? *Psychological Bulletin,* 1972, *78,* 70–71.

Belasco, J. A. The criterion question revisited. *British Journal of the Addictions,* 1971, *66,* 39–44.

Bigelow, G., Liebson, I., and Lawrence, C. Prevention of alcohol abuse by reinforcement of incompatible behavior. Paper presented at the meeting of the Association for Advancement of Behavior Therapy, Miami, December, 1973.

Billings, A. G., Weiner, S., Kessler, M., and Gomberg, C. A. Drinking behavior in laboratory and barroom settings. *Journal of Studies on Alcohol,* 1976, *37,* 85–89.

Blake, B. G. The application of behaviour therapy to the treatment of alcoholism. *Behaviour Research and Therapy,* 1965, *3,* 75–85.

Bowen, W. T., and Androes, L. A follow-up study of 79 alcoholic patients: 1963-1965. *Bulletin of the Menninger Clinic,* 1968, *32,* 26–34.

Caddy, G. R. Blood alcohol concentration discrimination training: Development and current status. In P. E. Nathan and G. A. Marlatt (Eds.), *Behavioral assessment and treatment of alcoholism.* New Brunswick: Rutgers Center for Alcohol Studies, 1977, in press.

Caddy, G. R., and Perkins, D. Alcoholics treated by individualized behavior therapy: A third year double-blind follow-up, 1977, in preparation.

Cahalan, D., Cisin, I. H., and Crossley, H. M. *American drinking practices: A national survey of behavior and attitudes.* Monograph No. 6. New Brunswick, N.J.: Rutgers Center of Alcohol Studies, 1969.

Cahalan, D., and Room, R. *Problem drinking among American men.* Monograph No. 7. New Brunswick, N.J.: Rutgers Center of Alcohol Studies, 1974.

Cantril, H. *The psychology of social movements.* New York: John Wiley & Sons, 1941.

Cautela, J. R. The treatment of alcoholism by covert sensitization. *Psychotherapy: Theory, Research and Practice,* 1970, *7,* 86–90.

Clark, W. B. Conceptions of alcoholism—consequences for research. *Addictive Diseases,* 1975, *1,* 395–430.

Clark, W. B. and Cahalan, D. Changes in problem drinking over a four-year span. *Addictive Behaviors,* 1976, *1,* 251–259.

Conger, J. J. Reinforcement theory and the dynamics of alcoholism. *Quarterly Journal of Studies on Alcohol,* 1956, *17,* 296–305.

Crawford, J. J., and Chalupsky, A. B. The reported evaluation of alcoholism treatments, 1968–1971: A methodological review. *Addictive Behaviors,* 1977, *2,* 63–74.

Davies, D. L. Normal drinking in recovered alcohol addicts. *Quarterly Journal of Studies on Alcohol,* 1962, *23,* 94–104.

Davies, D. L. Normal drinking in recovered alcohol addicts. (Comments by various correspondents), *Quarterly Journal of Studies on Alcohol,* 1963, *24,* 109–121; 321–332.

Davies, D. L., Shepard, M., and Myers, E. The two-year's prognosis of 50 alcohol addicts after treatment in hospital. *Quarterly Journal of Studies on Alcohol,* 1956, *17,* 485-502.

Davison, G. C., and Stuart, R. B. Behavior therapy and civil liberties. *American Psychologist,* 1975, *30,* 755–763.

DeRisi, W. J. and Butz, G. *Writing behavioral contracts.* Champaign, IL: Research Press, 1975.

Doherty, J. Controlled drinking: Valid approach or deadly snare? *Alcohol and Health Research World,* 1974, *Fall,* 2–8.

Edwards, G. The status of alcoholism as a disease. In R. V. Phillipson (Ed.), *Modern trends in drug dependence and alcoholism.* New York: Appleton–Century–Crofts, 1970.

Eisler, R. M., Miller, P. M., Hersen, M., and Alford, H. Effects of assertive training on marital interaction. *Archives of General Psychiatry,* 1974, *30,* 643–649.

Elkins, R. L. Aversion therapy for alcoholism: Chemical, electrical, or verbal imagery. *International Journal of the Addictions,* 1975, *10,* 157–209.

Emrick, C. D. A review of psychologically oriented treatment of alcoholism. *Quarterly Journal of Studies on Alcohol,* 1974, *35,* 523–549.

Engle, K. B., and Williams, T. K. Effect of an ounce of vodka on alcoholics' desire for alcohol. *Quarterly Journal of Studies on Alcohol,* 1972, *33,* 1099–1105.

Ewing, J. A., and Rouse, B. A. Failure of an experimental treatment program to inculcate controlled drinking in alcoholics. *British Journal of Addictions,* 1976, *71,* 123–134.

Feldman, D. J., Pattison, E. M., Sobell, L. C., Graham, T., and Sobell, M. B. Outpatient alcohol detoxification: Initial findings on 564 patients. *American Journal of Psychiatry,* 1975, *132,* 407–412.

Fillmore, K. Drinking and problem drinking in early adulthood and middle age. *Quarterly Journal of Studies on Alcohol,* 1974, *35,* 819–840.

Foy, D. W., Miller, P. M., Eisler, R. M., and O'Toole, D. H. Social skills training to teach alcoholics to refuse drinks effectively. *Journal of Alcohol Studies,* 1976, *37,* 1340–1345.

Gallen, M. Toward an understanding of follow-up research with alcoholics. *Psychological Reports,* 1974, *34,* 877–878.

Gerard, D. L., and Saenger, G. Interval between intake and follow-up as a factor in the evaluation of patients with a drinking problem. *Quarterly Journal of Studies on Alcohol,* 1959, *20,* 620–630.

Gerard, D. L., and Saenger, G. *Out-patient treatment of alcoholism.* Toronto: University of Toronto Press, 1966.

Gerard, D. L., Saenger, G., and Wile, R. The abstinent alcoholic. *Archives of General Psychiatry,* 1962, *6,* 83–95.

Gibbins, R. J., and Armstrong, J. D. Effects of clinical treatment on behavior of alcoholic patients: An exploratory methodological investigation. *Quarterly Journal of Studies on Alcohol,* 1957, *18,* 429–450.

Gillies, M., Laverty, S. G., Smart, R. G., and Aharan, C. H. Outcomes in treated alcoholics. *Journal of Alcoholism,* 1974, *9,* 125–134.

Goldfried, M. R., and Davison, G. C. *Clinical behavioral therapy.* New York: Holt, Rinehart & Winston, 1976.

Goldstein, A. P. Relationship enhancement methods. In F. H. Kanfer and A. P. Goldstein (Eds.), *Helping people change.* New York: Pergamon Press, Inc., 1975.

Goodwin, D. W., Davis, D. H., and Robins, L. N. Drinking amid abundant illicit drugs: The Vietnam case. *Archives of General Psychiatry,* 1975, *32,* 230–233.

Gross, M. M., Lewis, E., and Hastey, J. The acute alcohol withdrawal syndrome. In B. Kissin & H. Begleiter (Eds.), *The biology of alcoholism, Volume 3: Clinical Pathology.* New York: Plenum Press, Inc., 1974.

Harris, R. N., and Walter, J. Outcome, reliability and validity issues of alcoholism follow-up. Paper presented at the 27th Annual Meeting of the Alcohol and Drug Problems Association of North America, New Orleans, September, 1976.

Hill, M. J., and Blane, H. T. Evaluation of psychotherapy with alcoholics: A critical review. *Quarterly Journal of Studies on Alcohol*, 1967, *28*, 76–104.

Hollingshead, A. B., and Redlich, F. C. *Social class and mental illness*. New York: John Wiley & Sons, 1958.

Hunt, G. M., and Azrin, N. H. A community-reinforcement approach to alcoholism. *Behaviour Research and Therapy*, 1973, *11*, 91–104.

Jacobson, E. *Progressive relaxation*. Chicago: University of Chicago Press, 1938.

Jellinek, E. M. Phases in the drinking history of alcoholics. *Quarterly Journal of Studies on Alcohol*, 1946, *7*, 1–88.

Jellinek, E. M. Current notes: Phases of alcohol addiction. *Quarterly Journal of Studies on Alcohol*, 1952, *13*, 673–684.

Jellinek, E. M. *The disease concept of alcoholism*. New Brunswick, NJ: Hillhouse Press, 1960.

Johnson, V. E. *I'll quit tomorrow*. New York: Harper & Row, 1973.

Kalant, H., LeBlanc, A. E., and Gibbins, R. J. Tolerance to, and dependence on, ethanol. In Y. Israel and J. Mardones (Eds.), *Biological basis of alcoholism*. New York: Wiley-Interscience, 1971.

Kanfer, F. H., and Grimm, L. G. Behavioral analysis: Selecting target behaviors in the interview. *Behavior Modification*, 1977, *1*, 7–28.

Keller, M. On the loss-of-control phenomenon in alcoholism. *The British Journal of Addiction*, 1972, *67*, 153–166.

Kerlinger, F. N., and Pedhazur, E. J. *Multiple regression in behavioral research*. New York: Holt, Rinehart & Winston, 1973.

Kessler, M., and Gomberg, C. Observations of barroom drinking: Methodology and preliminary results. *Quarterly Journal of Studies on Alcohol*, 1974, *35*, 1392–1396.

Lazarus, A. A. Towards the understanding and effective treatment of alcoholism. *South African Medical Journal*, 1965, *39*, 736–741.

Lazarus, A. A. *Behavior therapy and beyond*. New York: McGraw-Hill Book Co., 1971.

Lloyd, R. W., and Salzberg, H. C. Controlled social drinking: An alternative to abstinence as a treatment goal for some alcohol abusers. *Psychological Bulletin*, 1975, *82*, 815–842.

Lovibond, S. H., and Caddy, G. Discriminated aversive control in the moderation of alcoholics' drinking behavior. *Behavior Therapy*, 1970, *1*, 437–444.

Lowe, W. C., and Thomas, S. D. Assessing alcoholism treatment effectiveness: A comparison of three evaluative measures. *Journal of Studies on Alcohol*, 1976, *37*, 883–889.

MacAndrew, C. On the notion that certain persons who are given to frequent drunkenness suffer from a disease called alcoholism. In S. C. Plog and R. B. Edgerton (Eds.), *Changing perspectives in mental illness*. New York: Holt, Rinehart & Winston, 1969.

MacAndrew, C., and Edgerton, R. B. *Drunken comportment*. Chicago: Aldine Publishing Company, 1969.

Madsen, W. Alcoholics Anonymous as a crisis cult. Paper presented at the meeting of the 3rd Annual Alcoholism Conference of the National Institute on Alcohol Abuse and Alcoholism, Washington, D.C., June, 1973.

Maisto, S. A., and Adesso, V. J. The effect of instructions and feedback on blood alcohol concentration discrimination training in non-alcoholic drinkers. *Journal of Consulting and Clinical Psychology*, 1977, *45*, 625–636.

Maisto, S. A., Sobell, L. C., and Sobell, M. B. Comparison of alcoholic and collateral self-reports of drinking behavior. Unpublished manuscript, 1977.

Mann, M. *New primer on alcoholism*, second edition. New York: Holt, Rinehart & Winston, 1968.

McNamee, H. B., Mello, N. K., and Mendelson, J. H. Experimental analysis of drinking patterns of alcoholics: Concurrent psychiatric observations. *American Journal of Psychiatry*, 1968, *124*, 81–87.

Meichenbaum, D., and Cameron, R. The clinical potential of modifying what clients say to themselves. In M. J. Mahoney and C. E. Thoresen (Eds.), *Self-control: Power to the person*. Monterey, CA: Brooks/Cole Publishing Co., 1974.

Mello, N. K., and Mendelson, J. H. Operant analysis of drinking patterns of chronic alcoholics. *Nature*, 1965, *206*, 43–46.

Mendelson, J. H. (Ed.). Experimentally induced chronic intoxication and withdrawal in alcoholics. *Quarterly Journal of Studies on Alcohol*, 1964, Supplement No. 2.

Miller, B. A., Pokorny, A. D., Valles, J., and Cleveland, S. E. Biased sampling in alcoholism treatment research. *Quarterly Journal of Studies on Alcohol*, 1970, *31*, 97–107.

Miller, P. M. The use of behavioral contracting in the treatment of alcoholism: A case report. *Behavior Therapy*, 1972, *3*, 593–596.

Miller, P. M. A behavioral intervention program for chronic public drunkenness offenders. *Archives of General Psychiatry*, 1975, *32*, 915–918.

Miller, P. M. *Behavioral treatment of alcoholism*. New York: Pergamon Press, 1976.

Miller, P. M., Hersen, M., Eisler, R. M., and Watts, J. G. Contingent reinforcement of lowered blood alcohol levels in an outpatient chronic alcoholic. *Behaviour Research and Therapy*, 1974, *12*, 261–263.

Miller, W. R. Alcoholism scales and objective assessment methods: A review. *Psychological Bulletin*, 1976, *83*, 649–674.

Mills, K. C., Sobell, M. B., and Schaefer, H. H. Training social drinking as an alternative to abstinence for alcoholics. *Behavior Therapy*, 1971, *2*, 18–27.

Moos, R., and Bliss, F. Difficulty of follow-up and alcoholism treatment outcome. Unpublished manuscript. Stanford University, Stanford, 1977.

Nathan, P. E., and Briddell, D. W. Behavioral assessment and treatment of alcoholism. In B. Kissin and H. Begleiter (Eds.), *The biology of alcoholism*, Volume 5. New York: Plenum Publishing Co., 1977.

Nathan, P. E., and O'Brien, J. S. An experimental analysis of the behavior of alcoholics and nonalcoholics during prolonged experimental drinking: A necessary precursor of behavior therapy? *Behavior Therapy*, 1971, *2*, 455–476.

Nathan, P. E., Titler, N. A., Lowenstein, L. M., Solomon, P., and Rossi, A. M. Behavioral analysis of chronic alcoholism. *Archives of General Psychiatry*, 1970, *22*, 419–430.

National Council on Alcoholism, press release, July 19, 1974.

Nunnally, J. C. *Psychometric theory*. New York: McGraw-Hill, 1967.

Oki, G. Alcohol use by skid row alcoholics: Part 1. Drinking at Bon Accord. Substudy No. 612. Toronto: Addiction Research Foundation, 1974.

Orford, J. A comparison of alcoholics whose drinking is totally uncontrolled and those whose drinking is mainly controlled. *Behaviour Research and Therapy*, 1973, *11*, 556–576.

Orford, J., and Hawker, A. Investigation of an alcoholism rehabilitation halfway house,

2. Complex question of client motivation. *British Journal of the Addictions*, 1974, *69*, 315–323.

Orford, J., Oppenheimer, E., and Edwards, G. Abstinence or control: The outcome for excessive drinkers two years after consultation. *Behavior Research and Therapy*, 1976, *14*, 409–418.

Orne, M. T. Demand characteristics and the concept of quasi-controls. In R. Rosenthal and R. L. Rosnow (Eds.), *Artifact in behavioral research*. New York: Academic Press, 1969.

Osborn, A. F. *Applied imagination*. (3rd Ed.) New York: Scribner's, 1963.

Paredes, A., Hood, W. R., Seymour, H., and Gollob, M. Loss of control in alcoholism: An investigation of the hypothesis, with experimental findings. *Quarterly Journal of Studies on Alcohol*, 1973, *34*, 1146–1161.

Paredes, A., Ludwig, K. D., Hassenfeld, I. N., and Cornelison, F. S., Jr. A clinical study of alcoholics using audio-visual self-image feedback. *Journal of Nervous and Mental Disease,* 1969, *148*, 449–456.

Pattison, E. M. Nonabstinent goals in the treatment of alcoholics. In R. J. Gibbins, Y. Israel, H. Kalant, R. E. Popham, W. Schmidt, and R. G. Smart (Eds.), *Research advances in alcohol and drug problems: Volume 3*. Toronto: John Wiley & Sons, 1976.

Pattison, E. M., Headley, E. B., Gleser, G. C., and Gottschalk, L. A. Abstinence and normal drinking: An assessment of changes in drinking patterns in alcoholics after treatment. *Quarterly Journal of Studies on Alcohol*, 1968, *29*, 610–633.

Pattison, E. M., Sobell, M. B., and Sobell, L. C. (Authors/Eds.) *Emerging concepts of alcohol dependence*. New York: Springer Publishing Co., 1977.

Pittman, D. J., and Tate, R. L. A comparison of two treatment programs for alcoholics. *The International Journal of Social Psychiatry*, 1972, *18*, 183–193.

Plaut, T. F. A. *Alcohol problems: A report to the nation*. New York: Oxford University Press, 1967.

Pokorny, A. D., Miller, B. A., Kanas, T., and Valles, J. Effectiveness of extended aftercare in the treatment of alcoholism. *Quarterly Journal of Studies on Alcohol*, 1973, *34*, 435–443.

Pomerleau, O., Pertschuk, M., and Stinnett, J. A critical examination of some current assumptions in the treatment of alcoholism. *Journal of Studies on Alcohol*, 1976, *37*, 849–857.

Popham, R. E., and Schmidt, W. Some factors affecting the likelihood of moderate drinking in treated alcoholics. *Journal of Studies on Alcohol*, 1976, *37*, 868–882.

Rachman, S., and Teasdale, J. *Aversion therapy and behavior disorders: An analysis*. Coral Gables: University of Miami Press, 1969.

Ravetz, J. *Scientific knowledge and its social problems*. New York: Oxford University Press, 1971.

Rhodes, R. J., and Hudson, R. M. Follow-up of tuberculous skid row alcoholics. I. Social adjustment and drinking behavior. *Quarterly Journal of Studies on Alcohol*, 1969, *30*, 119–128.

Robinson, D. The alcohologist's addiction—some implications of having lost control over the disease concept of alcoholism. *Quarterly Journal of Studies on Alcohol*, 1972, *33*, 1028–1042.

Roman, P. M., and Trice, H. M. The sick role, labeling theory and the deviant drinker. *The International Journal of Social Psychiatry*, 1968, *14*, 245–251.

Rosenthal, R. *Experimenter effects in behavioral research*. New York: Appleton-Century-Crofts, 1966.

Rosenthal, R. Interpersonal expectations: Effects of the experimenter's hypothesis. In R. Rosenthal and R. L. Rosnow (Eds.), *Artifact in behavioral research*. New York: Academic Press, 1969.

Schaefer, H. H., Sobell, M. B., and Mills, K. C. Baseline drinking in alcoholics and social drinkers: Kinds of drink and sip magnitude. *Behaviour Research and Therapy*, 1971a, *9*, 23–27.

Schaefer, H. H., Sobell, M. B., and Mills, K. C. Some sobering data on the use of self-confrontation with alcoholics. *Behavior Therapy*, 1971b, *2*, 28–39.

Schaefer, H. H., Sobell, M. B., and Sobell, L. C. Twelve-month follow-up of hospitalized alcoholics given self-confrontation experiences by videotape. *Behavior Therapy*, 1972, *3*, 283–285.

Sidman, M. *Tactics of scientific research*. New York: Basic Books, 1960.

Silver, M. J. Investigator effects, experimenter effects, and experimenter bias: A taxonomy and a clarification. *Journal Supplement Abstract Service*, 1973, *3*, Ms. No. 335.

Sobell, L. C. The validity of self-reports: Toward a predictive model. Unpublished doctoral dissertation. Irvine: University of California, 1976.

Sobell, L. C. A critique of alcoholism treatment evaluation. In P. E. Nathan and G. A. Marlatt (Eds.), *Behavioral Assessment and Treatment of Alcoholism*. New Brunswick: Rutgers Center of Alcohol Studies, 1977, in press.

Sobell, L. C., and Sobell, M. B. A self-feedback technique to monitor drinking behavior in alcoholics. *Behaviour Research and Therapy*, 1973c, *11*, 237–238.

Sobell, L. C., and Sobell, M. B. The erudite transient. *The International Journal of Social Psychiatry*, 1974, *20*, 242–256.

Sobell, L. C., and Sobell, M. B. Outpatient alcoholics give valid self-reports. *The Journal of Nervous and Mental Disease*, 1975c, *161*, 32–42.

Sobell, L. C., Sobell, M. B., and Christelman, W. C. The myth of "one drink." *Behaviour Research and Therapy*, 1972, *10*, 119–123.

Sobell, L. C., Sobell, M. B., and Schaefer, H. H. Alcoholics name fewer mixed drinks than social drinkers. *Psychological Reports*, 1971, *28*, 493–494.

Sobell, L. C., Sobell, M. B., and VanderSpek, R. Three independent comparisons between clinical judgment, self-report and physiological measures of blood alcohol concentration. Paper presented at the Annual Meeting of the Southeastern Psychological Association, New Orleans, March, 1976.

Sobell, M. B., Schaefer, H. H., and Mills, K. C. Differences in baseline drinking behaviors between alcoholics and normal drinkers. *Behaviour Research and Therapy*, 1972, *10*, 257–268.

Sobell, M. B., and Sobell, L. C. Individualized behavior therapy for alcoholics: Rationale, procedures, preliminary results and appendix. *California Mental Health Research Monograph, No. 13*. Sacramento: California Dept. of Mental Hygiene, 1972.

Sobell, M. B., and Sobell, L. C. Individualized behavior therapy for alcoholics. *Behavior Therapy*, 1973a, *4*, 49–72.

Sobell, M. B., and Sobell, L. C. Alcoholics treated by individualized behavior therapy: One year treatment outcome. *Behaviour Research and Therapy*, 1973b, *11*, 599–618.

Sobell, M. B., and Sobell, L. C. The need for realism, relevance and operational assumptions in the study of substance dependence. In H. D. Cappell and A. E. LeBlanc (Eds.), *Biological and behavioral approaches to drug dependence*. Toronto: Addiction Research Foundation, 1975a.

Sobell, M. B., and Sobell, L. C. A brief technical report on the Mobat: An inexpensive portable test for determining blood alcohol concentration. *Journal of Applied Behavior Analysis*, 1975b, *8*, 117–120.

Sobell, M. B., and Sobell, L. C. Second year treatment outcome of alcoholics treated by individualized behavior therapy: Results. *Behaviour Research and Therapy*, 1976, *14*, 195–215.

Sobell, M. B., Sobell, L. C., and Samuels, F. H. The validity of self-reports of prior alcohol-related arrests by alcoholics. *Quarterly Journal of Studies on Alcohol*, 1974, *35*, 276–280.

Sobell, M. B., Sobell, L. C., and Sheahan, D. B. Functional analysis of drinking problems as an aid in developing individual treatment strategies. *Addictive Behaviors*, 1976, *1*, 127–132.

Stuart, R. B. Challenges for behavior therapy—1975. *Canadian Psychological Review*, 1975, *16*, 164–171.

Tamerin, J. S., and Mendelson, J. H. The psychodynamics of chronic inebriation: Observations of alcoholics during the process of drinking in an experimental group setting. *American Journal of Psychiatry*, 1969, *125*, 886–899.

Tatsuoka, M. M. *Multivariate analysis: Techniques for educational and psychological research.* New York: John Wiley & Sons, 1971.

Verden, P., and Shatterly, D. Alcoholism research and resistance to understanding the compulsive drinker. *Mental Hygiene*, 1971, *55*, 331–336.

Vogler, R. E., Weissbach, T. A., and Compton, J. V. Learning techniques for alcohol abuse. *Behaviour Research and Therapy*, 1977, *15*, 31–38.

Weisman, M. N. Letter in *New and Views*, Newsletter published by the Alcoholism Council of Greater Los Angeles, January, 1975.

Williams, R. J. and Brown, R. A. Differences in baseline drinking behavior between New Zealand alcoholics and normal drinkers. *Behaviour Research and Therapy*, 1974a, *12*, 1–8.

Williams, R. J., and Brown, R. A. Naming mixed drinks: Alcoholics vs. social drinkers. *Psychological Reports*, 1974b, *35*, 33–34.

Wilson, G. T., Leaf, R. C., and Nathan, P. E. Aversive control of excessive alcohol consumption by chronic alcoholics in laboratory settings. *Journal of Applied Behavior Analysis*, 1975, *8*, 13–26.

Wolpe, J. *The practice of behavior therapy.* New York: Pergamon Press, 1969.

SELECTED READINGS

CONTROLLED DRINKING OUTCOMES

Anant, S. S. Former alcoholics and social drinking: An unexpected finding. *The Canadian Psychologist*, 1968, *9*, 35.

Arikawa, K., Kotorii, M., and Mukasa, H. The therapeutic effect of cyanamide on the alcoholic addicts in out-patient clinic. *Clinical Psychology (Japan)*, 1972, *14*, 219–227.

Bailey, M. B., and Stewart, J. Normal drinking by persons reporting previous problem drinking. *Quarterly Journal of Studies on Alcohol*, 1967, *28*, 305–315.

Baker, T. B., Udin, H., and Vogler, R. E. A short term alcoholism treatment program using videotape and self-confrontation techniques. Paper delivered at 80th American Psychological Association, Honolulu, 1972.

Barchha R., Stewart, M. A., and Guze, S. B. The prevalence of alcoholism among general hospital ward patients. *American Journal of Psychiatry*, 1968, *125*, 681–684.

Barr, H. L., Rosen, A., Antes, D. E., and Ottenberg, D. J. Two year follow-up study of 724 drug and alcohol addicts together in an abstinence therapeutic community. Paper presented at the 81st Annual Convention of the American Psychological Association, Montreal, 1973.

Bhakta, M. Clinical application of behaviour therapy in the treatment of alcoholism. *The Journal of Alcoholism*, 1971, *6*, 75–83.

Blake, B. G. The application of behaviour therapy to the treatment of alcoholism. *Behaviour Research and Therapy*, 1965, *3*, 75–85.

Bolman, W. M. Abstinence versus permissiveness in the psychotherapy of alcoholism. *Archives of General Psychiatry*, 1965, *12*, 456–463.

Caddy, G. R. Behaviour modification in the management of alcoholism. Unpublished doctoral dissertation. University of New South Wales, Australia, 1972.

Caddy, G. R., and Lovibond. S. H. Self-regulation and discriminated aversive conditioning in the modification of alcoholics' drinking behavior. *Behavior Therapy*, 1976, *7*, 223–230.

Cain, A. H. *The cured alcoholic.* New York: John Day, 1964.

Davies, D. L. Normal drinking in recovered alcohol addicts. *Quarterly Journal of Studies on Alcohol*, 1962, *23*, 94–104.

Davies, D. L., Scott, D. F., and Malherbe, M. E. L. Resumed normal drinking in recovered psychotic alcoholics. *The International Journal of the Addictions*, 1969, *4*, 187–194.

de Morsier, G., and Feldman, H. Le traitement de l'alcoolisme par l'apomorphien: Etude de 500 cas. *Schweitz. Archi. Neurolo. Psychiat.*, 1970, *70*, 434–440.

Dubourg, G. O. After-care for alcoholics—a follow-up study. *The British Journal of Addiction*, 1969, *64*, 155–163.

Evans, M. The Cardiff Plan and the Welsh Unit. *The British Journal of Addiction*, 1967, *62*, 29–34.

Faillace, L. A., Flamer, R. N., Imber, S. D., and Ward, R. F. Giving alcohol to alcoholics: An evaluation. *Quarterly Journal of Studies on Alcohol*, 1972, *33*, 85–90.

Faillace, L. A., *et al.* Unpublished manuscript, cited in Faillace, *et al.,* 1972.

Gallen, M., Williams, B., Cleveland, S. E., O'Connell, W. E., and Sands, P. A short term follow-up of two contrasting alcoholic treatment programs: A preliminary report. *Newsletter for Research in Mental Health and Behavioral Science*, 1973, *15*, 36–37.

Gerard, D. L., Saenger, G., and Wile, R. The abstinent alcoholic. *Archives of General Psychiatry*, 1962, *6*, 83–95.

Gerard, D. L., and Saenger, G. *Out-patient treatment of alcoholism.* Toronto: University of Toronto Press, 1966.

Gibbins, R. J. Unpublished manuscript, 1975.

Glatt, M. M. The question of moderate drinking despite 'loss of control.' *The British Journal of Addiction*, 1967, *62*, 267–274.

Goodwin, D. W., Crane, J. B., and Guze, S. B. Felons who drink: An 8-year follow-up. *Quarterly Journal of Studies on Alcohol*, 1971, *32*, 136–147.

Hacquard, M., Beaudoin, M., Derby, G., and Berger, H. Contribution a l'étude des résultats éloignés des cures de désintoxication éthylique. *Revue d'Hygiène et de Médecine Sociale*, 1960, *8*, 686–709.

Harper, J., and Hickson, B. The results of hospital treatment of chronic alcoholism. *Lancet*, 1951, *261*, 1057–1059.

Hedberg, A. G., and Campbell, L. III. A comparison of four behavioral treatments of alcoholism. *Journal of Behavior Therapy and Experimental Psychology*, 1974, *5*, 251–256.

Hyman, M. M. Alcoholics 15 years later. Presented at the 6th Annual Medical-Scientific Session National Council on Alcoholism, Milwaukee, 1975.

James, J. E., and Goldman, M. Behavior trends of wives of alcoholics. *Quarterly Journal of Studies on Alcohol*, 1971, *32*, 373–381.

Kendall, R. E. Normal drinking by former alcoholic addicts. *Quarterly Journal of Studies on Alcohol*, 1965, *26*, 247–257.

Kendall, R. E., and Staton, M. C. The fate of untreated alcoholics. *Quarterly Journal of Studies on Alcohol*, 1966, *27*, 30–41.

Kohrs, E. V. Behavioral approaches to problem drinkers in a rural community. *Behavioral Engineering*, 1973, *1*, 1–10.

Kraft, T., and Al-Issa, I. Alcoholism treated by desensitization: A case report. *Behaviour Research and Therapy*, 1967, *5*, 69–70.

Kraft, T., and Al-Issa, I. Desensitization and the treatment of alcohol addiction. *The British Journal of Addiction*, 1968, *63*, 19–23.

Lambert, B. E. V. "Social alkoholkonsumtion hos alkoholskadade? *Svenska Lakartidningen*, 1964, *61*, 315–318.

Lazarus, A. A. Towards the understanding and effective treatment of alcoholism. *South African Medical Journal*, 1965, *39*, 736–741.

Lemere, F. What happens to alcoholics. *American Journal of Psychiatry*, 1953, *109*, 674–676.

Levinson, T. The Donwood Institute—a five year follow-up study. Presented at the 31st International Congress on Alcoholism and Drug Dependence, 1975.

Lundquist, G. A. R. Alcohol dependence. *Acta Psychiatrica Scandinavica*, 1973, *49*, 332–340.

Marlatt, G. A. A comparison of aversive conditioning procedures in the treatment of alcoholism. Presented at the meeting of the Western Psychological Association, Anaheim, 1973.

Miller, P. M. The use of behavioral contracting in the treatment of alcoholism: A case report. *Behavior Therapy*, 1972, *3*, 593–596.

Miller, P. M. Training responsible drinking with veterans. Presented at the 83rd American Psychological Association annual conference, Chicago, 1975.

Monnerot, E. Cure hospitalière psychiatrique de l'alcoolomanie: Réflexions thérapeutiques sur un bilan, une enquête, un essai particulier. *Revue de l'Alcoolisme*, 1963, *9*, 114–128.

Moore, R. A., and Ramseur, F. Effects of psychotherapy in an open-ward hospital on patients with alcoholism. *Quarterly Journal of Studies on Alcohol*, 1960, *21*, 233–252.

Mukasa, H., and Arikawa, K. A new double medication method for the treatment of alcoholism using the drug cyanamide. *The Kurume Medical Journal*, 1968, *15*, 137–143.

Mukasa, H., Ichihara, T., and Eto, A. A new treatment of alcoholism with cyanamide (H_2NCN). *The Kurume Medical Journal*, 1964, *11*, 96–101.

Nørvig, J., and Neilsen, B. A follow-up study of 221 alcohol addicts in Denmark. *Quarterly Journal of Studies on Alcohol*, 1956, *17*, 633–642.

One of 7 patients has drinking problem, doctor team says. *Los Angeles Times,* November 20, 1972, p. 28.

Orford, J. A comparison of alcoholics whose drinking is totally uncontrolled and those whose drinking is mainly controlled. *Behaviour Research and Therapy,* 1973, *11,* 565–576.

Pattison, E. M., Coe, R., and Rhodes, R. J. Evaluation of alcoholism treatment: A comparison of three facilities. *Archives of General Psychiatry,* 1969, *20,* 478–488.

Pattison, E. M., Headley, E. B., Gleser, G. C., and Gottschalk, L. A. Abstinence and normal drinking: An assessment of changes in drinking patterns in alcoholics after treatment. *Quarterly Journal of Studies on Alcohol,* 1968, *29,* 610–633.

Pfeffer, A. Z., and Berger, S. A follow-up of treated alcoholics. *Quarterly Journal of Studies on Alcohol,* 1957, *18,* 624–648.

Pokorny, A. D., Miller, B. A., and Cleveland, S. E. Response to treatment of alcoholism: A follow-up study. *Quarterly Journal of Studies on Alcohol,* 1968, *29,* 364–381.

Popham, R. E., and Schmidt, W. Some factors affecting the likelihood of moderate drinking in treated alcoholics. *Journal of Studies on Alcohol,* 1976, *37,* 868–882.

Quinn, J. T., and Henbest, R. Partial failure of generalization in alcoholics following aversion therapy. *Quarterly Journal of Studies on Alcohol,* 1967, *28,* 70–75.

Quirk, D. A. Former alcoholics and social drinking: An additional observation. *The Canadian Psychologist,* 1968, *9,* 498–499.

Rakkolainen, V. and Turunen, S. From unrestrained to moderate drinking. *Acta Psychiatrica Scandinavica,* 1969, *45,* 47–52.

Reinert, R. E., and Bowen, W. T. Social drinking following treatment for alcoholism. *Bulletin of the Menninger Clinic,* 1968, *32,* 280–290.

Robson, R. A., Paulus, I., and Clarke, G. G. An evaluation of the effect of a clinic treatment program on the rehabilitation of alcoholic patients. *Quarterly Journal of Studies on Alcohol,* 1965, *26,* 264–278.

Rohan, W. P. A follow-up study of hospitalized problem drinkers. *Diseases of the Nervous System,* 1970, *31,* 259–265.

Rosengrem, E. Behandling av alkoholister med amtriptylin. *Lakartingningen,* 1966, *63,* 231–238.

Schaefer, H. H. Twelve-month follow-up of behaviorally trained ex-alcoholic social drinkers. *Behavior Therapy,* 1972, *3,* 286–289.

Schaefer, H. H., Sobell, M. B., and Sobell, L. C. Twelve month follow-up of hospitalized alcoholics given self-confrontation experiences by videotape. *Behavior Therapy,* 1972, *3,* 283–285.

Schuckit, M. A., and Winokur, G. A short term follow-up of women alcoholics. *Diseases of the Nervous System,* 1972, *33,* 672–678.

Selzer, M. L., and Holloway, W. H. A follow-up of alcoholics committed to a state hospital. *Quarterly Journal of Studies on Alcohol,* 1957, *18,* 98–120.

Shea, J. E. Psychoanalytic therapy and alcoholics. *Quarterly Journal of Studies on Alcohol,* 1954, *15,* 595–605.

Silverstein, S. J., Nathan, P. E., and Taylor, H. A. Blood alcohol level estimation and controlled drinking by chronic alcholics. *Behavior Therapy,* 1974, *5,* 1–15.

Skoloda, T. E., Alterman, A. I., Cornelison, F. S., and Gottheil, E. Treatment outcome in a drinking decisions program. *Journal of Studies on Alcohol,* 1975, *38,* 365–380.

Sobell, M. B., and Sobell, L. C. Individualized behavior therapy for alcoholics. *Behavior Therapy,* 1973a, *4,* 49–72.

Sobell, M. B., and Sobell, L. C. Alcoholics treated by individualized behavior therapy: One year treatment outcome. *Behaviour Research and Therapy*, 1973b, *11*, 599–618.

Sobell, M. B., and Sobell, L. C. Second year treatment outcome of alcoholics treated by individualized behavior therapy: Results. *Behaviour Research and Therapy*, 1976, *14*, 195–215.

Tomsovic, M. A follow-up study of discharged alcoholics. *Hospital and Community Psychiatry*, 1970, *21*, 38–41.

van Dijk, W. K., and van Dijk-Koffeman, A. A follow-up study of 211 treated male alcoholic addicts. *The British Journal of Addiction*, 1973, *68*, 3–24.

Vogler, R. E., Compton, J. V., and Weissbach, T. A. Integrated behavior change techniques for alcoholics. *Journal of Consulting and Clinical Psychology*, 1975, *43*, 233–243.

Index